CHILDHOOD AND EMOTION

How did children feel in the Middle Ages and early modern times? How did adults feel about the children around them? This collection addresses these fundamental but rarely asked questions about social and family relations by bringing together two emerging fields within cultural history – childhood and emotion – and provides avenues through which to approach their shared histories.

Bringing together a wide range of material and sources, such as court records, self-narratives and educational manuals, this collection sheds a new light on the subject. The coverage ranges from medieval to eighteenth-century Europe and North America, and examines Catholic, Protestant, Puritan and Jewish communities. Childhood emerges as a function not of gender or age, but rather of social relations. Emotions, too, appear differently in source-driven studies in that they derive not from modern assumptions but from real, lived experience.

Featuring contributions from across the globe, *Childhood and Emotion* comes a step closer to portraying emotions as they were thought to be experienced by the historical subjects. This book will establish new benchmarks not only for the history of these linked subjects but also for the whole history of social relations.

Claudia Jarzebowski is Associate Professor of Early Modern History at the Free University of Berlin, working in the field of social history, the history of emotions and early modern global history. She has published various articles and books on topics ranging from incest to childhood.

Thomas Max Safley is Professor of Early Modern European History at the University of Pennsylvania. A specialist in the economic and social history of early modern Europe, h⸢ has ⸥ LIVERPOOL JMU LIBRARY books covering the history of marriage and the f⸢amily⸥ ⸢ ⸥ity, and the history of labour and business.

'This is a strong collection which brings together a wide range of internationally renowned scholars, working in different historical traditions worldwide. The volume, unusually and significantly, provides links into current research not often available in English and addresses two areas of growing research – childhood and emotion. It offers thoughtful avenues and lenses through which we might approach their shared and dialogic histories.'

Susan Broomhall, *University of Western Australia, Australia*

CHILDHOOD AND EMOTION

Across cultures 1450–1800

Edited by
Claudia Jarzebowski and Thomas Max Safley

Routledge
Taylor & Francis Group

LONDON AND NEW YORK

First published 2014
by Routledge
2 Park Square, Milton Park, Abingdon, Oxon OX14 4RN

and by Routledge
711 Third Avenue, New York, NY 10017

Routledge is an imprint of the Taylor & Francis Group, an informa business

British Library Cataloguing in Publication Data
A catalogue record for this book is available from the British Library

Library of Congress Cataloging in Publication Data
Childhood and emotion : across cultures 1450-1800 / edited by Claudia
Jarzebowski and Thomas Max Safley.
pages cm
Includes bibliographical references and index.
1. Emotions in children. 2. Child psychology. I. Jarzebowski, Claudia, 1971-
editor of compilation. II. Safley, Thomas Max, editor of compilation.
BF723.E6C45 2013
305.2309–dc23   2013026254

ISBN: 978-0-415-83195-6 (hbk)
ISBN: 978-0-415-83196-3 (pbk)
ISBN: 978-1-315-85087-0 (ebk)

Typeset in Bembo
by Taylor & Francis Publishers

Printed and bound by CPI Group (UK) Ltd, Croydon, CR0 4YY

CONTENTS

CONTRIBUTORS

Arianne Baggerman, University of Rotterdam, The Netherlands.

Paola Baseotto, Insubria University, Italy.

Tali Berner, Program in Research of Child and Youth Cultures, Tel Aviv University, Israel.

Nicola Borchardt, University of Hamburg, Germany.

Claudia Jarzebowski, Free University of Berlin, Germany.

Marjo Kaartinen, University of Turku, Finland.

Philippa Maddern, University of Western Australia, Australia.

Thomas Max Safley, University of Pennsylvania, US.

Valentina Sebastiani, European University Institute, Italy.

Naoko Seriu, University of Lille II, France.

Claudia Ulbrich, Free University of Berlin, Germany.

Otto Ulbricht, University of Kiel, Germany.

Kelly J. Whitmer, The University of the South at Sewanee, US.

PREFACE

Childhood has entered the public consciousness with astonishing force since the digital revolution that began in the 1980s. Video gaming and internet access have transformed the experience and perception of childhood as have few historical events in the past. Never mind the subtle blending of fantasy and reality that computers make possible; they offer access to and participation in violence and pornography as readily as they transmit information and stimulate creativity. The innocence and latency of childhood seem under threat as much from new media, at least in the minds of many experts, as from child labour. These are emotional as well as material circumstances; the feelings associated with childhood and felt by children seem to be experiencing a phase-shift.

Under these circumstances, it is surprising to realize that the history of childhood as a cultural and emotional phenomenon has attracted so little scholarly attention. Scholars have addressed it in terms of the affective relations between parent and child but have yet to consider the emotional ties themselves as historically and socially constructed. This volume takes up childhood and emotion in the early modern world, when the understanding of both underwent a fundamental transformation. Using a wide variety of legal and personal records, the essays in this volume examine the relationship between childhood and emotion in the so-called "transition" to modern society.

These essays originated in a conference, held at the University of Pennsylvania, in 2010. The organizers wish to thank the University of Pennsylvania, its School of Arts and Sciences, its School of Medicine and its Graduate School of Education, as well as its Departments of Art History, English, German, History and Psychology for their support. Thanks are due as well to Routledge, especially its editors, Paul Brotherston, Laura Mothersole, Victoria Peters, Eve Setch and Michael Strang, without whose professional expertise and experience this volume could not have been completed.

INTRODUCTION

Claudia Jarzebowski and Thomas Max Safley

We are all young once and experience the phases of life associated with the passage of time and the aging of bodies. Yet, the commonality of human life and death obscures a complexity of meanings and interpretations. Among other things, it is a-historical.

This observation applies with particular force to the history of childhood and emotion. The biological fact of human development influences the categories, definitions and interpretations applied to different ages, but these categories, definitions and interpretations vary comparatively and historically. What a child is, when childhood begins and how it "feels" varies over time and space. In the West, for example, commentators have divided the lifecycle by age into different phases, according to which childhood was the first of four, lasting until sexual maturity, the second of seven, lasting from ages 7 to 14 in Ancient Greece, or the fourth, fifth and sixth of 12, lasting from ages 3 to 11, in modern North America.[1] According to Hindu teachings, by contrast, life consists of four *ashramas*, or stages, divided according to spiritual occupations: student, householder, hermit and wandering ascetic.[2] Clearly, the demarcation of various phases and the conceptions applied to each can be highly arbitrary and idiosyncratic, reflecting the societies and cultures that create them, rather than the biological fact of childhood itself.[3] Childhood, therefore, is not by itself meaningful or consistent. It is assigned meanings and consistencies, bridging multiple and culturally specific requirements of being a child and acting towards children. These culturally specific meanings have – putatively, as many chapters in this book will argue – less to do with age and body physicality and more to do with how age and body weave into cultural patterns and shifts.

In Western historiography, childhood and emotion mark two emerging fields within social and cultural history. Their study dates back to the 1960s, originating in 1962 with the seminal work of Philip Ariès, *Centuries of Childhood*,[4] a transparent attempt to integrate emotions into the history of childhood. Although much criticized and revised in succeeding decades, it remains incontestably the starting point for any discussion of the topic, as witnessed by the contributions to this volume, nearly all of which make reference to it. Ariès argues that in Western Europe, childhood is a modern construct, one that began to emerge first in the fifteenth century and developed more quickly from the eighteenth century. The Middle Ages had no notion of childhood. It is, moreover, an elite concept, becoming evident among well-to-do families who dressed, treated and considered their children as something other than "little adults". The rise of industrial production and nuclear families promoted the process in a number of ways, but especially by separating work and education from the household and, thus, insulating children from adult society. Thus, according to Ariès, notions of childhood mark the process of modernization, characterize modern society and emerge only in the presence of modern institutions and organizations.

His evidence provoked the first criticisms of his work as well as the further attempts to grapple with his subject. Ariès based his theory to a large extent on works of art, images of children, over time. He argued that pre-modern children were not considered persons fundamentally separate and different from adults because they were not represented in a visually distinct manner. They appear to look, dress and act the same as adults.

Yet, the resort to visual sources offers a much more nuanced view, an increased interest in depictions of children, especially portraits of children, beginning in the late medieval period.[5] Dutch and Italian paintings tend to include children in socially vivid settings, both private and public, such as games, meals and festivities, as well as parades, receptions and celebrations. These same visual sources often depict children as individuals engaged in individual occupations and pastimes: playing, working, walking and reading.[6] The careful study of children in Renaissance paintings yields another central insight: not only have children been a favoured subject of artists in early modern Europe, but their paintings reveal much about the social history of childhood and children. Especially Dutch paintings from the sixteenth and seventeenth centuries show children dressed in unique fashions, given their own toys and provided with appropriate furniture.[7] Jeremy Goldberg has lately shown on the basis of testamentary inventories that medieval English households contained a large variety of children's furniture and toy-like devices.[8] According to the last will of a craftsman, he had owned extra tables and chairs for his godchild because he was himself a childless and unmarried man.[9]

Beyond demonstrating that childhood was understood as such from a much earlier period, the re-examination of late medieval works of art, Ariès's favoured source for insight into the history of childhood, has given cause to reconsider gender and class issues related to the topic. Paintings show girls and boys playing together, rather than in segregated groups.[10] They depict encounters in public spaces, such as streets, plazas, playgrounds, parks and meadows, among young people of different social origins.[11] Parents' manuals of the sixteenth and seventeenth centuries encouraged such interaction, recommending that children of noble, even royal, status regularly play and study with children of lower status, whether in the household, neighbourhood or community.[12] Indeed, art work, particularly work that represents rural life, has emerged as one of the main sources in the social history of children and children's lives.

Lately, the material culture of childhood has also attracted scholarly interest. The books of children, their notebooks and sketches, their toys, their attire and, as has been mentioned above, their furniture have become the object of study. School grounds have been excavated and the remnants of sticks, tablets, notes and drawings preserved by archaeologists and displayed in museums.[13] The *Residenzschloss* of Dresden, Germany, displays full suits of armour for princelings as young as four years of age. These armour suits vastly outweighed the boys for whom they were intended and, so, could only be worn for minutes or by court dwarves pretending to be the royal child.[14] The *Rijksmuseum* in Amsterdam, The Netherlands, contains in its collections one potty chair from the seventeenth century, presumably still working. All of these sources, whether artistic or material, contradict longstanding notions that pre-modern children were ignored or unappreciated by the adults around them. Rather, they testify to a consciousness of children and childhood before the Industrial Revolution, the Enlightenment and the Renaissance.

Any study of the history of childhood must, therefore, begin with this realization – namely, with the knowledge that children were undoubtedly perceived as a social group with its own needs. Accordingly, this volume turns away from the theoretical presuppositions of the 1960s and 1970s that, in some instances, continue to shape historical scholarship on childhood and the emotions that did or did not attend it.

The contention that modern elites, especially the bourgeoisie, invented the love of children in the late-eighteenth century remains deeply engrained in the collective consciousness as recently as 2013.[15] Yet, this notion appears to serve modern needs more than it mirrors historical evidence, reflecting a teleology in which the historical process demonstrates constant improvement to the present, thus declaring and justifying contemporary society as the zenith of human development. By way of analogy, the historical process itself comes to resemble an organic process of growing and maturing, comparable to the growth of a child into adulthood. Such histories have trouble explaining departures from progress, to say nothing of the lapses into barbarism, that have plagued human history and inspired such noteworthy historians as Norbert Elias, who wrote his *The Civilizing Process* in the face of the rising fascism of the 1930s.[16] This is especially remarkable in the history of emotions.

The so-called father of the history of emotions, Lucien Febvre, followed impulses similar to those that drove Norbert Elias.[17] His call to include emotions in historical thought and study followed his experiences during the Second World War, including the loss of his close friend and colleague, Marc Bloch.[18] His now famous essay belongs to the intellectual setting of the French *Annales* school[19] that promoted radically new interdisciplinary approaches to the past, such as applying the theories and methods of sociology and psychology to historical study. Febvre understood society as a conglomerate of different forces, structures and interests. He considered emotions to be of primary interest due to the role they play shaping people's attitudes, perceptions and behaviours. The focus of his interest was clearly not the individual, but the collectivity in its social and political function, and he posed the question of what role emotions play in configurating collective behaviours. He wished to understand and explain what he had experienced in his own life as the tendency of crowds to follow leadership blindly to their own destruction. It made sense to him to imagine emotions as collectively rooted and collectively active. Emotions transformed individuals into masses that could be manipulated by charismatic holders of political power.[20]

Thus, Febvre and his colleagues in the *Annales* school asked the "how" questions: how do emotions influence historical processes, and how are they subject to manipulation? Such an approach is based on the assumption that certain emotions are always present in the human psyche: fear, anger, shame. Some scholars include love, too.[21] Quickly adopted by many historians, this approach seemed to explain the connection between the concept of a "civilizing process" and the susceptibility of crowds to manipulation.

The emotion that has attracted the most historical attention appears to be fear. In his then path-breaking study *La Peur en Occident*,[22] Jean Delumeau drew a picture of late medieval and early modern society in which people were driven by senseless fear, given to irrational behaviours at a very high level. This pattern has especially been imputed to the largest group in medieval and early modern society: the lower social strata. By attributing "irrationality" to the common folk, it became easy to construct a huge collectivity in pre-modern society that resembled an amorphous mass rather than a community of individuals, differentiated according to their origins, abilities, incomes, interests and situations. In the approach taken by Delumeau and other scholars,[23] the lower strata of pre-modern society emerged as a passive, immobile, irrational group, subject to and driven by instincts more than by reason. Reason became thus a characteristic of modern society, established by modern science and promulgated by modern education. As a result, the history of emotions came to be viewed as retrograde, a topic unworthy of study because it played no essential role in – was a hindrance to – human progress. It retained, at best, an antiquarian interest as a quality of pre-modern people.

This separation of emotion from progress – from the positive aspects of history – allowed the history of emotions to be detached from social history. If the population of pre-modern society were considered emotionally underdeveloped, irrational, passive and manipulable, then its emotional life, including any emotions attached to children or childhood, would certainly be uninteresting because it was under-developed. In this context, Ariès's work made perfect sense and, indeed, seemed to provide objective evidence to support the case. Pre-modern society showed a lack of visible emotion, especially with regard to its offspring.

Yet, as noted, by examining the collective and by privileging the visible, historians led themselves astray. The contributions to this volume take up the wealth of evidence – individual and written, as well as collective and visible – that argues for the emotional richness of the pre-modern. They begin with the assumption that most parents, then as now, love their children, celebrate their births and grieve their deaths, and that what changes over time is not the emotional content of parent–child relationships, but rather the ways in which that emotional content finds expression.

One needs some historiographical background in order to understand the explo-siveness of these bold questions. When the history of childhood emerged as a field of study in the 1960s, some scholars still clung to teleological assumptions and habits. They gathered information about living conditions, especially demographic data on life expectancies, family size, and natality and mortality, in order to demonstrate improvement over the past rather than to describe lived experience in the past. The numbers encouraged some historians, such as Edward Shorter, to conclude that the higher infant mortality rates of pre-modern Europe prevented parents from developing an emotional attachment − a loving and caring attitude − towards their own children.[24] Others contributed to this view by assuming that the resort to wet-nursing functioned in the same manner.[25] The reliance on wet-nurses appears to have been commonplace in early modern Europe, especially among elites and especially in southern France.[26] Though the evidence is patchy, the conclusion was similar: child-rearing practices created emotional distance between parent and child.[27] Some scholars argue, moreover, that wet-nursing served as a tacit means to dispose of unwanted children, claiming more girls than boys were sent to nurse.[28] In each instance, modern assumptions and standards were applied to pre-modern families, a problem of anachronism.[29]

Consider, for example, pre-modern assumptions about nursing.[30] Medical and family handbooks taught that a mother's milk was unfit for an infant to drink for the first four to eight weeks of its life because of the polluting effects of the birth process.[31] Humoral medicine assumed that milk, semen and blood were actually the same fluid albeit in different states.[32] Indeed, the new mother's milk remained tainted until she was churched, a period that lasted as long as eight weeks, suggesting not only humoral but also spiritual arguments against nursing. For these reasons, it made intrinsic sense for pre-modern parents to hire wet-nurses for the health and longevity of their new-born offspring.[33] From this perspective, wet-nursing emerges as a positive act of parental care and affection, a deliberate attempt to preserve children from early illness and death. Private notes from Italy during the fifteenth and sixteenth centuries show "the great pain that fathers took in selecting an appropriate wetnurse for their sons".[34] Erasmus of Rotterdam offered yet another argument in favour of wet-nursing. An educated and temperate nurse would provide not only physical but also emotional and intellectual sustenance. He argued as well that fathers should be similarly supplemented by a preceptor or tutor, appointed as early as the first day of the child's life.[35] These and other contemporary arguments for wet-nursing suggest that pre-modern approaches to child-rearing need to be considered on their own terms, rather than according to modern standards. The history of wet-nursing still awaits a serious revision.[36]

Beyond question, pre-modern society suffered higher infant and child mortality rates than modern societies. The question thus remains: did higher mortality rates among children affect parental attitudes towards them in former times? If parents lived in the expectation that their offspring would probably die in infancy, and if this created an emotional distance between parents and new-born children, when, if ever, did affection emerge? Historians long assumed that social and familial conditions delayed the ignition of parental love and care until the child reached the age of reason, roughly in his or her seventh year.[37] This age also marked the point at which the child became physically and mentally able to labour and thus to enter the world of work. The capacity to communicate and to labour in minor but meaningful ways might have inspired the parental care.[38] This reasoning applied with particular force to rural parents, who were thought to behave carelessly towards their children. Historical studies examined, for example, the numbers and occasions of accidental deaths, especially in pre-modern England. Not that England is particular in this regard.[39] German town chroniclers regularly recorded the perils that befell children: their accidental deaths by drowning in rivers, canals and races, by shooting with bullets or arrows, by trampling by horses or crowds.[40] On the one hand, the numbers of such fatalities might suggest parental carelessness. On the other hand, the very fact that these fatalities became the stuff of historical chronicles, to say nothing of legal procedures, might suggest that they were a matter of note, if not care.[41]

Early modern parents mourned the deaths of their children, as Marjo Kaartinen shows in Chapter 10. In retelling stories of the deaths of children from accidents or illnesses, all recorded in a variety of archival sources, she depicts a broad scheme of emotions as well as of social settings, including norms of emotional expression, to be considered when interpreting reactions to such deaths. In addition, Kaartinen more closely investigates gender-specific aspects of mourning. Her question, if and how mothers and fathers grieved differently, has major implications for the further studies of emotions in the past.[42] Indeed, how parents expressed or were expected to express their grief may have varied more over the course of time than whether they expressed it.

The history of childhood has long been understood as the history of attitudes towards children. This is partly due to an interest deriving from the history of education and partly to what has been labelled a lack of sources. A number of contributions to this volume rely upon sources that offer what might be called a child-centred perspective. Such a perspective requires, however, either that available sources be read in new ways or that new sources be exploited.

In Chapter 8, Philippa Maddern poses the question "How Children Were Supposed to Feel; How Children Felt" with reference to a variety of archival sources from late medieval and early modern England. Her reading succeeds, first, in reconstructing the normative and social contexts in which feelings and emotions have been permitted; and, second, in excavating how they were actually enacted. In addition, she manages to capture what she considers to be the otherwise unheard voices of children themselves.

Among newly examined sources, self-narratives take an important position. They offer insight into the thoughts and feelings of the author, a first-person testimony to emotional life. Yet, the matter of interpretation is by no means simple or straightforward.

In Chapter 4, Claudia Ulbrich presents her sources as texts that offer access to historically negotiated emotions and memories, recalled and reinterpreted by specific persons, in specific circumstances and for specific purposes. Self-narratives offer a couple of approaches to the topic of children and childhood: via writing about one's own childhood and via writing about one's own children. The differences between writing about childhood and writing about children emerge as indicators of emotion that are distinguished by gender, age, class and religion.

Otto Ulbricht, in Chapter 5, also relies on self-narratives, a collection of diaries and autobiographies to examine emotional socialization in early modern Germany. By adopting an explicitly social psychological approach to the topic of childhood emotions, he argues for the gradual exposure of boys to a regime of acceptable emotional behaviours that were defined for them and imposed upon them by adults. This raises profound theoretical and methodological questions about the degree to which childhood emotions in the past can actually be identified and studied.

The historical study of childhood has developed considerably during the last decade. All scruples concerning the value of Ariès's work and his theory aside, one aspect of it has remained unassailable: the "discovery of childhood" concerns not merely a biologically determined fact, but also a socially constructed phenomenon. Childhood varies according to cultural and social circumstances, among other things. Forms of socialization differ not only between cultures and societies, but also within them. And both cultural and social conditions directly affected the "feelings" associated with and expected of children.

Accordingly, any study of childhood and emotion requires a sensitivity to cultural and social context, a commitment to transcultural and trans-social perspectives and comparisons. There is a certain irony to this. One could argue that emotions have long been considered anti-social, something private, something out of place in public. Wild, uncontrollable and, most importantly for the West, irrational, they endanger social stability and disrupt social discourse, as noted above. Such thinking reflects not only the putative distinction between public and private spheres, but also the presumed biology of gender differences. The di-*vision de monde*, as Pierre Bourdieu described the invention of a dichotomous order of the world, can be traced back to the late-eighteenth and early-nineteenth centuries, when it became fashionable to assign emotions to a private female sphere, intellectually associated with nature and irrationality, in contrast to a public masculine sphere of society and rationality. The banishment of emotions to a private sphere or space is tantamount to their separation from reason. This dichotomous invention of modernity distorts how the present distinguishes itself from the past and how the West contrasts itself with the world.

Transcultural perspectives help to disentangle a highly intertwined complex of attitudes and practices, whether assigned to distant communities or one's own. Barbara Rosenwein coined the term "emotional community" in her now classic essay "Worrying about Emotions".[43] Inspired by Febvre's argument that emotions contribute to the creation of collectives, she seized upon the notion of communities as more elastic units in a wider social or communal setting. Following her basic idea, a person gained access to a community by employing or demonstrating the proper emotional behaviour. Accordingly, emotions become both opportunity and instrument in a process of social relationship and integration, and communities are distinguished not only by shared social interests, but also by shared emotional responses. Thus understood, emotions become a key to social acceptance in pre-modern societies. They become not merely reflections of subjective mental states that may vary according to gender, status or age, but realities for objective historical study.

Given the changing social construction of childhood and emotion over time, a comparative approach offers unique perspectives. It exposes how different cultures and societies possess different conceptions of childhood and the emotions appropriately associated with it. It demonstrates the range of concepts that can be associated with a particular phase of the life-cycle. It permits the examination of different behaviours related to childhood and, by so doing, contextualizes as well as compares it across cultures and societies.

In Chapter 3, Nicola Borchardt investigates the life of children raised in the Dutch colony of Batavia (now Indonesia) during the seventeenth and early-eighteenth centuries. Her findings suggest a tangle of child-rearing practices that combined local traditions and "Dutch" attitudes and institutions into a hybrid culture of children and child-rearing. The hybridity also stems from the many children of mixed relations.

A different type of transfer may come to mind when thinking of travelling concepts between Europe and Early America. People who went to the early American colonies came to the "New World" in order to establish a religious and social community that had not been possible in their respective home countries. As Paola Baseotto shows in Chapter 6, children assumed a central position in the symbolic and social order. The burden of a spiritual and physical perpetuation was laid squarely on their shoulders, with parents assuming full responsibility for seeing to it that the burden was carried.

The spiritual significance of children and childhood is not unique to puritanism, but is evident in other dissident, marginalized or deviant[44] religious cultures. As Tali Berner points out in Chapter 2, children revitalized relations across the boundaries of hierarchy, age and gender in religious and social communities through their capacity to experience and elicit joyous emotions, such as pleasure, love and excitement. Indeed, the fact that children, rather than adults, experience this ritual and social joy provides the very justification for it.

Emotional and cultural practices are closely interwoven. This applies to status groups as well as religious communities. The matter becomes harder to study the further down the social ladder one looks. But emotions attached to children played a crucial and, as Naoko Seriu elaborates Chapter 11, explicit role in social interaction. Her subjects deserve even more interest as they combine status and gender issues in unexpected ways: her study takes up soldiers who deserted from their military position in order to see their children. This justification made sense to deserters and, interestingly, occasionally found acceptance on the part of the authorities.

One of the most interesting recent shifts in the history of childhood stems from a re-evaluation of emotions in educational practices.[45] This shift is closely connected to a material history of education that rendered childhood education sensual – that is, based on hearing, smelling, touching, seeing and travelling. At the same time – the late-seventeenth and early-eighteenth centuries – education came to be viewed as crucial for the elevation and enlightenment of the population generally. The broadening of teaching media, to say nothing of the circle of those taught, had a direct impact upon the emotional experience of children and childhood.

Reading, in a general sense, is part of a sensual history of education as we learn from Arianne Baggerman in Chapter 7. Children were encouraged to read; children were read to; children were encouraged to reflect on what they read or heard. The result involved emotional arousal and its rational consideration as a means of education. At the same time, shared reading experiences emerge as a sign for a group identity: not all books were supposed be read by all children and not all books were read by all children. Indeed, as becomes clear, in the matter of reading and emotion, social standing could trump gender identity.

Children themselves could become the medium of emotionally driven religious identity and enthusiasm. As carriers of innocence, as living symbols of Christian piety, children in Protestant sects – such as the Pietists in eighteenth-century Germany – were thought capable of (perhaps uniquely suited to) prophecy. Those future prophets were deemed to be exceptionally gifted, as Kelly J. Whitmer explains in Chapter 1. In this context, the term "emotional intelligence" gains a new and specific early modern meaning.

This approach falls in line with what William Reddy has famously called "emotives"[46] in the broader framework of his influential study "Navigation of Feeling".[47] Children could be emotionally driven and, at the same time, emotionally driving. Their emotions were not viewed as irrational, however, if they were spiritually determined and bounded. The God-given rationality of emotions attached to or inspired by spirituality, which defy human understanding, undermines both the classical dichotomy of reason versus emotion and the conventional timelines for the triumph of the latter, such as 1800.

To reconstruct the history of emotions is not the same as to reconstruct emotions in history. It has long been argued that emotions in pre-modern society functioned as modes of social interaction and means of relationship-building. They are, therefore, integral to the social history of all groups in the period, not merely to the history of childhood alone. This becomes particularly apparent when we turn to the narration of emotions and query the sources as to how emotions worked in social interaction. Valentina Sebastiani has worked her way through the correspondence of the Amerbachs, a printing family of late medieval and early modern Basel. Her reading of the correspondence between sons and their parents, which she presents in Chapter 9, offers rich material for clarifying how emotions were at once narrated and woven into the process of relation-building among parents and children.

Childhood and emotion have been connected in the historical literature since their discovery by scholars. The chapters in this volume approach the topic from new standpoints and with new methods to address three essential concerns:

1 how emotions shape perceptions of children and childhood;
2 how emotions lend themselves to historical investigation;
3 how children can be understood through their experienced and assigned emotions.

This is a book not about early modern families, to clarify the basic difference to other approaches, but rather about children in multiple settings. It covers roughly the Early Modern Period, from the mid-fifteenth to the mid-eighteenth century, during which time children were closely attached not only to their families but also to a variety of spiritual and social communities.

Contributions to the current volume locate childhood and emotion through different sources, such as court records, self-narratives and educational manuals, and in different settings, such as schools, families, courts and orphanages, in different cultures and countries. The overarching line of questioning that binds the contributions together addresses the interaction of different notions of children, childhood and emotion.

Childhood and emotion emerge thus as radically historical:

> We cannot ignore, nor did the medieval parents and theorists ignore, the basic biology of a child, which has not changed over the four centuries we are discussing. To be sure, the cultural attitudes toward children and images of them change over time, but basic to any concept of childhood and childrearing are children themselves.[48]

Rather than assume the validity of general theories, the contributors examine historical realities, how childhood and emotions shaped and were shaped by norms and practices according to specific social and cultural contexts. Childhood and emotion achieved, therefore, radically different meanings and significances, even in the same historical time and place.

The results are original in at least two major respects. First, they suggest an approach to the history of childhood and emotion that is different from existing ones in terms of the wide variety of source materials and a focus on children's activities. The arguments are empirical in that they proceed from the sources rather than from *a priori* models or theories of development. As a result, childhood emerges as a function not of gender or age, but rather of social relations. Emotions, too, appear differently in source-driven studies in that they derive not from modern assumptions but from lived experience. Our contributors come a step closer to portraying emotions as they were thought to be and were experienced by the historical subjects. Second, they move away from a notion of childhood and emotion as historically constant and immutable. These chapters pay heed to normative sources, but set them in the context of real social structures, relations and situations, and the feelings behind and within them. The study of sources and their historical, discursive, normative and daily contexts lend urgency to the revision of the history of emotion and childhood.

Notes

1 P. Maddern and S. Tarbin, "Life-cycle", in S. Evangelisti and S. Cavallo (eds) *A Cultural History of Childhood and Family, Volume 3, Early Modern Period (1400-1650)* (Oxford, UK, 2010).
2 M. W. Muesse, *The Hindu Traditions: A Concise Introduction* (Minneapolis, MN, 2011), pp83–97.
3 B. A. Hanawalt, "The Child in the Middle Ages and the Renaissance", in W. Koops and M. Zuckerman (eds) *Beyond the Century of the Child: Cultural History and Developmental Psychology* (Philadelphia, PA, 2003), pp21–43, esp. p25.
4 P. Ariès, *L'enfant et la vie familiale sous l'Ancien Régime* (Paris, 1960); P. Ariès, *Centuries of Childhood: A Social History of Family Life* (New York, 1962).

5 K. Christiansen and S. Weppelmann (eds) *The Renaissance Portrait from Donatello to Bellini* (Berlin/New York, 2011), esp. pp157, 158, 160, 243, 289, 296, 303; M. Neumeister (ed) *The Changing Face of Childhood: British Children's Portraits and their Influence in Europe* (Frankfurt/Main, 2007).

6 Cf. L. Campbell et al (eds) *Renaissance Faces: From Titian to van Eyck* (New Haven, CT, 2008), esp. pp177–203, 264, 265.

7 P. de Hooch, *A Mother and Child with Its Head in Her Lap* (1658/1660) at the Rijks-museum, Amsterdam.

8 J. Goldberg, "At Home and Outdoors: A Material Cultural Perspective on the Experiences of Children in Later Medieval England", in P. Maddern et al (eds) *A Cultural History of the Emotions in the Late-Medieval, Reformation and Renaissance Age, vol 3* (London, 2014).

9 Ibid.

10 For examples, see K. Ertz (ed) *Pieter Breughel der Jüngere und Jan Breughel der Ältere: Tradition und Fortschritt* (Wien, 1997), pp119, 377.

11 "Pieter Bruegel the Elder's 'Children's Games' (Painting)", in Children and Youth in History, Item #332, http://chnm.gmu.edu/cyh/primary-sources/332 (accessed 1 July 2013); annotated by Miriam Forman-Brunell.

12 R. Chavasse, "Humanist Educational and Emotional Expectations of Teenagers in Late 15th Century Italy", in S. Broomhall (ed) *Emotions in the Household, 1200–1900* (Basingstoke, UK, 2008), pp69–85; for sources, see C. W. Kallendorf, *Humanist Educational Treatises* (Cambridge, MA, 2002).

13 A. Willemsen, *Back to the Schoolyard: The Daily Practice of Medieval and Renaissance Education* (Turnhout, 2007).

14 J. Baeumel, *Rüstkammer: Fuehrer durch die ständige Ausstellung im Semperbau* (Dresden, 2004).

15 For example, *The White Ribbon, a German Children's Story* [*Das weiße Band, eine deutsche Kindergeschichte*] directed by Michael Haneke (2009).

16 N. Elias, *The Civilizing Process: Sociogenetic and Psychogenetic Investigations* (Oxford, UK, 2000). It was first published in German in 1939 and went almost without notice. A revised edition was published in English in 1968/1969, at which point the book garnered the attention of scholars.

17 L. Febvre, "Sensibility and History: How to Reconstitute the Emotional Life of the Past", in P. Burke (ed) *A New Kind of History: From the Writings of Febvre* (New York, 1973), pp12–26.

18 Marc Bloch fought with the French Resistance and was executed by the Gestapo in 1944.

19 P. Burke, *The French Historical Revolution: The Annales School, 1929–89* (Stanford, CA, 1990).

20 For "charisma" and "power", see M. Weber, *Economy and Society: An Outline of Interpretive Sociology* (New York, 1968), ch. III.

21 Originally, Febvre put love on the agenda. It has long been overlooked by scholars and has only recently begun to attract historical study, often in the context of the new history of childhood, as promoted by the chapters in this book.

22 J. Delumeau, *La peur en Occident, XIVe–XVIIIe siècles: Une cite assiegée* (Paris, 1978).

23 See, for example, the works of Arlette Farge and Alain Corbin.

24 E. Shorter, *The Making of the Modern Family* (New York, 1975).

25 An early critique of this view was provided by V. Fildes, *Breasts, Bottles, and Babies: A History of Infant Feeding* (Edinburgh, 1987).

26 For Britain, see A. Borsay and B. Hunter (eds) *Nursing and Midwifery in Britain since 1700* (Basingstoke, UK, 2012); for France, see E. Badinter, *Mother Love. Myth and Reality: Motherhood in Modern History* (New York, 1981); J. R. Lehning, "Family Life and Wetnursing in a French Village", *Journal of Interdisciplinary History*, vol 12 (1982): pp645–656.

27 N. Dye Schrom and D. B. Smith, "Mother Love and Infant Death 1750–1920", *Journal of American History*, vol 73 (1986): pp329–353.

28 H. Newton, *The Sick Child in Early Modern England, 1580–1720* (Oxford, UK, 2012).

29 One should not forget that the "nursing question" in the 1970s centred on the issue of nursing as a necessary sign of motherly care and was highly contested by those who advocated other forms of nutrition for new-borns.

30 See "Wet-Nursing", in *Encyclopedia of Children and Childhood in History and Society*, vol 3, P. S. Fass (ed) (New York, 2004), pp884–887.

31 For Jewish customs, see D. G. Hundert, "Jewish Children and Childhood in Early Modern East Central Europe", in D. Kraemer (ed) *The Jewish Family: Metaphor and Memoir* (New York, 1989), pp81–94, esp. p87.

32 P. Quattrin, "The Milk of Christ – on Parzival's Herzeleyd", in J. C. Parsons and B. Wheeler (eds) *Medieval Mothering* (New York/London, 1996), pp25–39.

33 Apparently, mothers were encouraged to have new-born animals sucking their breasts in order to keep the milk flowing. In the Rijksmuseum one can find a relief showing a satyr mother nursing her satyr child, blurring the borders between humans and animals: https://www.rijksmuseum.nl/images/aria/bk/d/bk-nm-2934.d01?aria/maxwidth_590.

34 For references, see B. A. Hanawalt, "The Child in the Middle Ages and the Renaissance", p35. Hanawalt refers to the *ricordienze* that were originally studied by Christiane Klapisch-Zuber.

35 C. Jarzebowski, "Lieben und Herrschen. Fürstenerziehung im späten 15. und 16. Jahrhundert", *Saeculum*, vol 1 (2012): pp39–56.

36 See "Infant Mortality", in *Encyclopedia of Children and Childhood in History and Society*, Paula S. Fass (ed) (New York, 2004), pp474–478; B. A. Hanawalt, "The Child in the Middle Ages and the Renaissance", p35.

37 For a critique of this view, see R. Habermas, "Die Sorge um das Kind. Die Sorge der Frauen und Männer: Mirakelerzählungen im 16. Jahrhundert", in H.-J.Bachorski (ed) *Ordnung und Lust. Bilder von Liebe, Ehe und Sexualität in Spätmittelalter und Früher Neuzeit* (Trier, 1991), pp165–183.

38 B. A. Hanawalt, *Growing up in London: The Experience of Childhood in History* (Oxford, UK, 1993).

39 B. A. Hanawalt, "The Child in the Middle Ages and the Renaissance", p37.

40 Cf. H. Krafft, *Chronik aus dem Dreißigjährigen Krieg*, Hans Medick und Norbert Winnige (eds), http://www.mdsz.thulb.uni-jena.de/krafft/quelle.php.

41 Ibid.

42 Cf. C. Jarzebowski, "Loss and Emotion in Funeral Works on Children in Seventeenth-Century Germany", in L. Tatlock (ed) *Loss in Early Modern History* (Leiden, 2010), pp187–213.

43 B. H. Rosenwein, "Worrying about Emotions in History (Review Essay)", *The American Historical Review*, vol 107 (2002): pp821–845.

44 Deviant understood here in relationship to that which is perceived as the majority or mainstream culture.

45 C. Jarzebowski, "Lieben und Herrschen"; W. G. Ruberg, "Epistolary and Emotional Education: The Letters of an Irish Father to His Daughter, 1747–1752", *Paedagogica Historica*, vol 44 (2008): pp207–218.

46 W. M. Reddy, "Against Constructionism: The Historical Ethnography of Emotions", *Current Anthropology*, vol 38 (1997): pp327–351.

47 W. M. Reddy, *The Navigation of Feeling: A Framework for the History of Emotions* (Cambridge, MA, 2001).

48 B. A. Hanawalt, "The Child in the Middle Ages and the Renaissance", p41.

PART I
Communities

1

MODEL CHILDREN AND PIOUS DESIRE IN EARLY ENLIGHTENMENT PHILANTHROPY

Kelly J. Whitmer

Introduction

Accounts of child prophets and other spiritually gifted children played important roles in communities of Protestants in seventeenth- and eighteenth-century Europe. Among the most popular were accounts describing the "inspired discourses" of the "child prophets of Dauphine"; these were circulated in pamphlets among members of Huguenot communities in the French countryside after the revocation of the Edict of Nantes in 1685.[1] The pamphlets contained depositions and extracts of letters of individuals claiming to have witnessed hundreds of children prophesying in villages scattered along the River Drôme from 1686 to 1689.[2] Huguenots of the Camisard region of France, who took up arms to defend themselves immediately following the Nantes revocation, were also associated with child prophecy as a kind of phenomenon.[3]

English Puritans and other non-conformist religious groups circulated stories of child prophets and other spiritually gifted young people that duly served to document their activities and inspire young people to behave in similar ways. The most popular of these stories included James Janeway's very popular *Conversion, Holy and Exemplary Lives and Joyful Deaths of Several Young Children* (1670) and an octavo tract called *The Wise Virgin* that contained "A wonderfull Narration of the various dispensations of God towards a Childe of eleven years of age."[4] The young prophet was a girl named Martha Hatfield who, during severe bouts of illness for several months in 1652, went into trance-like states and foretold future events.[5] Accounts of Hatfield's activities appeared only a few years after a very popular account of the ministry of Sarah Wight, whose visions were recorded by the Baptist minister Henry Jessey in 1647.[6]

Groups of evangelical Lutherans, often referred to as Pietists, also worked to raise public awareness of the young prophets and other spiritually gifted children in their midst.[7] This chapter focuses on an account of a spiritually gifted child published by

Halle's controversial community of Pietists in 1708. Told from the perspective of his tutor, the account offered a hagiographical account of the life of a ten-year-old boy named Christlieb Leberecht von Exter.[8] That same year (1708), Christlieb's story was translated into English and published in London along with a related account of some "extraordinary pious motions and devout exercises observ'd of late in many children in Silesia" called *Praise out of the Mouth of Babes*.[9] The story of the Silesian children was based on actual reports of a youth movement that erupted during the campaigns of the Great Northern War and was recounted by radical Pietist Johann Wilhelm Petersen (1649–1727) in his 1709 book, *The Power of Children*.[10]

Part of what made the story of Christlieb particularly important was that immediately following its publication, an individual who was critical of Halle Pietism – a man named Johann Heinrich Feustking (1672–1713) – used it as an opportunity to attack the public face of the movement, a prominent professor of theology at the university named August Hermann Francke (1663–1727). Under the pseudonym Hieronymous Bahr, Feustking published a text called *The Highly Perverse Raising up of Children by Pietists* (*Höchstverderbliche Auferziehung der Kinder bey den Pietisten*) in which he lamented Francke's efforts to "canonize" ten-year-old Christlieb, in particular.[11] Christlieb's father, Johann Eberhard Exter, responded immediately with a defence of Francke and his efforts to promote awareness of his son's exemplary behaviour and piety.[12]

The debates surrounding the activities of Halle Pietists that Christlieb's story became associated with resulted largely from a public controversy that Francke had been involved in while teaching at the university in Leipzig.[13] Francke had insulted several prominent theologians there by encouraging theology students not to attend their lectures, to burn their theology textbooks and to meet together in private circles called conventicles to discuss the Bible on their own terms. In 1689, these offended "orthodox Lutheran" professors formally investigated Francke and several others, banned the conventicles and forced him to leave the city. Francke became famous and with the help of his mentor, the Lutheran theologian (and "father of German Pietism") Philipp Jakob Spener (1635–1705), was given a prominent position at Brandenburg-Prussia's new university, the University of Halle, when it was founded in 1695. Francke, who was committed to the reform of the university, and of education more generally, founded what he described as a "universal seminar": a new "city of schools" or suburban educational community that was organized around an orphanage building and staffed almost entirely by theology students. Through Spener and many others, he maintained a close and, for the most part, mutually supportive relationship with courtly circles in Berlin.[14]

Told from the perspective of his tutor, the story of young Christlieb was useful both to Halle Pietists and their critics in ways I will explain. However, my purpose here is not to focus on the significance of Christlieb's story for the history of German Pietism, but rather for the histories of childhood and emotion more generally – in keeping with the aspirations of this volume. The story of Christlieb offers one way of better understanding what were on-going efforts in this period to explain the emotional effects of certain practices of piety (*praxis pietatis*) on the mind – specifically the minds of young men. Pietist theologians, many of whom became involved in some official capacity in Halle's new university, found themselves in an enviable position among other Protestant groups in that they had their very own institutions within which they could explore and elaborate upon these effects. They had created their own unique "emotional community", which I define (following Barbara Rosenwein) as a group "in which people adhere to the same norms of emotional expression and value – or devalue – the same or related emotions."[15] The group of Pietists who had created their own community in Halle by 1700 used Christlieb's story to draw attention to the power of gifted male children – the main targets of their educational programming – and to demonstrate that certain kinds of emotions could affect young boys' abilities to perceive, to remember and to teach. Christlieb's story contained an argument about the meaning and potential of certain kinds of emotions to spark both rational and socially responsible (i.e. philanthropic) behaviour.

In sum, Christlieb's example offered proof that, first, young men could achieve forms of spiritual and emotional perfection; and, second, this perfection involved real forms of emotional intelligence, not spontaneous and potentially dangerous outpourings of emotion that were difficult to direct or appropriate. Christlieb's emotional intelligence – *not* his enthusiasm – was what made him worthy of emulation, even canonization (to borrow Feustking's term). Readers who encountered the story were presented with several recognizable characteristics of Christlieb's advanced affective state. They could then use this description to measure the quality of their own piety, to recognize forms of emotional intelligence they also possessed, and to apply this intelligence to the improvement of their communities in some tangible way. Francke said he hoped the story would make older readers "blush by what is to be seen in children" and also serve as a kind of manual for children so that "their Heart and Affections to God may thereby be raised and mounted up".[16]

Enthusiasm and emotional intelligence

Francke wrote a long introduction to the story of Christlieb's life in which he acknowledged the negative associations or assumptions people often had about young people. There would be many, he wrote, who might not bother to read the account since it related things that "concern only a Child, and are only the product of a Child." He acknowledged that the rest of the world might interpret the things related in the text:

> ... as childish Things and consequently deserving all Contempt and Disregard, as not worthy, that any one should spend his Time and Pains upon Reading them.[17]

In response, he reminded his readers of the Biblical dictum to "become as little Children" (Matt. 18:1–4) and what he described as God's tendency to choose "the weak Things of the world to confound the Things which are Mighty". He also insisted that he had seen Christlieb with his own eyes, establishing himself as a credible witness who stood by the account of his actions as retold by his tutor.[18]

Francke also emphasized Christlieb's age and lack of experience with the world – an empiricist position – as the key attributes that defined him as a child.[19] In his estimation, the combination of these attributes usually meant an undeveloped or simple mind, which made the evidence of Christlieb's emotional and intellectual maturity all the more striking. He explained that most of Christlieb's biography contained "edifying meditations which the Pious Child wrote and left according to the Measure of that Knowledge he had obtained from the Word of God, in such Hours as others of his Age trifle way with Childish Plays".[20] These meditations were especially noteworthy, Francke continued, because they are:

> … not of a Man, who has attained at length to an eminent Knowledge by many Years Labour, Industry and Experience, but of a Child, who thought that the Love of Christ surpass'd and transcended all Knowledge; who wrote in his Simplicity concerning true Christianity, no otherwise than he found it lively in his own Heart.[21]

The contrast between Christlieb's lack of experience in the world and what he actually knew is manifest throughout the story and serves as a way of drawing attention to the relationship between Christlieb's piety and his intelligence. Here was a child who possessed and retained as much knowledge as an experienced and well-travelled man of industry.

It was not just *what* young Christlieb knew, it was also *how* he knew it that mattered most to Francke and his circle. Critics, such as Feusting, associated Halle's community of Pietists with religious enthusiasm (*Schwärmerei*), which was roundly linked to spontaneous and highly emotive expressions of piety through ecstasies, prophetic visions or intensified outpourings of affection, and also anti-social or even irrational behaviour. "One really ought to think about what kind of people Francke and his accomplices in 'the Pietist enthusiasm' are", he wrote.[22] His entire treatise was devoted to providing evidence of their misuse, even abuse, of children in their midst. Among his concerns was how much attention Halle Pietists had paid to Christlieb as a model or example at the expense of directing readers' attention to the Scripture – and the example of Jesus, in particular. Feusting believed Halle Pietists were really ecstatic Calvinists, who were endangering young people through their institutionalization of false and fanatical teachings. He was also concerned about their interests in linking the study of theology to the study of medicine.[23]

Francke and other members of his circle were aware of Feusting's criticisms, particularly the links he and many others were making between Pietism and enthusiasm. More generally, they were aware of a general tendency to associate enthusiasm with the impulsive or disconcerting behaviour often reported in accounts of individual child prophets associated with non-conformist groups. What they also knew was that the best-known child prophets tended to be young girls, not boys, and were readily associated with a long tradition of female mysticism and piety.[24] In his analysis of the Martha Hatfield case, for example, Nigel Smith notes that her story is best understood in conjunction with the "extreme millenarianism" of the English Civil War and the phenomenon of female pietism and prophecy, more generally.[25] Halle Pietists needed a different kind of young role model, a male prophet, whose story they could use to dissuade people of the notion that they were dangerous religious radicals.

Part of the reason this was such a major concern was that Francke remained associated with the phenomenon of female prophecy and the still recent controversies over ecstatic women that had erupted throughout Protestant "middle Germany" in the 1690s.[26] Just as he was getting ready to move to Halle, he had published descriptions of three young maids whom he had met and observed in various states of ecstasy while working in Erfurt.[27] As Judd Stitziel explains:

> … a major issue in the public discussion about the women was their public behavior and the disturbances it caused. The Orthodox were quick to link the disorder to the Pietists as Spener and Francke took up defensive positions, privately worrying about the public and political consequences of their connections to the women as well feeling the need to determine the true nature of the women's inspirations.[28]

Whereas Spener tried completely to disassociate himself from these ecstatic women – worried about his and Francke's reputations – Francke stayed more engaged in the on-going public discussions, mostly insisting that their ecstasies were not necessarily anything to be concerned about.[29] He believed the women really did have special spiritual gifts that they had acquired from God and not the devil. He also linked their unique abilities to what he saw as their overly emotional, passive and irrational nature.[30]

Halle Pietists, it is true, became quite well known for their emphasis on the emotional dimensions of religious experience as the primary means through which the divine inspired and transformed the lives of his followers. However, they were equally aware of how easily signs of spiritual giftedness or divine inspiration could be misinterpreted and used as evidence of the disorderly and even dangerous qualities of their movement. What is more, their educational community in Halle was comprised mainly of young men, not women. How could they continue to emphasize the importance, even the necessity, of cultivating spiritual gifts without simultaneously suggesting their male charges adopt forms and expressions of piety associated with female prophets or the three "ecstatic maids"? Francke and his circle had to find a gifted male child whose example could help them communicate to the boys they educated how very carefully to cultivate certain kinds of pious emotions that were genuine, easily recognized and reinforced by other members of the community and that could be associated with rational and orderly behaviour – not the opposite.

The three ecstatic women Francke wrote about in 1692 were illiterate and during their ecstasies suddenly became able to read and interpret God's Word. Christlieb, on the other hand, did not move in and out of states or trances. He was a child who reportedly knew as much as someone two, three or four times his age – and this ability did not come and go or disappear. Unlike the maids, who could not consistently retain or remember the knowledge they possessed when their ecstasies were finished, Christlieb was entirely transformed. Arends insisted that he had acquired an unparalleled ability to understand, to grasp or to apprehend things because he had allowed "the love of Christ to actuate all his powers and faculties":

> The Gifts of Nature in this Child were easily discovered in his happy Memory, in his clear Understanding, and Readiness of Apprehension in any Matter. But when the Love of Christ began to actuate all his Powers and Faculties and prov'd now the Spring of all their Movements, he began to turn and apply whatsoever he learnt to the true Edification of his Soul.[31]

Arends portrayed "the love of Christ" in this passage as a kind of physical force that had very directly affected the "powers and faculties" of Christlieb's mind – including his ability to think, to remember and to understand.

This way of describing the power of love as a force that could produce unbelievable forms of emotional intelligence *in the mind* was entirely in keeping with conversations about religious experience, emotions and cognition that were on-going in Halle and elsewhere at exactly this moment. A growing number of philosophers, including Gottfried Wilhelm Leibniz, Baruch Spinoza and Nicholas Malebranche, had offered new "theories of emotions" that paid a great deal of attention to the role of love in decision-making and in human affairs, more generally.[32] There were several individuals working at the university in Halle who were very interested in these theories and also quite concerned about the prevalence of mechanistic accounts of human motivations and behaviour (still roundly associated with the writings of René Descartes). They worried that because of the pre-eminence of a "mechanistic world view", fewer people took as seriously the effects of other affective forces, tendencies, desires or passions that were long believed to be located in the body and the soul. Mechanical philosophy had rendered these forces mostly inert and lifeless and elevated the power of the mind. Francke's friend and colleague at the University of Halle, Christian Thomasius (1655–1728), suggested that the solution to the problem was to re-imagine something he called "rational love" as starting with an "honest passion" located in the soul that then affected the mind. "Rational love" – another way of referring to what I am calling "emotional intelligence" – emerged first and foremost as the result of "a desire or passion for a particular end".[33]

For Thomasius – and I think also for many Pietist intellectuals participating in a new "emotional community" – passions or desires were physical forces that interacted with cognition in powerful ways. Especially pious desires (*pia desideria*) had the potential to generate the higher forms or expressions of love detailed in the Christlieb account.[34] But triggering these desires – or, more specifically, ensuring that they were pious and not impious – was easier said than done. When Spener used the phrase *Pia Desideria* in one of his most widely circulated texts, he was communicating his awareness of the strategies other religious reformers and mystics had long been recommending in order to generate pious or holy desires. He knew that the phrase *Pia Desideria* had long been associated with Counter Reformation emblem books and treatises on the arts of meditation, in particular. One of the most popular of these emblem books was Herman Hugo's *Pia Desideria* (1624), in which this Jesuit father popularized what were then widely embraced as the three basic steps of meditation: seeing, reflecting and observing. This text was published at least 42 times in Latin, with several other editions appearing in Spanish, French, English, Dutch, German and Italian by the 1630s.

Meditating on powerful examples became a key part of the *praxis pietatis* advocated by Halle Pietists, which means that for them the story of Christlieb itself might effectively serve as a kind of trigger for generating pious desires – and ultimately higher forms of cognition in young men. Francke wrote and preached extensively about powers of meditation learning to see with the inner eye. He strongly advocated learning how to meditate both on sacred texts and sacred objects, such as models of sacred spaces. Consider, for example, how he described the emotional effect of observing a wooden model of the city of Jerusalem that he sent to the adolescent crown prince of Brandenburg-Prussia in 1720: "the frequent observation of it and the comparison of it with the Holy Scriptures," he wrote, "can yield all kinds of benefits, so that the word of God is approached with more and more desire".[35] Especially in his sermons, Francke attempted to explain the forms of love he hoped to see more of as the result of the triggering of these desires – including what he called *Philotheia*, love of the divine, and a better understanding of God's love of men, or *Philanthropia Dei*.[36]

Christlieb's philanthropy

Through the Christlieb account, Francke and his circle were able to provide easily understandable examples of how pious desires, philotheia and expressions of love and friendship toward others could be linked with reason, order and expressions of male solidarity in the form, especially, of instructing or teaching.[37] They also used the account to assert that they believed in the power of child prophets or spiritually gifted children while simultaneously discouraging people from using their emphasis on triggering people's desires as evidence that they were dangerous promoters of enthusiasm. Christlieb's story stressed that Halle Pietists were in the business of helping young men to realize and make use of their spiritual gifts – or enthusiasm – in such a way as to maximize their potential to help others learn in a serious and consistent way from the knowledge they possessed. It offered them a chance to reimagine the phenomenon of child prophecy and spiritual giftedness more generally according to the needs of their new educational community – and their preference for gifted boys.[38]

Part of how Francke participated in reimagining this phenomenon was by describing the Halle Orphanage as an "orderly medium" that was very much like the Temple of Jerusalem and the "prophet schools started by the prophet Samuel."[39] For help he turned to the prophet schools described by previous generations of Lutheran theologians as spaces exclusively reserved for male prophets in training, who were gifted and esteemed for their intelligence, knowledge and their love of others. In Nürnberg professor of theology and philosophy Johann Michael Dilherr's *Prophet School* (published in 1662), for example, prophets are described as truth-sayers, who receive knowledge directly from God.[40] Old Testament prophets such as Samuel, Isaiah, Jeremiah, Daniel and Ezekiel, he wrote, also reportedly made use of "external signs and ceremonies" and were called Seers or visionaries because they could see things that other people could not.[41] But they were not fanatics, Dilherr explained; rather, they were professors and resident visionaries who "instructed the youth in godliness and the free arts (*freie Künsten*) so that there would always be well educated people who could be useful to both God and the fatherland."[42] Because of the prophet's ability to make his powers visible, individuals looked to these "prophets of the heart" for advice and gathered in their houses or synagogues to partake in their wisdom.[43]

For Halle Pietists, ten-year-old Christlieb was a prophet because he, too, could see and feel things other people could not; more importantly, he could offer extemporaneous discourses that were both "affective and tautological", meaning (for a logician at least) that they were universally true.[44] He read, studied, prayed and meditated constantly but always in conjunction with his receiving of the Holy Spirit, which allowed him to "arrive" at extraordinary levels of "dexterity and discretion" that generated feelings of admiration in others. Arends explained the phenomenon in the following way:

> And since from his younger years he had already treasured up in his heart a good Stock of the Knowledge of God, it was now not difficult for him, to speak for half an Hour together on one and the same Subject, so that he needed to be advertised of the End. In these ex-temporaneous Discourses there did not appear either Want of Judgment or Tautology or Affectation. He spoke so fluently, that to every one's Admiration he would propose and explain without any Hesitation a text with Scriptural and Theological Expressions and with proper Similitudes. He was never tired of Reading, Praying, Studying and Meditating; as the Means by which, under the Blessing of God and the gracious Operation of his Holy Spirit, he arrived to that extraordinary Dexterity and Discretion.[45]

Christlieb's giftedness, or virtuosity, seemed to reside in his heightened ability to perform exegesis, the intensive, highly critical and technical readings of sacred texts the Halle Pietist theologians came to be known for. More importantly, he made people admire him and want to be around him – they did not fear him or feel they had to puzzle over his statements, which were clear, reasonable and logically sound.

Arends emphasized that the boy had an especially profound effect on his servants and on other children, who became enamoured and inspired in his presence. More importantly, he was very careful about how he spent his time, preferring only to use it to engage in socially responsible or philanthropic activities. He went to school but "never cared for sport or other childish recreations". Instead, during his "leisure hours", Arends wrote:

> ... he was frequently found with the Servants of the House, awakening and animating them through the Word of God and Prayer. ... He made himself so

entirely beloved through his engaging and hearty expressions that they ...
would with a hearty desire, hear, and receive from him the word of God; and
often joined with him in prayer and devotion. Hereby this child accustomed
the domesticks to pouring out themselves and their hearts before God.[46]

Arends also reported that Christlieb regularly engaged in "ardent discourse" with his
eleven-year-old sister, whom he entreated to pray with him while she observed the
"inward state of his soul". Of "his own free motion", he wrote a treatise of 25 chapters
called *True Christianity* (a very direct reference to Francke and the orphanage) as well as
several hymns, which were appended to the story for readers to apply in their own
spiritual praxis. Arends's account of Christlieb's life exhorted readers to allow themselves to feel Christlieb's message and to take it as a "strengthening encouragement,
the better to hold out here in Christian warfare under so many anxieties, calamities,
persecutions and afflictions".[47]

Conclusion

The example of ten-year-old Christlieb was supposed to serve as a kind of tonic,
which could strengthen, fortify or at the very least improve the quality of a reader's
inner life, including their intelligence. That said, his story was mainly – or at least
initially – intended to be consumed by the young men associated with Halle's Pietist
community, a community that was in the process of creating its own unique "norms
of emotional expression and value".[48] Francke and his circle could not recommend
that their new charges, some of whom were the sons of gentry or noblemen, emulate
the examples of the ecstatic female prophets who had initially been associated with
Francke in the 1690s. They had to create a new kind of model who could offer
young men a mainstream and masculine archetype of the learned, emotionally intelligent or wise, youthful prophet. This model or archetype better corresponded with
the new identities Francke and his followers had assumed in Halle as academicians
and professors, deeply concerned with the epistemological issues of their day and, at
the practical level, with how to encourage more people to engage in philanthropic or
socially responsible behaviour.

For the communities of benefactors, parents, teachers and professors who
supported and participated in the Halle Pietist community, spiritually gifted male
children were revered not for their innocence or humility, but for their strength and
their "rational love" – that is, their emotional intelligence. With the help of the
Christlieb account, they could turn the cultivation of pious desires into something
normative and reasonable – something that promised to uphold and improve the
social order rather than to undermine it.

Notes

1 G. Cosmos, *Huguenot Prophecy and Clandestine Worship in the Eighteenth Century: The
Sacred Theatre of the Cevennes* (London, 2005), pp28, 155.

2 Ibid, p28.

3 W. R. Ward writes: "In the Camisard rebellion schools of child prophets were produced who were attached to the Protestant commandos and prophesied as to the killing of prisoners and other matters." In W. R. Ward, *The Protestant Evangelical Awakening* (Cambridge, UK, 1992), p43; see also H. Schwartz, *The French Prophets: the History of a Millenarian Group in Eighteenth Century England* (Berkeley, CA, 1980).

4 J. Fisher, *The Wise Virgin, or A wonderfull Narration of the various dispensations of God towards a Childe of eleven years of age* (London, 1653); J. Janeway, *A Token for Children; Being an Exact Account of the Conversion, Holy and Exemplary Lives and Joyful Deaths of Several Young Children* (London, 1670).

5 N. Smith, "A Child Prophet: Martha Hatfield as The Wise Virgin", in G. Avery and J. Briggs (eds) *Children and Their Books: A Celebration of the Work of Iona and Peter Opie* (Oxford, UK, 1989), pp79–94; B. R. Dailey, "The Visitation of Sarah Wight: Holy Carnival and the Revolution of the Saints in Civil War London," *Church History*, vol 55 (1986): pp438–453.

6 M. Mascuch, "The Godly Child's 'Power and Evidence' in the Word: Orality and Literacy in the Ministry of Sarah Wight", in A. Immel and M. Witmore (eds) *Childhood and Children's Books in Early Modern Europe, 1550–1800* (New York, 2006), pp103–126.

7 For Pietism as part of a general movement of Protestant evangelical awakening, see W. R. Ward (1992) and C. Lindberg, *The Pietist Theologians: An Introduction to Theology in the Seventeenth and Eighteenth Centuries* (Oxford, UK, 2005). For an introduction to debates around defining Pietism broadly or narrowly (i.e. as an evangelical Lutheran movement), see J. Strom, "Problems and Promises of Pietism Research," *Church History*, vol 71 (2002): esp. pp537–538. For an introduction to radical Pietism in Germany, see H. Schneider, *German Radical Pietism*, translated by G. T. MacDonald (Lanham, 2007). For Pietists' contributions to an emerging "public sphere," see J. Van Horn Melton, "Pietism and the Public Sphere in Eighteenth-Century Germany", in J. Bradley and D. Van Kley (eds) *Religion, Politics and Enlightened Europe* (Notre Dame, 2001).

8 W. E. Arends, *Eines zehen-jährigen Knabens Christlieb Leberecht von Exter, aus Zerbst, Christlich geführter Lebens-Lauff: Nebst dessen angefangenen Tractätlein vom Wahren Christenthum, ingleichen seine Briefe und Lieder, &c.* (Halle, 1708).

9 W. E. Arends, *Christlieb Leberecht von Exter of Zerbst … Account of his life compiled by his Tutor. The remaining part of this Book contains the edifying Mediations, which the Pious Child wrote and left according to the Measure of that Knowledge he had obtained from the Word of God in such Hours as others of his Age trifle away with Childish Plays: whereto are likewise adjoined his Christian letters, hymns and prayers* (London, 1708); Anonymous, *Praise out of the mouth of babes: or, a particular account of some extraordinary pious motions and devout exercises, observ'd of late in many children in Silesia*, translated by A. W. Böhme (London, 1708).

10 See J. W. Petersen, *Die Macht der Kinder in der letzten Zeit: auf Veranlassung der kleinen Prediger, oder der betenden Kinder in Schlesien* (Frankfurt/Leipzig, 1709) and Ward (1992), p43: "Early in 1708 … children began to hold camp-meetings like those which the Swedish troops had held, praying all day for the restoration of Protestant schools and churches."

11 H. Bahr, *Höchstverderbliche Auferziehung der Kinder bey den Pietisten, durch Gelegenheit des von dem hällische Professore M. August Herrmann Francken canonisirten zehen-jährigen Kindes Christlieb Leberecht Exters* (S. I., 1709). Feusting was certainly not the first person to criticize Pietist approaches to early childhood education and their interest in child prophets. For more criticism see Casparis Sagittarius, *Untheologische und abgeschmackte Lehrsätze von Pietismo* (S. I., 1691).

12 J. E. Exter, *Kurtze Nachricht was von der unter dem Nahmen Hieronymi Bahr herumgeflogenen Charteque zu halten so derselbe wider das von meinem seeligen Kinde Christlieb Leberecht geschriebene und von … Herrn Prof. Avgvst. Herman. Francken zu Halle edirte Büchlein aus boßhafftigem und vergälleten Gemüthe ausgeschüttet* (Zerbst, 1709).

13 For more, see M. Gierl, *Pietismus und Aufklärung. Theologische Polemik und die Kommuni-kationsreform der Wissenschaft am Ende des 17.Jahrhunderts* (Göttingen, 1997).

14 There is a vast literature on Halle Pietists' special relationship to the Prussian state. Key works include C. Hinrichs, *Preussentum und Pietismus. Der Pietismus in Brandenburg-Preußen als religiös-soziale Reformbewegung* (Göttingen, 1971); J. Van Horn Melton, *Absolutism and the Eighteenth-Century Origins of Compulsory Schooling in Prussia and Austria* (Cambridge, UK, 1988); C. Clark, *The Iron Kingdom: the Rise and Downfall of Prussia, 1600–1947* (Cambridge, MA, 2007); and B. Marschke, *Absolutely Pietist: Patronage, Factionalism and State-Building in the Early Eighteenth-Century Army Chaplaincy* (Tübingen, 2005). For more on the theology students as teachers, see A. La Vopa, *Grace, Talent, Merit: Poor Students, Clerical Careers and Professional Ideology in Eighteenth-Century Germany* (Cambridge, UK, 1988).

15 B. Rosenwein, *Emotional Communities in the Early Middle Ages* (Ithaca, NY, 2006), p2.

16 Rather than translating the original German version of Christlieb's story, I have derived most quotations from the English edition. See A. H. Francke's "Dedication", in W. Arends, *Christlieb Leberecht von Exter of Zerbst* (London, 1708): "But I would not here be misunderstood, as if this Writing did therefore afford no manner of Edification for old and adult People. Before it was Printed, many were edified already from the Manuscript, insomuch that even Teachers confess'd their being specially touched by the reading of it. It is therefore not doubted, since it is gone forth in Print and laid open to every one's Eye; the number of such, even among Adult Persons, will be encreas'd, as many freely own the good Edification that have from thence received."

17 Ibid.

18 Ibid, "I have been very far from thinking it a Shame, or Disgrace, to let it go abroad under my Name", Francke continued. "For if the Custom of the World had here pre-vail'd, her rash and inconsiderate Judgment would doubtless have been this: That because we have nothing better, we are therefore serving up such Childish things."

19 Halle Pietists adapted empiricist approaches to their educational programming in innovative ways, most famously through their use of real objects (or *Realien*) in lessons. See J. Jacobi, "Anthropologie und Pädagogik: Empirische Aspekte der Erziehung im Halleschen Waisenhaus (1695–1769)", in idem (ed) *Zwischen christlicher Tradition und Aufbruch in die Moderne: Das Hallesche Waisenhaus im bildungsgeschichtlichen Kontext* (Tübingen, 2007), pp59–74; T. Müller-Bahlke, "Der Realienunterricht in den Schulen August Hermann Francke", in *Schulen Machen Geschichte: 300 Jahre Erziehung in den Franckeschen Stiftungen zu Halle* (Halle, 1997), pp43–65.

20 A. H. Francke's "Dedication", in W. Arends, *Christlieb Leberecht von Exter of Zerbst* (London, 1708).

21 W. Arends, *Eines zehen-jährigen Knabens Christlieb Leberecht von Exter*, p5. The German version of the above cited passage reads: "Denn es ist der Lebens-Lauff nicht eines Grossen in der Welt, sondern eines Kindes, und zwar eines solchen, welches nicht wegen einiges weltlichen und äusserlichen Vorzuges, sondern wegen seiner Gottseligkeit gerühmet wird. So sind es auch Meditationes nicht eines Mannes, der durch vieler Jahre Fleiß, Arbeit und Erfahrung endlich zu einer sonderbaren Wissenschafft gelanget, sondern eines Kindes, welches Christum lieb zu haben für viel besser gehalten als alles Wissen, welches in seiner Einfalt vom Wahren Christentum so geschrieben, wie es ihm ums Herz gewesen … ."

22 H. Bahr, *Höchstverderbliche Auferziehung der Kinder* (1709), p21: "Mann soll denken, was doch Franck und sine Mitarbeiter in der Pietistischen Schwermerey für treffliche Leute seyn vor jenen."

23 Ibid, p23: "Worüberman sich eben nicht groß zu verwundern hat, indem die Pietisten, die doch immer von Vereinigung mit den Reformirten schwatzen, auch hierinnen dem Exempel der Calvinisten nachfolgen, welche sich in Theologischen Dingen der Ärzte und Medicorum gebrauchten." For more on Halle Pietists' efforts to develop medical institutions and a trade in pharmaceuticals, see the work of R. Wilson, esp. *Pious Traders in Medicine: A German pharmaceutical network in eighteenth-century North America* (University Park, PA, 2000).

24 E. Petroff, *Body and Soul: Essays on Medieval Women and Mysticism* (Oxford, UK, 1990); S A. Brown (ed) *Women, Gender and Radical Religion in Early Modern Europe* (Leiden, 2007).

25 N. Smith, "A Child Prophet", p80; D. L. Parish, "The Power of Female Pietism: Women as Spiritual Authorities and Religious Role Models in Seventeenth-Century England", *Journal of Religious History*, vol 17 (1992): pp33–46.

26 J. Stitziel, "God, the Devil, Medicine, and the Word: A Controversy over Ecstatic Women in Protestant Middle Germany, 1691–93", *Central European History*, vol 29 (1996): pp309–337.

27 A. H. Francke, *Eigentliche Nachricht von Dreyen Begeisterten Maegden* (S. I., 1692).

28 J. Stitziel, "God, the Devil, Medicine, and the Word", p317.

29 Ibid, p322.

30 Ibid, p326.

31 W. E. Arends, *Eines zehen-jährigen Knabens Christlieb Leberecht von Exter*, pp5–6.

32 G. Boros, H. De Dijn and M. Moors (eds) *The Concept of Love in 17th and 18th Century Philosophy* (Leuven, 2007), pp6–7. "According to the seventeenth century theories, it is precisely through the emotions, and especially love, that the explicitly or implicitly made assumptions concerning basic values enter the field of both our everyday concerns and the principally value-free scientific-philosophical investigation. Love is what directs the steps of the Spinozean philosopher to real wisdom; love of a God who creates and maintains order and harmony in the world is the cornerstone of the philosophy of Malebranche and Leibniz."

33 For more on Thomasius's ideas about "rational love", see T. Ahnert, *Religion and the Origins of the German Enlightenment: Faith and the Reform of Learning in the Thought of Christian Thomasius* (Rochester, MN, 2006), p30.

34 The phrase *Pia Desideria* was associated with Pietism during this period because Spener used it as the title of a widely read essay he wrote as an introduction to the sermons of Johann Arndt. The essay was called "Pia Desideria or Heartfelt Desires for an Improvement of the True Evangelical Church Pleasing to God" (Frankfurt, 1675).

35 Quoted in D. G. Kramer, *August Hermann Francke: Ein Lebensbild*, Part II, first edition, 1880 (Hildesheim, 2004), pp326–327.

36 A. H. Francke, *Schriftmäßige Betrachtung von Gnade und Wahrheit: ... : Dem in dieser neuen Edition noch beygefüget worden die vorhin besonders gedruckte Betrachtung von der Philanthropia Dei oder Liebe Gottes gegen die Menschen* (Halle, 1705); idem, *Philotheïa: Oder die Liebe zu Gott* (Halle, 1706, 1723). Reprinted in D. G. Kramer, *A. H. Francke's Paedagogische Schriften* (Langesalza, 1876), pp169–180.

37 L. Gowing, M. Hunter and M. Rubin, *Love, Friendship and Faith in Europe, 1300–1800* (Basingstoke, UK, 2005); A. Bray, *The Friend* (Chicago, IL, 2003).

38 S. Brockerhoff, "Begabtenförderung bei August Hermann Francke am Beispiel der Lateinischen Schule", in J. Jacobi (ed) *Zwischen christlicher Tradition und Aufbruch in die Moderne: Das Hallesche Waisenhaus im bildungsgeschichtlichen Kontext* (Tübingen, 2007), pp87–110.

39 A. H. Francke, *Project zu einem Seminario Universali oder Anlegung eines Pflanz-Gartens ...* [1701] (Halle, 1881), p21.

40 J. M. Dilherr, *Propheten Schul. Das ist Christliche Anweisung zu Gottseliger Betrachtung des Lebens und der Lehre heiliger Propheten Altes Testaments; derer Bildnussen, in schönen Kupferstichen mit sind beygefüget. Allerlei Stands Personen erbaulich zu lesen* (Nürnberg, 1662), pp2–3. See F. van Ingen, "Johann Michael Dilherr (1604–69)", in U. Sträter (ed) *Orthodoxie und Poesie* (Leipzig, 2004), pp47–48.

41 J. M. Dilherr, *Propheten Schul*, p4.

42 Ibid, p4: "Es ist wissens wohl werth, dass in den Alten Testament, die Priester und öffentliche Lehrer der Kirchen Gottes auch Professores gewesen. Denn die Synagogen wahren nicht allein Kirchen und öffentliche Gotteshäuser; in welchen man zu bethen und die Predigen pflegte anzuhören: sondern man hatte auch Auditoria, oder solcher Gemächer und Losamter dabei in welchen dei Priester Schule hielten und die Jugend in der Gottesfurch und freien Künsten unterrichteten: Damit immer mögten Leute erzogen werden; welche Gott dem Herrn und dem gemeinen Vatterland könnten nützlich seyn."

43 Ibid, p201.
44 Tautology can also imply excessive wordiness or redundancy; but I think that here it is meant to connote Christlieb's astounding abilities to offer statements that were true in every possible interpretative setting in which they were placed.
45 W. E. Arends, *Eines zehen-jährigen Knabens Christlieb Leberecht von Exter*, pp5–6.
46 Ibid, pp6–7.
47 Ibid, pp6–7.
48 B. Rosenwein, "Emotional Communities", p2.

2

"FOR THE PLEASURE OF BABIES"

Children and emotions in early modern Jewish communities

Tali Berner

> Children are joy,
> children are a blessing.
> And you have a heart of gold
> It is written in the Bible
> Perhaps in the *Talmud*
> Go ask the rabbi![1]

This popular Israeli song was written as a satire criticizing the Israeli pro-natal policy in the early years of the state. Nevertheless, while the writer intended to ridicule the ancient foundation of the popular notion that "children are [a source of] joy", it *is*, indeed, grounded in Jewish texts, if not in the Bible then in rabbinical writings from late antiquity, continuing well into the Middle Ages and the Early Modern Period.

In this chapter I will discuss the issue of children and joy on two levels: first, children as a source of joy; and, second, the importance of ensuring children's pleasure and joy, especially on festive occasions. I will argue that children appear in a large variety of texts and in different situations as a source of joy to their parents and communities and that the pleasure that people extract from children competes with other activities and distracts them from fulfilling religious obligations. In the second part, I will demonstrate how, in order to maintain children's pleasure and adults' pleasure from children, Jewish laws and customs have been adapted to popular norms and behaviours and to the needs and feelings of both adults and children.

Terminology and definitions

This chapter is concerned with positive emotions, more precisely with joy (*simhah*), and the verb from which it is derived: "to rejoice" (*sameah*). Both are also often translated as "happiness", "content", "gladness" and "pleasure". In this chapter I will use the English nouns "joy" and "pleasure" and the verb "to rejoice" to replace the Hebrew. "Happy" and "happiness", often used in colloquial language as a translation of *simḥah*, should really be translated as *'osher*.

The English word "joy" as well as the Hebrew equivalent *simḥah* can mean both joy in a religious, transcendent sense and in a human, everyday sense.[2] The double meaning of this term will prove to be important in this chapter, as both types of joy derive from each other and complement one another.

The term used for children in most sources in this chapter is babies (*tinoqot*), which, in traditional Jewish texts, can also mean "children", and even "adolescents" or "unmarried young adults", depending upon the context.[3] Nevertheless, the context implies that, in most cases, the sources refer to young children of approximately 3 to 13 years old, children who are under the age of religious maturity (12 for girls and 13 for boys). Although most texts refer to children in the male grammatical form, one can assume that, in most cases, they refer to girls as well.

Most of the texts discussed in this chapter are either Jewish legal writings (*Halakha*) or books of customs (*Minhag*) documenting local Jewish traditions and daily behaviours that assumed obligatory status. While legal codices and, to some extent, books of customs are usually regarded as prescriptive and not descriptive, we shall see that many of the sources used in this chapter reflect daily behaviours or respond to them and, therefore, can be used to understand and analyse human interactions.

The use of these sources is not accidental: legal sources happen to be the prime media for discussing emotions and emotion-related issues in medieval and early modern Jewish communities in Central Europe. Surprisingly, legal sources provide a richer and larger discussion of emotions than other sources, such as autobiographical documents or books of moral and daily conduct.

This makes this chapter a case study in the relations between Jewish traditions and emotions. As these texts are mostly concerned with the public and communal sphere, rather than personal behaviour, they also enable us to examine the discussion of emotions in the public realm. The nature of the text, therefore, gives us a unique view into the discussion of children and emotions in the pre-modern world, both in the Jewish context and the European context, in general.[4]

The sources used in this chapter, excluding biblical and rabbinic sources from late antiquity, which provide a background for the discussion, range from the High Middle Ages to the end of the Early Modern Period (circa 1100–1750 CE). The geographical area is what in Jewish historiography is called "Ashkenaz", or the "Ashkenazic communities", Jews living in German-speaking lands in Western and Central Europe.[5] This wide timeframe and geographical area allows us to collect a critical mass of sources.

Joy and pleasure in Jewish festivals

That Jews were interested in happiness may appear odd to most people: according to conventional thought, its pursuit hardly seems like one of the major tenets of our religion.[6]

With these words, Tirosh-Samuelson opens her discussion on happiness in Jewish traditions. She reflects on the common view that Jews have little to do with positive emotions or with happy, joyful and pleasing events, in general. This misconception, she argues, is based on a misunderstanding of the word "happiness", on the view of the Jewish religion as based on awareness of human sin, reward and punishment, and on how Jewish history is usually depicted. This last reason, I would like to argue, is the prime cause of this misconception. The tradition of "the lachrymose conception of Jewish history", a term coined by Salo Baron,[7] still looms large in the image of Jewish history, and especially in that of medieval and early modern Ashkenaz.

Only in recent years have scholars of Jewish studies and Jewish history, in particular, turned their attention to positive emotions and the joyous side of Jewish life in the past. Tirosh-Samuelson's work on happiness, as well as the publication of a volume on love in Jewish tradition and the work of Anderson on joy, mark the change in this field.[8]

In medieval and early modern history, the works of Weinstein on weddings and studies of the synagogue initiation ritual[9] have proved that the Jews knew how to celebrate, rejoice and maybe even be happy. Indeed, we shall see that being joyful and ensuring pleasure were important values, if not on a daily basis, at least on special occasions.

The point of departure for the discussion on joy in Jewish tradition is often the commandment for the description of the holiday of Tabernacles:

> Rejoice during your festival, you and your son and your daughter, your male and female slaves, as well as the Levites, the strangers, the orphans, and the widows resident in your towns. Seven days you shall keep the festival to the Lord your God ... and you shall surely celebrate.
>
> *(Deuteronomy 16: 14–15)*

This quotation is useful in many ways. First, it can be employed to understand the meaning and context of the verb "to rejoice" (*sameaḥ*) and the noun derived from it: joy (*simḥah*). These terms appear 16 times in the Pentateuch. In most cases, as in this quote, it is strongly connected to the celebration of festivals and rejoicing before God.[10] However, it also appears in the context of human relationships. Like this quote, most of the biblical quotations refer to "rejoice before the Lord" in the Temple or the bringing of sacrifices. After the destruction of the Second Temple in 70 CE, this concept had to be modified, and it was transformed into the celebration of the holiday itself, as manifested in the rabbinic idiom of the "joy of the feast day".[11] This chapter, therefore, is concerned with two specific contexts of rejoicing: one is joy and pleasure in the human, social context. The second is in the context of the commandment to rejoice on festive days.

This commandment and the question of how one can be commanded to rejoice was the subject both of rabbinic enquiry and scholarly research.[12] The quote above teaches us that rejoicing is not a spontaneous act but, rather, a commandment. As a commandment, it cannot be left to the random, subjective understanding or state of mind of the individual. Indeed, in his study of the role of joy in rabbinic literature, Anderson argues that "the experience of 'joy' is often not an amorphous subjective feeling but rather a set of discrete behaviors which were thought to create the proper sentiment or feeling".[13] Anderson goes on to show that rabbis associated joy with the performance of specific acts, such as eating and drinking, engaging in sexual intercourse, festive attire, anointing with oil and the study of the *Torah*. These prescribed acts demonstrate, Anderson argues, the way in which joy can be commanded and performed in a non-spontaneous way.[14] As he shows, the ultimate way of rejoicing became, in late antiquity, the learning of the *Torah*.

Rejoicing in the world of commandments and learning were important elements in Jewish mystical thought. Fishbane points to the extensive discussion of the role of joy in divine worship in sixteenth-century Jewish discourse, mostly in mystical and Kabalistic literature.[15] He also discusses the liturgical power of joy, as described in the book of *Zohar*. However, people still found pleasure in other activities and drew pleasure from their social contacts. To this meaning, along with the role of children as being a source of joy on holidays, as well as other occasions, we shall dedicate the first part of this chapter.

The quote from Deuteronomy is telling in another sense: the joy of holidays should include everybody, and the text is careful to mention all groups of society, including children. How is this commandment translated into daily life and to children, in particular? While some scholarly attention was given to rejoicing in learning and mystical acts, very little attention, if any, was given to the daily acts that created the sense of joy – those acts of eating, drinking, sex and others that Anderson mentions. No attention is given to the ways in which children are included in this commandment either. This will be the focal point of the second part of the chapter.

Children as a source of joy

> When one's heart is in sorrow on the Sabbath, he should speak to a youngster and thus remove the sorrow from his heart.[16]

A conversation with a child – this is the cure that the author of *Sefer Hasidim* prescribes for a "heart in sorrow." The presence of children is an antidote to grief, pain and sorrow but also, in the eyes of the writer, who reflects the customs of the extremely pious groups of medieval Ashkenaz, one of the great dangers that stand in the way of a man who wishes to dedicate all his time to the study of the *Torah*:

> Playing with children and women, laughing with friends, pleasure walking and the re-visiting of idle things, all these cause a neglect of *Torah* study ... and this same love (of *Torah* study) prevents a man from neglecting it for vanities, for the amusing of his children and the love of watching women, and for idle talk, and for pleasure walking.[17]

The pious man is instructed to refrain from spending time with his children, playing and amusing himself with them. The man who is able to dedicate himself to the study of the *Torah* and keep himself from spending time with his children and drawing pleasure from playing with them will be rewarded "considerably" (in the world to come).[18] Children, therefore, are depicted as one of the main, if not the prime, sources of joy and of distraction from other activities. Playing with children is a temptation at the same level as looking at women, which the pious should avoid.

However, most medieval and early modern Ashkenazic Jews were not pious in this sense and allowed themselves to enjoy the presence of their children. In this section, I will refer to various sources that represent laws and customs that reflect the fact that children bring much joy and pleasure to those surrounding them.

The fact that children are a source of joy appears in the most prominent way in the instruction not to bring children to the house of the mourner and the instruction to the mourner to refrain from playing with children. This instruction first appears in *Tractate Smaḥot*, a source dated to the ninth century CE that deals with death and mourning.[19] It later appears in a variety of medieval and early modern sources:

> One [a mourner] should not hold a baby, lest this cause light-heartedness on his part; likewise one should not enter a house of happiness, such as the house of a groom or a house of feasting, etc.[20]

Holding a baby appears, in the source, to be one of the prime activities that cause joy and pleasure to a person. Holding a child has the potential to bring a person to a state of laughter or joy (*shoq*) – while the mourner is forbidden to rejoice during the period of the *Shivah* (seven days of ritual mourning) and, to a certain extent, for the next 30 days and a full year after the death of a close relative.[21]

The sources from *Sefer Hasidim*, as well as those dealing with the mourner, list playing with children, among other activities and interactions that amuse people and give them joy. The mourners, as well as the pious man who wishes to dedicate his life to study, should refrain from the company of children, but for different reasons, of course. The pious, according to the author of *Sefer Hasidim*, should replace the daily, earthly joys with the joy derived from learning. The mourner, on the other hand, should refrain from the mundane activities associated with joy. In both cases, we see that playing with children is among those mundane, commonplace activities. The case of the mourner is important: as Anderson demonstrated, rabbinic literature juxtaposes joy and mourning and constructs it such that the acts that mark joy are those that are forbidden for the mourner.[22] Therefore, the inclusion of children in this list emphasizes their prominent role as a source of joy.

More about the joy that children can potentially create appears again in rituals of mourning. This time, the *Talmud* discusses the rituals of mourning the death of children:

> And what status do they have with regard to eulogizing them? Rabbi Meir says in the name of Rabbi Yishmael: in the case of the deceased child of the poor, eulogies are delivered for three year olds and those older; in the case of the wealthy, eulogies are delivered for the five year olds and those older. Rabbi

Yheuda says in [Rabbi Yishmael's] name: in the case of the poor, eulogies are offered for five years and those older; in the case of the wealthy, for six year olds. And the children of the elderly are like the children of the poor in this regard.[23]

The burial customs for children, and especially those for babies, were different from those for adults; yet, as the age of the deceased increased, more of the burial rituals of adults applied.[24] This text discusses the question of the age at which one says a eulogy over children. Both sages make a distinction between the children of the rich and the children of the poor (and the second adds the elderly). The medieval commentator Rashi explains this difference in the fact that children are the only source of joy for the poor, so the poor grieve more the deaths of their children.[25] Here again, medieval and early modern sources create this identification between children and joy, seeing children as a source of pleasure, or at least a potential source of joy, for their parents.

Children were not considered a source of joy for their parents alone, however, and the joy and pleasure they create can be also found in more positive contexts. They created joy and gave pleasure to the community as a whole:

> And the Mahari Segal [Rabbi Yaacov ben Moshe Mulin] said that it was beyond wonderment in his eyes from whence stemmed the bad habit of bringing babies to the synagogue to hear the blowing of the *shofar*; when it came to bringing them for the reading of the *Megillah* it was for the sake of joy.[26]

This source, from the custom book of Rabbi Yaacov ben Moshe Mulin (circa 1360–1427), refers to the practice of bringing children to the synagogue on various occasions. The writer concedes to those who bring children on the holiday of *Purim*, due to the joyful character of the day, but he cannot tolerate the presence of children on more serious occasions. Many other sources support the observation of the writer: when children were present in the synagogue, they not only created a disturbance among the adults, but also pleased and amused them. They distracted people from the liturgy, as they preferred playing with the children over participating in the service:

> When people bring small children who are younger than three and have not yet reached the age of education to synagogue, and who have no speech in their mouths or words on their tongues, and play with them in the synagogue between the prayer of *Baruch She'amar* and the *She'moneh Esreh*, or during the cantor's repetition of the *She'moneh Esreh*, and by this they cause the congregation to sin as well, since they joke around, whistle and nod at the children, thereby pausing in their prayer and neglecting it.[27]

Another indication of the fact that children were a source of joy was their prominent role in holidays and occasions that were associated with joy, especially on the holidays of *Purim* and the holiday of Rejoicing in the *Torah* (*Simchat Torah*). On these occasions, not only were children welcomed into the synagogue but they were also given roles: on both holidays, for example, girls danced in the synagogue. On *Simchat Torah*, boys were called to the *Torah*, an honour usually reserved for adult men only. Children of both sexes were given candy and sweets that were thrown to them in the street to increase their pleasure.[28]

Children, therefore, appear in a variety of sources and cases as a source of joy. One who is not allowed to rejoice and those who wish to refrain from earthly pleasures should avoid the company of children. On the other hand, when one wishes to be joyful or when the joy is great, children appear as the prime vehicle for creating joy and pleasure.

Before concluding this section, I would like to address the relationship between parents and children and the specific pleasure parents and children take from spending time together. Here, too, legal sources prove to be an excellent source for learning about this issue. The legal (*halakhic*) issue discussed here is the prohibition of carrying items, including babies who cannot walk, from the private space to the public space and back on a holiday:

> And [playing ball on the holiday, discussed below] it is not similar to carrying a child, as his father takes joy in him, and his missing of his son is also part of his *Yom Tov* [holiday] joy, that he shouldn't be saddened for his son. And the Rosh [Rabbi Asher Ben Yehiel, 1250–1327] wrote verbatim: that if he needs to go to synagogue, or take a pleasure walk on *Yom Tov*, and cannot leave his small child alone at home, he can carry him with him. But nevertheless it seems that the dispensation is not only in the case where he cannot leave the small child, etc., but even in the case where he can leave him with his mother, even then he is allowed to carry him, as I explained.[29]

And in the customs book of the Maharil, Jacob ben Moses Mulin (1360–1427):

> Indeed, taking a baby for a walk on a holiday is permitted since one is supposed to rejoice on these days, and otherwise one would be like a prisoner in his home and there would be no joy.[30]

These two sources make a legal exception for the sake of family happiness and the pleasure of both father and child. Rejoicing on a holiday is an important value, but what is emphasized here is rejoicing with one's family and celebrating the holiday in a familial setting. The sources concentrate mostly on the pleasure of the father, yet the joy of children was not ignored. Special arrangements and rulings were made for them, as we shall see in the next section.

Children and the right to be joyful

Having discussed the role or position of children as a source of joy and pleasure, we shall now turn to the pleasure and joy of the children themselves. The point of departure for our discussion is, again, the commandment in Deuteronomy and the demand that all members of the household should rejoice on festival days. How should one ensure that? This issue is first discussed in the *Babylonian Talmud*. The context of the discussion is engaging children in holiday rituals:

> All are obligated in the *mitzvah* of drinking these four cups[31] – men, women and children. Rabbi Yehuda said: but what purpose is there for children to drink wine? Rather, we distribute to them parched grain and walnuts on *Pesach* [Passover] eve, so that they should not fall asleep and they should ask questions ... the rabbis taught in the *Baraita*: a person is obligated to gladden his children and members of his household on the festivals, as it is stated: "and you shall rejoice on your festival – you, your son, your daughter, your slave etc." With what does one gladden them? With wine! Rabbi Yehuda says: men with what is suitable for them, and women with what is suitable for them. Men with what is suitable for them – with wine, and with what does one gladden women? Rav Yosef taught a *Baraita*: in Babylonia one gladdens them by providing them with colored garments, and in the land of Israel with pressed linen garments.[32]

The text begins with a discussion of how to engage children in holiday celebrations and how to teach them the values and the history of the festival. The sages acknowledge that drinking wine is not suitable for children, yet still wish to encourage them to participate in the main ritual of the evening, the *Passover Seder* that includes the telling of the historical story of the Exodus from Egypt. Therefore, they replace the wine with parched grain and walnuts, which were perceived as treats for children. The *Talmud* goes on to offer other acts that encourage children to ask questions, participate in and think about the meaning of the day; but we are mostly concerned with the second part of the discussion: what helps people rejoice on the holiday? The sages go on to discuss how one should please the members of his household on the holiday. We should note that they see it as the obligation of the head of the household to ensure that everybody is enjoying and celebrating the holiday, and, most importantly, they assume that each group celebrates in different ways and that special treatment should be given to each one of them. This is the guideline that connects the two discussions – the understanding that children deserve special treatment on the holiday – both in the way the message is carried out to them and in the ways to enjoy and celebrate the holiday.

Women can be pleased by clothes. But what about children? The source here does not specify how one should please his children. A variety of sources refer to customs and rituals that children performed on different holidays. I will give a few examples here before analysing the common themes and ideas.

On *Hoshana Rabbah*, the last day of the holiday of Tabernacles, it was customary to beat the willow branches that were used during the holiday:

> And since the *mitzvah* is to beat the *aravah* [a leafy branch of the willow tree] and there is disagreement on how to fulfill it – there are those who say that

shaking it is sufficient, and there are those who say that one must hit it on the floor, therefore we do both together – we shake the *aravah*, and after we finish saying the *hoshanot* [poetical prayers], we hit the ground with it five times, and that is enough. And the custom of hitting the ground until all of the leaves of the *aravah* fall out is a children's custom, to cause joy.[33]

Here we have an example of a ritual that the entire community (or at least the adult men) take part in. The text states that the adults should not overdo the hitting: five times is enough. However, children can hit the branches until all the leaves fall off, as it gives them joy. There is no religious reason for allowing children to behave in this way. It does not even have an educational value and does not teach them anything. It is pure joy for the children. Other rites included both joy and an educational element.

The ritual of the day of *Purim* included the reading of the book of Esther. As we have seen above, children were brought to the synagogue on that event to increase the joy. However, the children themselves had to be entertained as well, so special customs were created. The first was the reading out loud of four verses from the book:

> And Rabbi Calonimus said further, the practice of Jewish communities to say the phrases "A Jewish man was in Shushan," "and Mordechai went out from before the king" and "for the Jew Mordechai ... " out loud during the reading of the *megillah* [scroll], is neither a requirement nor a custom, but only for the amusement of the children.[34]

This unique custom that became part of the liturgy of the day entertained the children but also carried educational value: the verses were not chosen at random; rather, they are key verses, marking the highlights of the book. They could serve as markers for the children and help them to follow the story of Esther.

Other customs were created to increase the awareness of children of the customs of the day. One of these is the use of the rattle during the reading of the book of Esther. It seems that some did not value this custom very much, as rabbis had to defend it, and claimed that "and nobody should disregard or ridicule this ritual, as it was not constituted in vain".[35]

Sometimes, however, the daily practices and ways that children made themselves joyous during the week contradicted various laws and commandments for holidays. One of the most popular games among Jewish children, as well as non-Jewish children, was, of course, playing ball.[36] Playing ball was considered problematic on the Sabbath and on holidays, and there was a debate regarding whether it should be allowed or not:

> And it is surprising that it should be permissible to play ball games on *Yom Tov* [holiday], since this is not a necessity of *Yom Tov* at all; but since it is for the amusement of children, who have not reached the age of requirement for *mitzvoth* [children under the age of legal responsibility, 12 for girls and 13 for boys], it is allowed. But for older people, this seems to me a bad custom, since it is not a stroll[37] but rather children's conversation and frivolity.[38]

What would remain of the pleasure of children if their favourite games and activities were denied to them on the holiday and they remained confined to their houses? Yet, adults even encouraged children to participate in activities that were not only legally (*halakhically*) problematic but also caused much upheaval and disorder, as the following description from this fifteenth-century book of customs shows:

> The Mahari Segal said that the practice of young men to take the wood covering the *succah* [tabernacle] and light a fire on *Simchat Torah* [holiday of Rejoicing in the Torah] is a good practice for *Yom Tov* joy, and there is no prohibition of the taking apart of the *succah*, as the taking apart is not considered problematic unless it is with the purpose of rebuilding, and the burning is likewise not problematic, even though it is without a purpose … . But this is an inappropriate thing for adults to do, to take apart the *succah* and make a fire; and he also said that his father, the Maharam Segal, used to reprove him in his youth not to take a *succah* apart or make a fire on *Simchat Torah*. (And I – who am but a gleaner in the words of the great – saw my father the Mahari Segal take great joy and pleasure in watching the young men run from house to house on *Simchat Torah* to take apart and plunder the planks from the *succah* and bring the wood to make a fire, and he himself allowed them to take from his *succah* and incited them to plunder the wood from those who didn't want to give them to them.)[39]

Like *Purim*, *Simchat Torah* was a holiday of joy, with a strong emphasis on dancing, eating and drinking. Celebrated immediately after the feast of tabernacles, it marked the end of the holiday season of the autumn and the end of the yearly reading cycle of the *Torah* and, therefore, was an occasion of great celebration. As we saw above, children took part in the celebrations; yet, this was apparently not enough, and they looked for ways to manifest their own joy. The wooden booths, put up for the feast of the tabernacle, that were to be torn down in any case, were a great temptation. Burning them was the right thing to do, in the eyes of the young. It is important to note that the practice of tearing down the tabernacle and burning the wood was limited to children and youth. As in the case of playing ball, adults were not supposed to take part in these activities. This fact emphasizes the unique nature of children's customs and the fact that certain activities were reserved for children, and they were allowed to participate because it was their special way to celebrate the holiday. These activities were problematic from a legal point of view but nevertheless important for children.

Children, therefore, celebrated certain holidays in their own special ways. They participated in adult activities and maybe even enjoyed them, but also (or mainly) took pleasure in special activities. If we look for the common features of these activities, we can see that they tend to be strongly connected with physical objects, with sound and disturbance of the public order. Rabbis and community leaders acknowledged the fact that these are the things that make children rejoice and contribute to their pleasure on the holidays and that these are their unique ways to celebrate on the holiday.

The other side of ensuring the happiness of children is taking their sorrow and pain into consideration. The discussion of negative emotions – sorrow, pain, sadness and so forth – is beyond the scope of this chapter. Nevertheless, I wish to discuss a few sources that refer to the same issues brought up here. This first source deals, this time, not with the clash between the law (*Halakha*) and the pleasure of children but, rather, between the pleasure of children and that of adults:

> It seems to me that those who prolong walks and conversations, even if they are on holy subjects, and delay the meal and thus cause discomfort to their families and small children, who thereby need to fast longer on *Shabbat* than on a week day, are not acting in a good manner; for it is surely a big prohibition, for the *Torah* was very stringent regarding causing suffering to animals, how much more so the suffering of people, his children, and even more so on *Shabbat*, which was given for pleasure and not for misery.[40]

While part of the pleasure of adults during the Sabbath was to converse with friends and neighbours, stroll and learn, children suffer due to the delay in meal times. The author here reminds the reader that one should feed his household animals before eating himself, and if such a command exists regarding animals, one should even be more careful regarding his very own creations. Here, again, we see the emphasis on the celebration of the Sabbath and the prevention of sorrow on that day. It is also clear that adults did not always take into consideration the needs of children and often preferred their own pleasure to that of their children.

One cannot, however, easily be happy when a suffering child is present. While, at weddings and other joyous occasions, one blesses those "in whose dwelling lies joy," this blessing is not said in the case of a circumcision:

> But at a circumcision feast, even though joy is mentioned, as it says: "I rejoice at your words," despite this we do not recite the blessing "In whose dwelling lies joy" due to the misery of the circumcised baby.[41]

These last two sources, from custom books from early modern Ashkenaz, both reflect and encourage a special sensitivity to the needs and feelings of the young. The fact that these recommendations appear in reference to religious conduct makes these recommendations of almost obligatory value and emphasizes their importance. It also makes them a matter of communal concern, as they refer to activities that belong to the public and social sphere.

Conclusion

In search of the ways in which children's pleasure and joy were secured, we have unveiled some of the ways in which the entire community celebrated and enjoyed holidays and joyous occasions. We have seen that joy was strongly connected with holidays and festive days, and, as adults celebrated, it was important for them not only to include children, but also to make sure that children celebrated in their own ways. Special legal (*halakhic*) considerations were made to ensure the pleasure of children and enable them to rejoice on the holiday. This, I would like to argue, manifests the sensitivity of medieval and early modern Jews towards the unique character of childhood and, especially, to the specific need to take special care for the emotional well-being of children.

This chapter has dealt mostly with the care of emotions in the public sphere. Rather than something confined to the family, emotions and the balance between different sentiments and needs were expressed and practised in communal spaces. We have seen that children were a source of joy for the community as a whole and even served as a competing value, something that could overshadow the importance of learning and prayer in the synagogue. This was true not only for parents but for the community as a whole, which gave much space to the customs of the children and took their emotional needs into consideration, even when other values were at stake.

Emotions are not only spontaneous: children's emotions, as well as adults' emotions, were a public matter and something to be regulated and prescribed. They were appropriate on some occasions and restricted on others. They were evoked and encouraged, both in adults and children.

This chapter has dealt with the pleasure of children during very specific occasions. What about their pleasure and joy, in general? Ensuring their happiness? It seems that these topics are not discussed in explicit ways in contemporary literature. Children's contentment on a regular basis might have not been a value for medieval and early modern Ashkenazic Jews. Nevertheless, it was important for them to ensure the well-being and pleasure of children when all others were celebrating, and not leave them behind.

Notes

1 This song was part of the play *Kriza*, written by Yehoshua Sobol and performed in 1976. It was adapted by the Israeli ethnic-world music band *Habrera Hativeet* (The Natural Choice) and became a beloved song, often played at weddings, celebrations for new babies and other fertility-related occasions, contrary to the original meaning of this satirical, critical song.

2 According to the Oxford English Dictionary, "joy" is: (1) "a pleasurable state or condition; a state of happiness or felicity; esp. the perfect bliss or beatitude of heaven; hence, the place of bliss, paradise, heaven"; or (2) "a vivid emotion of pleasure arising from a sense of well-being or satisfaction; the feeling or state of being highly pleased or delighted; exultation of spirit; gladness, delight." *Oxford English Dictionary Online*, http://www.oed.com, last accessed 18 January 2013.

3 For the definitions of age and terms used to describe children, see E. Kanarfogel, *Jewish Education and Society in the High Middle Ages* (Detroit, MI, 1992), p37, fn. 30. See also T. Meacham, *Sefer Ha-Bagrut Le-Rav Shmuel Ben Khofni Gaon Ve-Sefer Ha-Shanim Le-Rav Yehuda Rosh Ha-Seder* (Jerusalem, 1999), pp11–14.

4 During recent years, there has been a growing tendency to utilize legal sources for historical research and analyse them to depict daily life and other topics. For the use of legal sources as historical sources, see E. Baumgarten, *Mothers and Children: Jewish Family Life in Medieval Europe* (Princeton, NJ, 2004); E. Shoham-Steiner, *Involuntary Marginals: Marginal Individuals in Medieval Northern European Jewish Society* (Jerusalem, 2008) [Hebrew].

5 For an early definition of Ashkenaz, see J. Katz, *Tradition and Crisis: Jewish Society at the End of the Middle Ages* (New York, 1993), pp6–9. Recent scholarly discussions reaffirmed this definition. See J. David, "The Reception of the Shulchan Arukh and the Formation of Ashkenazic Jewish Identity", *Association of Jewish Studies Review*, vol 26 (2002): p257.

6 H. Tirosh-Samuelson, *Happiness in Premodern Judaism: Virtue, Knowledge and Well-Being* (Cincinnati, OH, 2003), p1.

7 S. W. Baron, *A Social and Religious History of the Jews*, vol II (New York, 1937), p31.

8 On love, see, *Studies in Jewish Civilization*, p18 (2008). The entire volume is dedicated to the concept of love in Jewish traditions. On joy: G. Anderson, "The Expression of Joy as a Halakhic Problem in Rabbinic Sources", *Jewish Quarterly Review*, vol 80 (1990): pp221–252; G. Anderson, *A Time to Mourn, a Time to Dance: The Expression of Grief and Joy in Israelite Religion* (University Park, PA, 1991); M. Fishbane, "The Inwardness of Joy in Jewish Spirituality", in L. S. Rouner (ed) *In Pursuit of Happiness* (Notre Dame, IN, 1995), pp71–88. Yochanan Muffs also contributed to the discussion of the tension between law and joy through a comparative dimension. See Y. Muffs, "Joy and Love as Metaphorical Expressions of Willingness and Spontaneity in Cuneifom, Ancient Hebrew, and Related Literature: Divine Investitures in the Midrash and in the Light of Neo-Babylonian Royal Grants", in J. Neusner (ed) *Christianity, Judaism and Other Greco-Roman Cults* (Leiden, 1975), pp1–36. Ohrenstein discusses the terms "the benefit of a pleasure" *tovat hana'ah* and "mutual benefit" *zeh neheneh vezeh lo' ḥaser* in Talmudic literature in the context of psycho-economic values. See R. A. Ohrenstein, "The Talmudic Doctrine of 'The Benefit of a Pleasure': Psychological Well-Being in Talmudic Literature", *American Journal of Economics and Sociology*, vol 664 (2007): pp661–680.

9 R. Weinstein, *Marriage Rituals Italian Style: A Historical Anthropological Perspective on Early Modern Italian Jews* (Leiden, 2004); N. Feuchtwanger-Sarig, "'May He Grow to the Torah … ': The Iconography of the Torah Reading and Bar Mizvah on Ashkenzi Torah Binders", in R. Langer and S. Fine (eds) *Liturgy in the Life of the Synagogue: Studies in the History of Jewish Prayer* (Winona Lake, IN, 2005), pp161–176; B. Kirshenblatt-Gimblett, "The Cut that Binds: The Western Ashkenazic Torah Binders as Nexus Between Circumcision and Torah", in V. Turner (ed) *Celebrations: Studies in Festivity and Ritual* (Washington, DC, 1982), pp201–204.

10 For example: Leviticus 23:40; Numbers 10:10; Deuteronomy 12:7, 12:12, 12:18, 14:26.

11 G. Anderson, "The Expression of Joy", p252.

12 Similar questions were raised concerning the commandment to love both one's creator and one's neighbour. L. H. Schiffman, "Commandment or Emotion? Love of God, Family, and Humanity in Classical Judaism", *Studies in Jewish Civilization*, vol 18 (2008): p13.

13 G. Anderson, "The Expression of Joy", p224.

14 G. Anderson, "The Expression of Joy", pp224–225.

15 M. Fishbane, op. cit., pp71–88.

16 *Sefer Hasidim*, J. Wistinetzki (ed) (Jerusalem, 1988), p194.

17 Ibid, p206.

18 See also ibid, p15.

19 *Tractate Smaḥot*, ch. 1:2.

20 *Sefer Kolbo* (Jerusalem, 1997), para. 114.

21 This instruction appears in other medieval sources, as well as early modern sources, both from the East and from Ashkenaz. See Joel ben Samuel Sirkis, *Bayit Chadash* Yoreh Deah, mourning, p391; Yosef Karo, *Shulchan Arukh* Yoreh Deah, mourning, p391; Moses b. Issac Mintz, *She'elot U-Teshuvot Rabbenu Moshe Mintz* (Jerusalem, 1991), para. 86.

22 G. Anderson, "The Expression of Joy", p226.

23 *Babylonian Talmud*, Tractate Moed Katan, 24b.

24 N. Rubin, *The End of Life: Rites of Burial and Mourning in the Talmud and Midrash* (Tel Aviv, 1997), pp203–204 [Hebrew].

25 Rashi on the *Babylonian Talmud*, Moed Katan, 24b. This distinction appears in later text as well and became an obligatory law: Yosef Karo *Shulchan Arukh,* Yoreh Deah, mourning, p344.
26 Jacob b. Moses Mulin, *Sefer Maharil: Minhagim* (Jerusalem, 1988), p287.
27 Yehuda Leib b. Moshe Minden, *Shirei Yehudah* (Amsterdam, 1697) 24a.
28 See T. Berner, *Children and Childhood in Early Modern Ashkenaz* (PhD thesis, Hebrew University of Jerusalem, 2010), pp175–178, 194–196 [Hebrew].
29 Solomon Luria *Yam Shel Shlomo*, Beitzah, ch. 1.
30 Jacob b. Moses Mulin, *Sefer Maharil: Minhagim* (Jerusalem, 1988), p167.
31 Four cups of wine drunk during the Passover *Seder*.
32 Babylonian Talmud Tractate Pesahim, 108b–109a.
33 A. Danzig, *Sefer Hayyei Adam* (Jerusalem, 2007), II–III, p153.
34 *Sefer Hapardes*, H. J. Ehrenreich (ed) (Budapest, 1924), p254.
35 M. Isserles, *Rema on the Shulchan Arukh*, Orach Haim para. 590:27.
36 K. Thomas, "Children in Early Modern Europe", in G. Avery and J. Briggs (eds) *Children and Their Books* (Oxford, UK, 1989), pp45–77.
37 The word "stroll" is used in rabbinic texts for a recreational activity permitted on the Sabbath and festive days. M. Sley, "Ha-Tiyul Be-Sifrut Ha-ShuT", *Ha-Maayan*, vol 16 (1976): pp17–35.
38 S. Luria, *Yam Shel Shlomo*, Beitzah, ch. 1.
39 Jacob b. Moses Mulin, *Sefer Maharil: Minhagim* (Jerusalem, 1988), pp376–377.
40 Y. Yospa Han Neurlingen, *Sefer Yosef Ometz* (Frankfurt, 1928), p141.
41 A. Khildig, *Sefer Haminhagim* (Jerusalem, 2006), marriage customs, p220.

3

GROWING UP IN VOC BATAVIA: TRANSCULTURAL CHILDHOOD IN THE WORLD OF THE DUTCH EAST INDIA COMPANY

Nicola Borchardt

In 1641, seven-year-old François Caron[1] first set foot on Batavia. He was born in Hirado, Japan, to a French-Huguenot father and a Japanese-Catholic mother. The father, François Caron senior,[2] was employed by the Dutch East India Company (VOC). As the Japanese government closed their country to foreign influences, the European-Asian family was forced to leave. The family headed for the headquarters of the VOC in Asia, Batavia. On the Island of Java in modern day Jakarta the father would soon rise to become one of the most influential members of the Indian Council.[3] François Caron junior stayed in Batavia for only two years. By the age of nine he lost his mother. Shortly afterwards, his father took him and his siblings to The Netherlands for schooling.

Unlike François Caron, Johanna Maria Van Riebeeck[4] spent her entire childhood in Batavia. She was born in Batavia in 1679 to a high-ranking VOC official, Abraham Van Riebeeck.[5] Unlike François, she had a European mother, Elisabeth Van Oosten,[6] making Johanna a European child[7] in Asian surroundings. Since there was a lack of European women,[8] her wet nurse was most likely of Asian origin, as were most of the children with whom she used to play. She learned to walk, talk, read and write in Asian surroundings. As a girl she wasn't sent to The Netherlands for schooling; girls promised to be married to other VOC officials helping to promote their father's and husband's careers. Johanna was first married by the age of 16. Her husband, Gerrit de Heere,[9] 22 years older, was soon promoted to VOC governor of Ceylon. After his death in 1702, Johanna returned to Batavia. At the age of 28, she married Governor-General Joan Van Hoorn.[10] When he resigned in 1709, Johanna's father became his successor. Her second marriage thus resulted in her father's promotion. Abraham Van Riebeeck became governor-general of the VOC.

Johanna Van Riebeeck and François Caron were considered by the VOC as *Anak Kompenie*, the Malay word for children of the company. They were children of European employees of the Dutch East India Company and, as in the case of

François, Asian women or very seldom European women, as in the case of Johanna. These children grew up in a multicultural environment. At the time, many different Asian and European cultures met in Batavia. Even before the VOC transformed Jayakarta forcefully into the Dutch trading base Batavia in 1619, traders from all over Asia met at this port city, among them Chinese, Arabs and Indians. In addition, slaves were imported mainly from Portuguese settlements on the Indian Malabar and Coromandel Coast and from the islands east of Java. All these different cultures thus influenced the childhood of the *Anak Kompenie* along with the Northern European culture of their fathers.

This chapter will argue how the cultural and social heritage as well as the gender of the *Anak Kompenie* influenced their childhood experience at an individual level. The roles played by the parents, wet nurses and social institutions, such as the orphanage and the schools, during the childhood of the *Anak Kompenie* will also be considered.

Although the *Anak Kompenie* can be considered cultural migrants within the VOC realm, in most cases this chapter will focus on Batavia. The social history of the VOC headquarters in Asia is the best researched among all VOC outposts.[11] In addition, a large variety of sources, such as legal documents,[12] have been published in The Netherlands since the late nineteenth century. Paintings, ego-documents and travel reports from seventeenth-century Batavia were taken into account as necessary.[13] These different sources will help to recreate an image of the childhood of the *Anak Kompenie*.

This research focuses on Batavia during the seventeenth century, with special focus on the period from 1619 to 1733. Batavia came into existence only by 1619, after VOC troops invaded the Banten principality Jayakarta. Batavia changed quite significantly during the eighteenth century. While the VOC trade of the seventeenth century was mainly based on spice monopolies on the Moluccas, the influence of the plantation industries on Java and other outer islands grew during the eighteenth century. In 1733, malaria became endemic in Batavia, raising immensely the death rate of Europeans and children, both without the necessary immunity. Surviving Europeans took their families and abandoned Batavia for the healthier suburbs.[14] After 1733 Batavia transformed from a "beautiful colonial town" into what travel writers of the time called a "graveyard for Europeans".[15]

The cultural influences on the childhood of the *Anak Kompenie* in seventeenth-century Batavia are difficult to describe. These depended, in part, on the cultural heritages of the child's parents and wet nurse. Most Asian mothers of the *Anak Kompenie* were not, as in the case of François Caron, local women but (former) slaves. The wet nurses were usually house slaves.[16] Most of the mothers and wet nurses taking care of the children thus were of Indian origin or came from islands east of Java. The fathers came from different parts of Europe. François's father was a French-Huguenot; Johanna Van Riebeeck's father descended from the famous Dutch family that founded the Cape Colony.

Besides the ethnic heritage of the parents and wet nurses, religion figured as well. The sources of the VOC Batavia distinguish between legitimate (*echte*) and illegitimate (*onechte*) children.[17] Legitimate children were either born into a Dutch-reformed

Christian marriage, like Johanna Van Riebeeck, legalized by their European fathers, like François Caron, or adopted by their Christian fathers and their lawfully wedded wives. Dutch-reformed education and baptism were a primary requirement for legalization and adoption of illegitimate children. Hence, all the children in this chapter were educated in a Dutch-reformed way. Nevertheless, due to the different religions of their wet nurses and others around them, Hinduism, Islam and other religions might have influenced them as well.

Status further determined the transcultural childhood experience of *Anak Kompenie*. In VOC Batavia, the rank of the father within the VOC mirrored the social status of the family. Johanna and François were both children of higher-ranking VOC officials. If François's father had not been a high-ranking VOC official, he would not have been able to legalize his children.[18] The cost of legitimizing children was affordable only to elites.[19] Moreover, the lower-ranking officials left Batavia sooner. Their children experienced less the transcultural, European-Asian childhood of other *Anak Kompenie* because they remained in the ethnic groups of their mothers. Some children of these lower-ranking officials were taken away from their mothers to be educated in the Batavian orphanage,[20] while others lived with their mothers in the poor-house of the Dutch Reformed Church. These were, however, the minority.

Besides legitimizing their illegitimate children, higher-ranking VOC officials could also afford to send their sons to Europe for rearing and education. Sons of lower-ranking VOC officials, like the boys of the orphanage, were educated in the local schools and studied to become craftsmen for the company or free burgers. For girls, status mattered less for their future. The lack of "European"[21] women in Batavia created a demand for daughters of the company, rich like Johanna Van Riebeeck and poor like the nameless girl in the orphanage, to become future wives of company employees. Gender thus determined the kind of education that *Anak Kompenie* received.

The fate of the girls also demonstrates that a Christian education was considered to be more important than the ethnic origin of the children. Racism, as known in the nineteenth century, did not rule in VOC Batavia. During the first half of the seventeenth century, European-Asian children, such as François Caron, could study in The Netherlands and secure a successful career outside the VOC. After returning a second time from East India, François Caron became a well-known pastor in The Netherlands. His childhood friend Pieter Hartsinck,[22] who also had a Japanese mother and a European father, started his studies in Leiden the same year as François Caron. He stayed in Europe and became a highly regarded mining engineer in the Harz region of Brunswick.

François Caron, Pieter Hartsinck and, to a lesser extent, also Johanna Van Riebeeck's father Abraham migrated between different worlds. Their fathers' promotions exposed them to new cultures and places. This was even truer for the daughters, as they usually stayed with their fathers until they were married. Johanna's aunt, Elisabeth Van Riebeeck,[23] was born at the Cape. Unlike her brother Abraham, who went to The Netherlands for his education, she left with the family for Malakka and Batavia, following the career path of her father.

Finding childhood in Batavia

Anak Kompenie, like children elsewhere, very seldom left diaries or toys behind. If a child dies at an early age, the parents may choose to keep some of his or her belongings as mementos. The children portrayed here left nothing that captured or recorded their childhoods.

Childhood as defined by third-party sources has not been considered in depth thus far. It is hard to find evidence on childhood in VOC records. Considering the wide range of these sources, the actual hints at childhood and children are quite few. Of the legal or normative sources, the *Plakaatboek* edited by the Batavian archivist Chijs contains the most information on childhood, its duration, and major institutions such as the schools and the orphanage.[24] Portraits and other images of European-Asian families and children in Batavia offer visual representation of childhood.

The normative sources of the VOC do not contain the old Dutch word for childhood (*kintsheyd*). Only the terms youth (*jeught*) and children (*kinderen*) appear. Interestingly, those terms are used as synonyms. They define a group of under-age persons and do not describe a period of life. Nevertheless, the laws governing under-age persons and edicts defining the time of maturity provide an idea of some of the difference between adults and children.

In normative sources, this difference is defined more than once. As early as 1619, before the establishment of Batavia, the VOC ruled that children in the fort of Jaya-karta could eat free of charge.[25] Thus, as early as 1619 there were children present in VOC forts. They could also sail (back) to The Netherlands at no cost.[26] Different rules thus apply for children and adults.

Further differences appear in rites of passage. The regulation of funerals from 1684 demonstrates, when a child dies, that different rules applied to children and adults. Children were to be buried during the day, but could be buried also at night, whereas adults were only to be buried at night.[27] The death of a child was treated and valued differently than the death of an adult. This difference is not easily explained. One explanation could be that because more children than adults died, their deaths were of less significance, so the funeral took less time for preparations and thus could take place at any time. But it could also mean that the funeral of a child was something so private that the public was not invited. Hence, it could take place at any time.

In a portrait of the family Cnoll[28] from the VOC era, children wear the same clothes as adults. Yet, they appear not only smaller, but also with certain icons that define them as children. In the family portrait by J. J. Coeman, both daughters are portrayed alongside puppies. In Dutch art of the Golden Age, dogs, especially puppies alongside children, symbolized "teachability" (*leerzugtigheid*)[29] – that is, as Simon Schama puts it: "Christian aptitude, and belongs to a tradition in which the instruction of children is reinforced by the visual analogue of training dogs in obedience."[30]

On the engraving of the Batavian orphanage in Joan Nieuhof's travelogue, *Remarkable Voyages & Travalls into the best Provinces of the West and East Indies*, children wear different clothes than adults.[31] This engraving is one of the few pictures that depict children in Batavian city life. The orphanage is shown in the background. In front of the orphanage many children with different attire and skin complexions are shown playing, laughing and talking. Some adults are portrayed as well. In the centre of the engraving a man with a raised index finger is talking to some children. A darker man on the left side of the picture makes similar gesture. He appears to be teaching badminton to two of the children. On the right side of the picture a group of women in European dress, accompanied by slaves are giving donations to some of the children.

The differences between children and adults in this engraving are not only reflected in their different heights and clothing, but more importantly by their different social roles. The adults are portrayed as teachers and sponsors, the children as pupils and beneficiaries who, not unimportantly, spend their time in recreation as well as instruction. They are playing badminton and other games. The image of childhood presented here is thus defined by social relations.

The childhood shown in this engraving appears less ordered than the one shown in the former portrait; these children still need to be educated. The engraving appears in a travelogue written for a European audience. It is possible that this picture was included in the report to raise funds for the orphanage. These children still need the guidance of the teachers shown in this picture. Nevertheless, some progress in the children's education is shown: in the foreground an Asian looking child is patting a dog, not eating it. This shows what Europeans should think of Batavian children, but it also shows an awareness of Batavian childhood in Europe and – through the institution of the orphanage – also in Batavia.

The awareness of childhood as a period of the lifecycle before maturity is further mirrored in normative sources that define the different stages leading to adulthood. During the 1620s different edicts were released concerning the guardianship of children. The 1621 conditions for the emigration of orphaned girls state that girls under the age of 20 need a guardian as long as they are not married.[32] The 1624 statutes for the masters of the orphanage established that children under the age of 21 were "under age and unable to be their own guardian" (*onmondich ende niet bequaem haer eygen voocht te wesen*).[33] The 1642 statutes of Batavia set age 25 as the boundary of legal adulthood.[34] Under-age persons (*minder jaerige persoonen*[35]), however, were allowed to marry without the explicit consent of a parent or guardian by age 21 for boys and 18 for girls.

The obligation to support one's children further determined the moment of maturity. Sons had the right to receive clothing and nutrition from their parents until the age of 18, daughters until the age of 15.[36] In the poorhouse, children were supported by the deaconry until age 16 regardless of gender.[37]

The end of childhood is thus defined by normative sources over a time span of ten years. It is important to note that sources distinguish between the maturity of a man and that of a woman. Women were considered adults earlier, but they never became lawful citizens. Women were not allowed to serve as a child's guardian; they were themselves to be guarded and guided by their husbands, fathers or other men, if they were orphaned and/or widowed.[38]

Places of childhood

As stated above, representations of childhood and children only very seldom appear in portraits and other pictorial sources of VOC Batavia. Additionally, descriptions of houses of VOC personnel do not mention special rooms for children.[39] We know from the sources cited above, however, that awareness of children and their needs existed in Batavia. Childhood was not limited to one special room in the household; it took place everywhere: in the home, in the streets, in the markets, in the churches, in the schools and in the institutions.

The family as a place of childhood

It is useful to think of the European-Asian family as a place of childhood. These families fluctuated a great deal. Even before 1733 there was a high death rate in Batavia. The before-mentioned Japanese mother of François Caron died within two years after her arrival in Batavia. Johanna Van Riebeeck was widowed twice. In all marriages, her husbands brought children from previous marriages into the family. She considered those children as her own.[40]

Besides death, promotion and repatriation could also alter the size and shape of a European-Asian family. François Caron and his siblings were taken to The Nether-lands to be educated after their mother's death in 1643. Six years later employees of the VOC were forbidden to take their Asian-European family with them once they repatriated.[41] Thereafter, many VOC employees took only temporary wives, leaving their families behind when they returned to The Netherlands or were transferred to another VOC outpost. The mothers of these abandoned families often remarried. By the beginning of the eighteenth century this law was strengthened. From 1716 onwards, company personnel with illegitimate families in the East were not allowed to repatriate at all.[42]

Divorce was also known in Batavia. Leonnard Blussé narrates in rich detail the story of the trials of Cornelia van Nieuwenrode,[43] the mother in the aforementioned family portrait, and her later husband Joan Bitter.

The research of Henk Niemeijer in the church archives of Batavia shows that legitimate and illegitimate children grew up together in many families. The author discusses among others the case of Cornelia Theulings who accepted her husband's illegitimate children as her own after his death.[44]

The structure of the European-Asian family was thus always changing. It could consist of parents, step-parents, (step-) children, legitimate, illegitimate, and/or adopted, house slaves and their children. Most of these family members came from different ethnic backgrounds. If the slaves and their children are included in this picture, some even came from a different social background. Death of one or more of these family members, migration and adoption or legitimation of illegitimate children altered the composition of those families.

Each member of the family confronted certain social expectations and legal limitations in this setting. Several Batavian laws and instructions stress the parents' duty to care for their children, to educate and discipline them.[45] In all of these sources, children are objects of adults' acts.

The surgeon and traveller Nicholaus de Graaf, who visited Batavia during the latter part of the seventeenth century, especially criticizes the mothers of these families as being too lazy to educate their children.[46] As a result, these children were unable to speak the Dutch tongue. De Graaf only spent a few weeks in Batavia. He seems to have expected to find Dutch family structures and values in VOC East India.[47]

Normative sources from Batavia support a more traditional European idea of motherhood. Following the 1621 legal requirements for the emigration of orphaned girls, it was the mothers' task to care for the girls and to teach them to read, write and sew.[48] The Batavian orphanage employed *Binnenmoeders* and *Buitenmoeders* (roughly translated: inside and outside mothers).[49] The *Binnenmoeders* lived with the orphans. They were to educate the girls to become good wives. The *Buitenmoeders* oversaw this education from the outside. A traditional European idea of motherhood was thus always present in VOC Batavia.

Not surprising in this context, de Graaf's account does not criticize the fathers for not taking care of their children. A VOC law of 1716 that forbade fathers of illegitimate children in Batavia to repatriate shows, however, that VOC officials understood parental neglect of children as a problem.[50] This was probably the case because those children left behind by repatriated employees created a social problem in Batavia and therefore a financial problem for the VOC. Hence, the law indirectly required the father to care even for his illegitimate children.

Repatriation was not the sole cause of neglect, however. Soon after seven-year-old François Caron arrived in Batavia, his father was promoted to Formosa (Taiwan). His family stayed behind in Batavia. The aforementioned Cornelia Van Nieuwenrode wrote in a letter to her mother that her husband was very busy.[51] It can be assumed that lower-ranking employees were frequently absent as well. As soldiers they were sent to war; as sailors they sailed with the monsoons.

Historians of social life in VOC Batavia argue that daughters had a higher standing within the European-Asian family than sons.[52] As has been noted above, Johanna Van Riebeeck's second marriage afforded her father the opportunity to become governor-general. Sons of elite families, such as François Caron, received their education in The Netherlands, but most sons with a mixed heritage were not so fortunate as to be granted a comparable chance of social advancement. Normative sources show that the VOC did not trust them.[53] They could not reach a higher position in the VOC than that of a clerk, which mirrored their position within the family.

They still, however, ranked higher than the house slaves. In 1697 the Batavian government ruled that slaves could only go outside the house if accompanied by their masters or the masters' children.[54] This resulted in a very ambivalent relationship between the slaves as caregivers and the children as their masters.

From a letter written by Johanna Van Riebeeck, however, we learn that this relationship could be very important to both parties. On 16 March 1710, she wrote from the Cape to her father about a meeting with his former wet nurse Ansiela.[55] Abraham Van Riebeeck himself, we learn from this letter, had met this woman again

16 years after he had left the Cape as a child. When the letter was written another 34 years had passed. A relationship between the indigenous caregiver and the *Anak Kompenie* could thus endure over half a century.

Childhood outside of the family

When parents died or fathers repatriated, the European-Asian family could be restructured or dissolved. In the latter case, childhood could take place in the institutions of the Dutch Reformed Church or among the members of the mother's ethnic group. In 1635, the Batavian government declared that all orphans and poor citizens were to be cared for by the church council.[56] Accordingly, children, especially girls, staying with their European-Asian family, spent at least part of their childhood in these institutions.

Until 1724, the orphanage and the poorhouse shared the same premises. According to Niemeijer, between 50 and 80 children lived in the orphanage at any given time.[57] Most of these children were of mixed origin. As stated above, they were not always orphans. In 1709, for example, the VOC took nine European-Asian children from their Javanese mothers to be educated in the orphanage.[58] The "orphans" lived with a "father" and a "mother" from the orphanage. Together with a comforter and up to 26 slaves, these "orphan-parents" took care of the children.[59]

The agency of Christian norms was the first goal for deaconry institutions such as the orphanage. Providing orphaned children with food, clothing and shelter was a basic means to achieve this goal. As stated in the rules of the deaconry, the children in these institutions should be educated "in good upbringing and with good manners" (*in goede tucht en manierlycheyt*).[60] Schools in Batavia were open to orphaned and non-orphaned children alike and taught them to read and write. The girls would stay home in the afternoon to learn how to spell and how to sew. Overseers would provide for Christian prayers to be read in the morning and at night. Children were to be sent to church on Sundays, and to study the catechism on Tuesday mornings. They were to go to bed early and dress neatly.

It was forbidden to hit or push children.[61] This latter aspect demonstrates that taking care of *Anak Kompenie* in Batavia entailed more than just providing children with primary care and sufficient clothing, food and religious education. Children were, furthermore, considered to be in need of protection against physical harm as well.

The engraving of the orphanage described above draws a very idyllic picture of the orphanage.[62] In 1723, Deacon Volkman revealed a different situation. The bedroom of the adolescent girls was, according to Volkman, especially repulsive. The girls did not sleep in proper beds, but on the ground with a small dirty cushion.[63] From Niemeijer we learn that the orphanage received 32 Stuivers to feed 32 children and 48 slaves.[64] The cost of living was very high in Batavia.[65] Thus, the money could not have provided sufficient nourishment for everyone. Growing up in the orphanage does not appear to have been as idyllic as Nieuhof's engraving teaches.

Affiliated with the orphanage was a school for the orphaned children. This school was one of six primary schools in Batavia, all administered by the church council. As stated by the Batavian government in 1624, these schools taught Christian belief to "tender and ignorant" youth.[66] They served thus not primarily to educate the *Anak Kompenie*, or what the Batavian government called the "Netherlandish youth" (*Nederlantsche* [...] *jeucht*),[67] but Asian children as well. Presumably, more Asian Christians attended these schools than *Anak Kompenie*. The community of Asian Christians was much larger in Batavia than the European (-Asian) community,[68] and most European and, until 1649, the European-Asian children could be sent to The Netherlands for their education.

The structure of Batavian schools was similar to those in the Dutch Republic. Girls and boys attended classes together, but were seated apart.[69] The pupils learned to read and write from Dutch spelling books.[70] Religion and mathematics were also taught. The language of instruction was Dutch.[71]

The schools in Batavia were not purely religious institutions, however, though the church council supervised classes and readings.[72] The VOC paid the teachers' salaries.[73] Unlike in other VOC settlements, children in Batavia learned to calculate in school.[74] The VOC was interested in Batavian offspring who could later work as clerks for the VOC.

That the VOC, nevertheless, mistrusted the locally born and raised *Anak Kompenie* is proven by its hesitation to establish a high school in Batavia. Furthermore, by 1713, the VOC stopped taking these children into the service of the company.[75] It accused them of being lazy and stupid and corrupted by their close contact with the slaves.[76]

Higher education for girls, in the form of instruction in domestic skills, was provided at the parents' houses and at the orphanage. Girls from poorer families could also end up as servants in the households of the elite families.[77]

Conclusion

No matter where the childhood of the *Anak Kompenie* took place, whether in the house of the family or in the Dutch Reformed institutions, such as the orphanage and the schools, the children were always in contact with elements of European and Asian cultures alike. The transcultural experience differed for each child, depending on their individual ethnic and social backgrounds, as well as their immediate environment. Religion and migration further influenced the ever-evolving hybrid culture in which the *Anak Kompenie* grew up.

The first steps in life, including birth and christening, were the same for boys and girls alike. Their later roles, however, determined their education. Although both girls and boys attended the primary schools of Batavia, girls later on also learned domestic skills to prepare them to be "good" housewives and servants. Their childhood ended earlier as well. Daughters could marry without their parents' consent by the age of 18, sons only by the age of 21. Johanna Van Riebeeck was first married by the age of 16. François Caron only married when he returned to the East Indies after 1667; accordingly, he was older than 33. Jean Gelman Taylor notes a general tendency among daughters to marry earlier than sons.[78]

Marriage was only one step towards adulthood; lawful maturity was another. Women of Batavia never became lawful citizens; they always depended on a male guardian. Nevertheless, the standing of daughters within the family was regarded as rather high. A daughter such as Johanna Van Riebeeck could become the key to the social advancement of the whole family if they were to marry a VOC official higher in rank than their fathers. Sons, on the other hand, married women from the same social stature or even of a lower stature.

The father's rank within the VOC significantly influenced the childhood of the *Anak Kompenie*. First it determined whether children of European fathers and Asian mothers could become *Anak Kompenie*. Lower-ranking VOC officials seldom could afford a legitimate European-Asian family. In addition, most often, the lower-ranking officials stayed in Batavia only for a short time. François Caron's father was financially able to legitimize and support his children. Lower-ranking officials were unable to do the same. It is hard to find biographical evidence from children of lower-ranking officials. Their fates appear in the records of the orphanage, among others, in which they tended to remain nameless.

The social class of the children was most often closely connected to their ethnic background. Higher-ranking VOC officials were allowed to bring their European wives to Batavia. Thus, some children from the elite, such as Johanna Van Riebeeck, had European mothers. As the case of François Caron shows, a European-Asian origin did not necessarily have to lead to poverty. François Caron became a well-known pastor, first in the Moluccas, and then in The Netherlands. Dirk Van Cloon, another *Anak Kompenie*, even rose to become governor-general of the VOC in 1731.[79] It can be assumed, however, that most of the European-Asian children in Batavia were not legitimized by their fathers and thus were never raised as *Anak Kompenie*. The engraving of the orphanage shows that the darker complexioned children wore fewer clothes than the lighter complexioned. This is confirmed by Niemeijer's study of the orphanage. It has been pointed out further that the VOC mistrusted these children of mixed heritage. By 1713 it stopped taking them into its service and supported their higher education only for a short while. According to the VOC, those children were too influenced by the Asian culture surrounding them.

It is hard to judge whether such regulations reflect a tendency towards racial discrimination. On the one hand, Eurasian children suffered an increasing burden of legal disadvantages. On the other hand, they could still rise on occasion to become governor-general, the highest-ranking VOC official in Asia, or marry high-ranking VOC officials and become influential women. Race had not yet become essential, though it seemed to move in that direction. Individual fortune and ability still mattered.

Notes

1 François Caron (1634–1705). See "Caron (François)", in *Digitale Versie Nieuw Neder-landsch Biografisch Woordenboek* (1910–1937), <http://www.historici.nl/retroboeken/nnbw/> (accessed 11 September 2012); J. G. Taylor, "Meditations on a Portrait from Seventeenth-Century Batavia", *Journal of Southeast Asian Studies*, vol 37 (2006): pp23–41, 33f.

2 François Caron Senior (1600–1673) was a well-known traveller of the East. He spent more than 30 years for the VOC in Japan, Batavia and Formosa (Taiwan). In his 60s he transferred to the French East India Company. For the French he went to islands of the Indian Ocean and India. See Van Dalen, "Caron (François)", in *Digitale Versie Nieuw Nederlandsch Biografisch Woordenboek*.

3 The Indian Council, also known as the High Government of Batavia, was the highest governmental institution in the Indies. It passed laws and reported to the VOC head-quarters in The Netherlands. It was headed by the governor-general. See F. S. Gaatra, *The Dutch East India Company: Expansion and Decline* (Leiden, 2003), pp66–70.

4 Johanna Maria Van Riebeeck (1679–1759). See D. B. Bosman (ed) *Brieve van Johanna Maria van Riebeeck en ander Riebeeckiana* (Amsterdam, 1952); M. Peters, "Riebeeck, Johanna Maria van", in *Digitaal Vrouwenlexicon van Nederland*, <http://www.historici.nl/Onderzoek/Projecten/DVN/lemmata/data/Riebeeck> (accessed 10 September 2012).

5 The future governor-general of the VOC, Abraham Van Riebeeck (1653–1713), was also born to a VOC official. His father was Jan Van Riebeeck, the founder of the Cape Colony. Abraham thus grew up at the Cape Colony, leaving to be educated in The Netherlands by the age of 11. See D. B. Bosman, *Brieve van Johanna Maria van Riebeeck en ander Riebeeckiana*; "Abraham Van Riebeeck", in VOC website, <http://www.vocsite.nl/geschiedenis/personalia/vanriebeeck.html> (accessed 10 September 2012).

6 Elisabeth Van Oosten (1660–1740) was born in Delft, although the name may suggest differently. See D. B. Bosman, *Brieve van Johanna Maria van Riebeeck en ander Riebeeckiana*.

7 In sources such as *censi* all legitimate children of European fathers were considered European or Dutch, as nationality was passed from the father in Dutch Roman law.

8 E. Jones, *Wives, Slaves, and Concubines: A History of the Female Underclass in Dutch Asia* (DeKalb, IL, 2010), p6.

9 Gerrit de Heere (1657–1702); see M. Peters, "Riebeeck, Johanna Maria van".

10 Joan Van Hoorn (1653–1711) came as a child of nine years to Batavia; soon orphaned, he entered the VOC service by the age of 12 and rose to the highest rank within 39 years. He served as governor-general from 1704 until 1709. See J. G. Taylor, *The Social World of Batavia* (Madison, WI, 1983), p72; "Joan Van Hoorn" in VOC website, <http://www.vocsite.nl/geschiedenis/personalia/vanhoorn.html (accessed 21 May 2013).

11 Since the 1980s, a number of historians, such as Leonard Blussé, Jean Gelman Taylor, Eric Jones, Henk Niemeijer and Remco Raben, among others, have already been researching the social and cultural history of Batavia. See L. Blussé, *Strange Company: Chinese Settlers, Mestizo Women and the Dutch in VOC Batavia* (Dordrecht, 1986); J. G. Taylor, *The Social World of Batavia*; E. Jones, *Wives, Slaves, and Concubines*; H. Niemeijer, *Batavia: Een koloniale samenleving in de zeventiende eeuw* (Amsterdam, 2005); U. Bosma and R. Raben, *De oude Indische wereld 1500–1920* (Amsterdam, 2003).

12 As early as the late nineteenth century, Batavian and Dutch historians started editing VOC legal sources. Thus, many normative sources are easily accessible: J. A. Van der Chijs (ed) *Realia. Register op de generale resolutiën van het Kasteel Batavia 1632–1805*, 3 vols (The Hague, 1882–1886), an alphabetical selection of all resolutions of the Batavian government; J. A. Van der Chijs (ed) *Nederlandsch-Indisch Plakaatboek 1602–1811*, Deel 1–4, 1602–1749 (Batavia, 1885–1887). The most evidence on childhood, its duration and major institutions, such as the schools and the orphanage, is to be found here. Unfortunately, we do not always learn which institution – the Indian Council, the church council or other Batavian institutions – actually released these laws and edicts. Only the writings of the *Heeren XVII* are marked especially. In addition, the selection often lacks evidence as to which of the formulations are original and which added or changed by the editor. See, for example, W. Ph. Coolhaas, *Generale Missiven van Gouverneurs-Generaal en Raden aan Heren XVII der Verenigde Oostindische Compagnie*, vols I–VIII (The Hague, 1960–1985), containing the instructions of the governor-general and the Indian council; P. Van Dam, *Beschryvinge van de Oostindische Compagnie*, vols I–IV

(The Hague, 1927–1954), first published 1701–1703; J. K. J. de Jonge (ed) *De opkomst van het Nederlandsch gezag in Oost-Indië: Verzameling van onuitgegeven stukken uit het oud-koloniaal archief* (The Hague, 1870–1877), a selection of sources of resolutions of the *Heeren XVII* and the High Government of Batavia, and various decrees and laws from Batavia. Despite the flaws of these source editions, their selections appear to be widely accepted by the academic community. Major historians on the social history of the VOC make use of them.

13 As the research provided here derives from a Master's thesis, archival sources were not studied. N. Borchardt, *Euro-asiatische Kindheit im Batavia der VOC (1619–1733)*, *Wissenschaftliche Hausarbeit zur Erlangung des akademischen Grades eines Magister Artium der Universität Hamburg* (MA thesis, Universität Hamburg, 2008).

14 P. H. van der Brug, *Malaria en malaise: De VOC in Batavia in de 18de eeuw* (Amsterdam, 1994); E. Jones, *Wives, Slaves, and Concubines*, pp33–35.

15 E. Jones, *Wives, Slaves, and Concubines*, pp33–35.

16 P. Van Dam, *Beschryvinge van de Oostindische Compagnie I.1*, p564; N. de Graaf, *Oost-Indise Spiegel* (The Hague, 1930), p14.

17 For example: "1705. 1 September. Magtiging op Weesmeesteren de renten van gelden, onder hun beheer en met fidei-commis bezwaard, te doen ophouden, gerekend van ultimo Februarij 1705; eveneens te handelen ten aanzien van gelden, toekomende aan onechte kinderen en haar vrij gegeven slaven of hunne kinderen, 'maar die van de bekende te laten strecken tot derselver alimentatie, voor soo verre zy dat onvermydelyk mogten benodigt zyn, of anders renteloos te houden, totdat meerder jarigh werden", in J. A. Van der Chijs, *Nederlandsch-Indisch Plakaatboek III*, p561; "1716. 16 October. Bepaling, dat aan Compagnie's dienaren, die bij inlandische vrouwen onechte Kinderen hadden verwekt, geene verlossing naar Nederland zoude verlend", in J. A. Van der Chijs, *Nederlandsch-Indisch Plakaatboek IV*, p89.

18 J. A. Van der Chijs, *Realia II*, p114.

19 To legitimize three bastard sons, European men had to pay 1000 *Rijksdalers*. A normal soldier earned approximately 50 *Rijksdalers* a month, of which only half was paid in Batavia. To legitimize a child was thus not an option for the lower VOC ranks. See J. A. Van der Chijs, *Realia II*, p148; P. Van Dam, *Beschryvinge van de Oostindische Compagnie III*, p244.

20 J. A. Van der Chijs, *Realia II*, p114.

21 In this case, daughters of part-Asian extraction were considered "European" as well, provided they had an official European father.

22 Pieter Hartsinck, also Petrus Hartsing (1633/1637–1680). See Bartels, "Hartsinck (Pieter)", in *Digitale Versie Nieuw Nederlandsch Biografisch Woordenboek;* I. Seiichi, "The Life of Piter Hartsinck, the Japanner (1637–80); 'Grand-Pupil' of Descartes", *The Transactions of the Asiatic Society of Japan*, vol 20 (1985): pp145–167; H. Dennert, *Bergbau und Hüttenwesen im Harz vom 16. bis 19. Jahrhundert dargestellt in Lebensbildern führender Persönlichkeiten* (Clausthal-Zellerfeld, 1986), p135.

23 Elisabeth Van Riebeeck (1659–1704). See J. G. Taylor, "Europese en Euraziatische vrouwen in Nederlands-Indië in de VOC-tijd", in J. Reijs et al (eds) *Vrouwen in de Nederlandse koloniën* (Nijmegen, 1986), pp10–33, 30.

24 J. A. Van der Chijs, *Nederlandsch-Indisch Plakaatboek I-IV*. This source selection appears to be widely accepted by the academic community as major historians on the social history of the VOC use it – for example, U. Bosma, *De oude Indische wereld 1500–1920;* J. G. Taylor, *The Social World of Batavia;* H. F. Niemeijer, *Batavia.*

25 "1619. 6 Julij. Regelment op de rantsoenen voor de 'swarten, Chinesen, haere vrouwen ende kinderen, die al rede in grote menichte in 't fort Jaccarta syn, voor de soldaten, ambachtslieden ende jongens", in J. A. Van der Chijs, *Nederlandsch-Indisch Plakaatboek I*, p599.

26 "1648. 29 September. Bepaling van kostgeld en vracht voor repatriërende vrijlieden, – het laatste ook voor hunne goederen", in J. A. Van der Chijs, *Nederlandsch-Indisch Plakaatboek II*, p128; J. A. Van der Chijs, *Realia II*, p114.

27 "1684. 26 Mei/6 Junij. Bepaling nopens den tijd, voor begrafenissen toegestaan", in J. A. Van der Chijs, *Nederlandsch-Indisch Plakaatboek III*, p133.

28 J. J. Coeman: *Pieter Cnoll (gest. 1672). Eerste opperkoopman te Batavia, zijn echtgenote Cornelia van Nieuwenrode (1629–1692) en hun dochters Catharina (geb. 1653) en Hester (geb. 1658)* (Amsterdam, 1665), oil on canvas (https://www.rijksmuseum.nl/en/collection/sK-A-4062); discussed in: J. G. Taylor, "Meditations on a Portrait from Seventeenth-Century Batavia", *Journal of Southeast Asian Studies*, vol 37 (2006): pp23–41.

29 S. Schama, *The Embarrassment of Riches: An Interpretation of Dutch Culture in the Golden Age* (London, 1988), p547.

30 Ibid.

31 "The Hospital for Children of Batavia", printed copper engraving (http://ebooks.library.cornell.edu/s/sea/pages/s/e/a/sea174/00190-l.gif), reproduced in J. Nieuhof, *Remarkable Voyages & Travalls into the best Provinces of the West and East Indies* (London, 1703), p306.

32 "Bijlage I. Conditiën ende voorwaerden, waarop eenige eerlycke personen met haare kinderen, mitsgaders eenige meyskens sonder haare ouders, in dienst van de Vereenighde Compagnie sullen mogen by alle Camerenaangenomen werden omme met haare woonstede te nemen in de stad Batavia, in T' rijck van Jacarta, gelegen in 't eylant van Java-mayor, om voorsch. stadt ende lant te peupleren", in P. Van Dam, *Beschryvinge van de Oostindische Compagnie III*, p363.

33 "1625. 16 Junij/ 23 Augustus. Instructie voor de Weeskamer", in J. A. Van der Chijs, *Nederlandsch-Indisch Plakaatboek I*, p179.

34 "1642. 5/8 Julij. Statuten van Batavia", ibid, p518.

35 Ibid, p539.

36 Instructie voor de Weeskamer, 180f.

37 "1686. 24 Mei. Regelment voor het nieuwe armen-huis", in J. A. Van der Chijs, *Nederlandsch-Indisch Plakaatboek III*, p179.

38 Instructie voor de Weeskamer, 182f.; Statuten van Batavia, p521.

39 That might be because there was no such room or because when the descriptions were written in the late nineteenth century, children's bedrooms were not considered important enough to be mentioned. See F. De Haan, *Oud Batavia. Gedenkboek uitgegeven door het Bataviaasch Genootschap van Kunsten en Wetenschappen naar aanleiding van het drie-honderdjarig bestaan der stad in 1919*, vol 2 (Batavia, 1922), p52, 61f.

40 J. Van Riebeeck, "Brief No. 05. Johanna Maria aan haar ouders", [13 January 1710] in D. B. Bosman, *Briewe van Johanna Maria van Riebeeck en ander Riebeeckiana*, p68; J. Van Riebeeck, "Brief No. 08. Johanna Maria aan haar ouders", [30 January 1710] in D. B. Bosman, *Briewe van Johanna Maria van Riebeeck en ander Riebeeckiana*, p77.

41 "1649. 30 September/6 October. Regeling van het muntwezen. – Verbod tegen het vertrekken naar Europa van inlandsche vrouwen en van mannen, 'met iemandt derselve in huwelyck synde'", in J. A. Van der Chijs, *Nederlandsch-Indisch Plakaatboek III*, 133f.

42 "1716. 16 October. Bepaling, dat aan Compagnie's dienaren, die bij inlandische vrouwen onechte Kinderen hadden verwekt, geene verlossing naar Nederland zoude verlend", in J. A. Van der Chijs, *Nederlandsch-Indisch Plakaatboek IV*, p89.

43 Cornelia Van Nieuwenrode (1629–1692), also Van Nijenroode. Van Nieuwenrode was, like François Caron, born in Hirado to a Japanese woman and a European employee of the VOC. Unlike François's case, her father died before she could be legalized. In his will, however, he made sure that his daughters were provided with a Christian education in Batavia. In 1637 Cornelia and her sister Hester reached Batavia having left their mother behind. By the age of 23 she had married the father in the above-mentioned portrait. As chief merchant of the VOC, Pieter Cnoll was one of the richest men in Batavia. When he died after 20 years of marriage he made Cornelia one of the richest and most influential women in Batavia. Four years later she remarried. From 1678 until her death, she then lived separated from Joan Bitter trying to get a divorce. See L. Blussé, *Rosenkrieg. Ein Scheidungsdrama um Besitz, Macht und Freiheit im 17. Jahrhundert* (Frankfurt, 2000).

44 Niemeijer mentions the family Van Meteren. The legitimate son of Magdalena Smitsert and Abraham Emanuel van Meteren grew up with his bastard half-siblings, offspring of a house slave. See H. F. Niemeijer, "8. Slavery, Ethnicity and the Economic Independence of Women in Seventeenth Century Batavia", in B. W. Andaya (ed) *Other Pasts: Women, Gender and History in Early Modern Southeast Asia* (Honolulu, 2000), 179f.

45 Duty of caregiving: "1625. 16 Junij/ 23 Augustus. Instructie voor de Weeskamer", in Van der Chijs, *Nederlandsch-Indisch Plakaatboek I*, 180f.; Statuten van Batavia, p520; duty to educate: "Regelment voor het nieuwe armen-huis", p184; duty to discipline: "1714. 24 December. Vernieuwd verbod tegen het maken, verkoopen en afsteken van vuurwerk", in J. A. Van der Chijs, *Nederlandsch-Indisch Plakaatboek* IV, p60.

46 N. de Graaf, *Oost-Indise Spiegel*, p14.

47 The idea of the mother of these families behaving like a Javanese princess presages present day research on the social history of Batavia. See S. Abeyasekere, *Jakarta: A History* (Singapore, 1989); J. G. Taylor, "Meditations on a Portrait from Seventeenth-Century Batavia"; P. D. Milone, "Indian Culture, and its Relationship to Urban Life", in *Comparative Studies in Society and History*, vol 9 (1966), p411; H. F. Niemeijer, *Batavia*.

48 "Conditiën", p362.

49 "1685. 27 Februarij. Aanstelling van twee 'gequalificeerde' vrouwen tot buiten-moeders van het weeshuis te Batavia", in J. A. Van der Chijs, *Nederlandsch-Indisch Plakaatboek III*, p146; H. F. Niemeijer, *Batavia*, pp319, 328.

50 "1716. Bepaling", p89.

51 L. Blussé, *Rosenkrieg*, p59.

52 U. Bosma, *De oude Indische wereld 1500–1920*, p64; J. G. Taylor, *The Social World of Batavia*, p45.

53 "1727. 28 Augustus. Bepaling, dat te Batavia buiten functie zijnde onder-kooplieden, zoo spoedig mogelijk, geplaatst en 'in alle manieren geprefereerd moesten worden boven Indische kinderen', die slechts 'bij de uytterste noot en by gebrek van andere, bequame stoffe' in dienst mogten worden aangenomen. – Verbod tegen het gebruiken van soldaten 'aan de penne'", in J. A. Van der Chijs, *Nederlandsch-Indisch Plakaatboek* IV, p199.

54 "1697. 12 April/31 Mei. Renovatie en ampliatie van vroegere bepalingen nopens het dragen van krissen, licht, tjap's en verbijf van inlandsche vreemdelingen te Batavia", in J. A. Van der Chijs, *Nederlandsch-Indisch Plakaatboek III*, 424f.

55 J. Van Riebeeck, "Brief No. 18. Johanna Maria aan haar ouders" [16 September 1710], in D. B. Bosman, *Briewe van Johanna Maria van Riebeeck en ander Riebeeckiana*, p104.

56 J. A. Van der Chijs, *Realia II*, p111.

57 H. F. Niemeijer, *Batavia*, p406.

58 Ibid, p322; J. A. Van der Chijs, *Realia III*, p357.

59 H. F. Niemeijer, *Batavia*, pp319, 406.

60 In "1638. 7 December. Regelment voor het Diaconiehuis te Batavia", in J. A. Van der Chijs, *Nederlandsch-Indisch Plakaatboek I*, p427.

61 Ibid, p428.

62 "The Hospital for Children of Batavia", f. 32.

63 H. F. Niemeijer, *Batavia*, p320. A year after Volkman's report a new orphanage was built. The report thus might have been exaggerated to achieve this goal. The engraving, on the other hand, might have shown a very idyllic picture to raise money from European readers, as stated above.

64 Ibid.

65 L. Blussé, *Rosenkrieg*, p81.

66 "IX. Resolutie van den Gouverneur-Generaal en Rade van Indie, betreffende het onderwijs te Batavia", in J. K. J. de Jonge, *De opkomst van het Nederlandsch gezag in Oost-Indië* V, p55.

67 "XIII. De Gouverneur-Generaal Pieter de Carpentier en Rade van Indie aan Bewindhebbers der gener. O.I. Comp. (Heeren XVII)", in J. K. J. de Jonge, *De opkomst van het Nederlandsch gezag in Oost-Indië* V, p92.

68 U. Bosma, *De oude Indische wereld 1500–1920*, p74; H. F. Niemeijer, *Batavia*, p400.

69 "1684. 4 April. School-reglement", in J. A. Van der Chijs, *Nederlandsch-Indisch Plakaatboek III*, p129.

70 Ibid, p127; "1643. 7 December. Kerk-ordening voor de Batavische gemeente (Reglement voor de predikanten, krankenbezoekers, schoolmeesters, enz., alsmede op de middelen tot bekeering van heidenen)", in J. A. Van der Chijs, *Nederlandsch-Indisch Plakaatboek II*, p52; J. Nieuhof, *Remarkable Voyages & Travalls into the best Provinces of the West and East Indies*, p310.

71 "1684. 4 April. School-reglement", p128.

72 Ibid.

73 P. Van Dam, *Beschryvinge van de Oostindische Compagnie III*, pp218, 247, 263.

74 I. J. Brugmans, *Geschiedenis van het onderwijs in Nederlandsch-Indië*, (Groningen, 1938), p36.

75 "1715. 17 December. Verbod voor de buiten-kantoren tegen het in dienst nemen van kinderen, in Indië geboren of uit Nederland derwaarts aangebragt", in J. A. Van der Chijs, *Nederlandsch-Indisch Plakaatboek IV*, p74.

76 "Carel Reniers, Joan Maetsuyker, Carel Hartsinck, Joan Cunaeus, Cornelis Caesar en Dirck Jansz. Steuer, Batavia 31 jan 1653", in W. Ph. Coolhaas, *Generale Missiven van Gouverneurs-Generaal en Raden aan Heren XVII der Verenigde Oostindische Compagnie II*, p661; "De (provision.) Gouverneur-Generaal Joan Maetsuyker en Rade van Indie, aan de Bewindhebbers der Gen. O. Ind. Comp. (Heeren XVII.)", in J. K. J. de Jonge, *De opkomst van het Nederlandsch gezag in Oost-Indië VI*, p43. This last argument, however, also justified the reopening of the Latin school in Batavia. The school existed only from 1642 to 1656 and again from 1666 to 1670/1671.

77 J. G. Taylor, *The Social World of Batavia*, p27; H. F. Niemeijer, *Batavia*, p323.

78 J. G. Taylor, "Europese en Euraziatische vrouwen in Nederlands-Indië in de VOC-tijd", p22.

79 Dirk Van Cloon (1684–1735), Governor-General 1731–1735: J. G. Taylor, *The Social World of Batavia*, p5; "Dirk Van Cloon", in VOC website, <http://www.vocsite.nl/geschiedenis/personalia/vancloon.html> (accessed 16 June 2007).

PART II
Narrations

4

SELF-NARRATIVES AS A SOURCE FOR THE HISTORY OF EMOTIONS[1]

Claudia Ulbrich

In her essay from 2001, "Die Tränen des Jungen über ein vertrunkenes Pferd. Ausdrucksformen von Emotionalität in Selbstzeugnissen des späten 16. und 17. Jahrhunderts",[2] Benigna von Krusenstjern emphasizes that while primary sources such as contracts, testaments, speeches, sermons or court documents are worth consulting, self-narratives are the kinds of texts in which the articulation of emotions can be found with relative frequency. As an expert in the self-narratives from the Thirty Years' War, she challenges the thesis Werner Mahrholz put forward in 1919 that those who lived during this period had lost the ability to express their emotions.[3] Against Mahrholz, she contends that he did not take adequate account of historically variable forms of emotionality. She points to the significance of poems, prayers and songs in which suffering, mourning or gratitude are communicated and examines prose texts for indirect emotional clues. When Peter Hagendorf, the author of a sparsely worded mercenary diary,[4] mentions that something weighs heavily on his heart (*von Herze leidt*) or that he can still recall after many years a boy who cried on a particular occasion, von Krusenstjern detects unambiguous proof of human feeling even under the conditions of the Thirty Years' War. She ultimately concludes that emotionality is manifested in self-narratives in a way that makes them unique. She moreover calls on researchers to explore the objects and expressions of people's joy and frustration, gratitude and resentment, indignation and despair to examine the causes and articulations of their pride and anger, fear and grief.[5]

Those familiar with self-narratives will surely recognize that these sources are useful for answering a number of the issues raised by von Krusenstjern. The extent to which it is possible to write a history of emotions with the help of self-narratives, however, is unclear. Three of the most notable problems will be mentioned here. First, it is not certain whether reliable patterns and processes can be recognized and derived from individual personal histories that allow meaningful conclusions to be drawn that transcend any single case. This is a methodological problem that is today still largely unresolved.[6] Second, the selection, arrangement, weighing and evaluation of the communicated details of an individual's life are subject to perceptual and behavioural concepts that need to be decoded before self-narratives can be assessed thematically.[7] Recollections alone are not enough to explain why an author describes specific events or emotional responses, while leaving other details aside. Only an analysis of the writing situation can reveal the intentions behind it and allow for an under-standing of why a certain emotion appears in a self-narrative as an actualized memory. Third, it is important to note in this connection the inherent difficulty of interpreting described gestures, which are associated today with certain feelings, in their respective contexts. When writers of self-narratives mention tears, for instance, it is hardly conclusive proof that they were sad.[8] By the same token, when they fail to mention tears, it is not necessarily indicative of an absence of feeling. It is more likely that stylistic principles were at play that were informed by rhetorical rules.[9] In many personal histories, authors chose a documentary style that permitted them to present their own stories authentically. The autobiography genre and the proximity of auto-biographical writing to historical writing set strict limits on emotional expression.[10] The communication of feelings in writing was also influenced by changing customs, such as the manner of dealing with grief.

Andrea Kammeier-Nebel has shown on the basis of numerous sources that writing about death, mourning and personal pain changed after the Reformation.[11] This includes writing about the death of children, in reference to which she is able to cite numerous single documents. The intercessions for grace and mercy for the soul of the deceased described in the self-narratives gave way to appeals for the blessing of the resurrection and the family's reunion on Judgement Day.[12] Until then, the shared burial of the family grave was meant to provide comfort. Konrad Pellikan, for instance, describes how his nine-year-old daughter was laid to rest alongside her mother: "(a small consolation for our pain), put to rest at her mother's side" (*Wir betteten sie (ein kleiner Trost in unserm Schmerz) an der Seite ihrer Mutter zur Erde*).[13] At first, Kammeier-Nebel encountered more expressive descriptions of individual suffering in letters than in autobiographical records. Martin Luther describes his deep suffering over the death of the eight-month-old Elizabeth (1520) and the nine-year-old Magdalena in letters to his friends. He remarks that his love for his child is so great and his remorse so profound that he does not have the strength to pray without bursting into tears.[14] In general, Kammeier-Nebel observes an emotionalization of death announcements in her sources from the second half of the sixteenth century onward. She explicitly links her findings to the transformation of a culture of mourning, while also positing that "the repression of emotions in the private realm" caused individuals to "seek out new pri-vate modes of expression for their suffering".[15] This assertion, however, is slightly at odds with her description of the development of a new public mourning ritual around 1600, at least in Lutheran territories, which included funeral sermons, memorializations, epicedia and epitaphs – in other words, a public form of commemorating the dead that had found its way into private family chronicles.[16]

Private family chronicles already clearly show that the representation of emotions and self-narratives could meet very different objectives, which can only be deduced in context. A synchronic, rather than a diachronic, comparison would be helpful: contrasting different types of text (sermon texts, funeral sermons, self-narratives, dictionaries, etc.) would permit emotional constellations to be identified and thus shed light on the significance of certain emotions for individual writers. Since experiences and emotions are always dependent upon historically defined expectational patterns and forms of expression, this approach would also open access to discourses about feelings.[17] Emotional courses of action, forms of expression and coping mechanisms in certain life situations can only be recognized in terms of the tension between normativity discourses and self-descriptions – a tension which further allows clear delineations to be made with the present. Historicization reveals the normativity of individual concepts. Such a focus, though, would be directed more at the "other" of the Early Modern Period than at developments and ruptures (other sources would prove more fruitful here or at least easier to interpret than self-narratives).[18] At the same time, the question about the emotional character of self-narratives should not be limited to those feelings that are often designated as basic emotions, such as love, joy, grief, fear, anger or even jealousy, pride or compassion. If feelings are modes of relationships, as Claudia Jarzebowski suggests, then one should not look for a predefined feeling, but rather enquire into relationship constellations.[19]

There has long been a consensus in the field that self-narratives are excellent sources for investigating relationships. Writers of autobiographical texts generally value mentioning people to whom they are connected. As Gabriele Jancke has emphasized, they describe themselves above all as social persons who live within various relationships. Among the types of relationships that are often thematized in self-narratives are friendship, teacher–student relationships, parent–child relationships and marital relationships.[20] I would like to follow up on this approach and argue that written emotional expressions should not be understood as "actions within a relational network" (Jancke) and that they should not only be investigated in the context of the history of emotions, but that the writing itself should be ascribed the status of an emotional expression.[21]

To get a sense of the emotional character of self-narratives, it is important to first distinguish three areas relating to the subject "childhood and emotion":

1 writing about one's own childhood;
2 writing about one's own children;[22]
3 writing for one's own children.

Whereas the first point concerns a clearly demarcated life stage, the second and third points relate to childhood as a social relation. The children who are being written about might have already reached adulthood a long time ago. The same might also be said about the children for whom one is writing. Childhood is also described in diverse ways in each of these three areas. This does not mean, however, that the texts can be differentiated according to whether they have been written about one's own childhood or about or for one's own children. Frequently, both types of writing can be found in the same text. James Amelang thus stresses with regard to popular autobiography: "To a large extent, popular autobiography was an individualized expression of the experience of a broad range of overlapping circles, circles that began with the past and present of the author's family, and which quickly expanded to embrace a wider social universe." Be that as it may, I find that in responding to the question about the relation between "childhood and emotion in self-narratives", one would do well first to separate the distinct levels analytically.

Writing about one's own childhood

When Johanna Eleonora Peterson (1644–1722) recorded her life story in 1689, she was 45 years old. Her "Leben von ihr selbst mit eigener Hand aufgesetzet"[23] represents a coherent autobiography extending from her fourth year to her early years as a wife and mother. Her text is one of the few autobiographies from women that was published during the writer's lifetime and also attracted public notice.[24] As Prisca Gugliemetti, who has edited a new edition of the autobiography, emphasizes, Johanna Eleonora Peterson gives priority to those incidents from her childhood, puberty and adolescent years that could be characterized as experiences of deprivation. She laments, above all, that after her mother died, she did not experience enough protection or care, was not understood and did not receive any recognition.[25] Even if Peterson selects those childhood experiences that allow her to reveal the early effects of divine goodness, her text is a superb example of the emotional demands that children place on their parents, and the disappointments that they can endure. Peterson could only convince her readers of the authenticity of her story of God's grace if the connection between the described childhood experiences and the examples of divine grace were comprehensible – in other words, if the experiences of deprivation could be brought into relation with her readers' own experiences (for example, with regard to child-rearing). The extent to which the representation of emotions had to be oriented towards historically defined expectational patterns and forms of expression becomes clear precisely in terms of the relationship to the reader.[26]

Like Peterson, many male and female authors depicted their childhood and adolescence in a critical manner.[27] To cite a further example, Heinrich Bosshard von Rümikon complains that his parents frequently quarrelled because they were too poor to clothe their children sufficiently. He had been so inadequately attired himself that his fellow students both mocked and despised him, causing him finally to stay at home for his lessons. He was beaten by his parents because he preferred to read in silence rather than out loud.[28] Accounts like these are always ambiguous: a reference to solitude as a child, for instance, also reflects a narrative component that was used by writers to present themselves as authors.[29] Other writers, like Matheus Miller, emphasize (all the difficulties that they had with their family notwithstanding) the care with which they were raised by their parents and, in agreement with the normative requirements, write deferentially about their childhood.[30] Typically, particular attention is paid to one's birth, education and upbringing and to relating unfortunate incidents involving a rescue.[31] For Dwight Reynolds, who has also identified these themes in Arabic autobiographies, this discovery is clear evidence of the fact that childhood and education were individual life stages that could be distinguished from adulthood. He recognizes an opportunity for authenticating one's own life story (or "authenticating power") in the anecdotes from childhood and, above all, in the accounts of unfortunate incidents. As mentioned with regard to Peterson, these narratives could also be embedded in a Christian context and in stories of the influence of divine grace. Augustin Güntzer, who relates in his text "Kleines Biechlin von meinem gantzen Leben" numerous unfortunate incidents from which he was rescued, is a compelling example of this.[32] His accounts, which he embeds in prayers, convey his belief that he had been born to suffer. After his story of falling into water and being given up for dead, he writes quite predictably: "My parents were sad and afflicted, for I was their only son; they were fond of me, and they believed that I was dead and had drowned in the water" (*Meine Eltern wahren traurig und betriept, dan ich wahr ein eintziger Son, hatten mich lieb, dan sie vermeinen, ich woehre dodt und im wasser ertruncken*).[33] In this sentence, it becomes obvious at once that emotions and material interests cannot be separated.[34] As the only son, he was supposed to perpetuate the lineage and pass on the family's wealth; he was also a beloved child.

To sum up, the following is worth noting: because recollections of childhood and adolescence are an inherent feature of many autobiographies, autobiographical texts are excellent sources for research on childhood. Although they do not offer direct access to actual childhood experience or to experienced emotions, they usually provide information about the emotional demands that children can place on their parents over an extended period of time. By the same token, it is important to keep in mind that self-narratives have an exemplary function: they communicate – even with a view to one's own childhood – emotional behavioural standards.

Writing about one's own children

The writers of most biographies usually go into less detail about their own children than they do about their childhood. Births and deaths are frequently, although not always, noted, and sometimes the accounts can be quite comprehensive. In this context, one of the most intriguing questions is why certain emotions are recalled or actualized in the moment of writing. Here, I would like to mention the autobiography of the Berne Pastor Johann Heinrich Hummel (1611–1674).[35] Hummel composed the text, available only in transcription, shortly before his death in 1673 under the title "Ein kurzer Entwurf der Histori des Lebens Joannis Henrici Humelij, Brugensis".[36] Lorenz Heiligensetzer, who has carefully analysed this self-narrative, suggests that the text was prepared as a template for the author's funeral sermon. Hummel describes his professional career, the pinnacle of which was his appointment as church dean in Berne, the history of his family, illnesses and deaths. On the one hand, Hummel's self-presentation is, in accordance with the genre, oriented towards the normative ideal of a religious leader. Thus, as Heiligensetzer stresses, it can also be read as a "model book" (*Musterbuch*).[37] On the other hand, there was also room for the writer to elaborate his own individual life story. Hummel began writing when he was already seriously ill and could thus anticipate that his life was coming to an end.

In this situation, he recalled his son Hans Heinrich, who had become gravely ill and died at the age of six. He describes his efforts to care for the child, and how he tearfully tended to his son in his final hours: "God knows that the father's and the child's heart both broke" (*Gott ist bekannt, dass des Vaters und des Kindes Herz zugleich gebrochen*).[38] Hummel's grief over the death of his son remained with him his entire life. He mentions that not a single day had passed in which he did not cry over his loss. Although there were limitations on expressions of intense mourning, his account gave him the opportunity to depict his life and to portray his own suffering. By writing about the loss he suffered in detail, Hummel was able to document his own hardships. His emotionality here also serves as a kind of self-fashioning.[39] It is also an expression of a close father–son bond that Hummel wants to elaborate as fully as possible. It is precisely because of the prohibition against transgressing certain boundaries in writing that the spaces of the expressible can become known.

Emotional writing about one's children is not limited to the commonly portrayed loss, but also relates, for instance, to the writer's daily interactions with them. Fathers, and sometimes also mothers, write about how much they valued teaching their children and preparing them for life.[40] "Writing that is for one's own children" has particular importance in this regard.

Writing for one's own children

"[A]nd I write not for the sake of my reputation, for praising oneself is punishable, but only so that my children have an example and recognize the honor that is due to God" (*und das schreyb ich darumb an, nicht von rombs wegen, denn es streflichen ist, sich zu rüme, allein das meine kinde daran einen spiegel haben und sehen an die ere gottes*).[41] Here, the Nuremberg councilman Niklaus Muffel (1410–1469) justifies writing his memorial book in December 1468, a few months before he was hung for misappropriating city funds. By that time, his children were already adults and had had their own children. In describing his life, he hopes that his descendants "will take pleasure in it and thus also be inspired to similarly dedicate themselves to good works" (*davon ein ergetzlichkeit haben, domit sie auch zu sollichen guten wercken dester ee gereytzet warden*).[42]

It is often assumed that remarks like these, found in many self-narratives, primarily served the purpose of self-legitimation: "The egocentric undertaking of writing down one's life story is presented in terms of the socially relevant task of child rearing."[43] This interpretation rests on the view that the depiction of the individual is always primary in autobiographical writings. Such a view has long been questioned in self-narrative research, however. It has moreover been demonstrated that the vast majority of self-narratives do not, in fact, correspond to this model. In 1996, in her essay "Autobiographische Texte – Handlungen in einem Beziehungsnetz. Überlegungen zu Gattungsfragen und Machtaspekten im deutschen Sprachraum von 1400–1620", Gabriele Jancke emphasizes that male and female authors of autobiographical texts view themselves as anchored within a network of social relations, both as writing selves and described selves. They understand their autobiographical text in terms of a specific action inside of this relational network.[44] In her discussion of the limitations of the self in sixteenth-century France, Natalie Zemon Davis has pointed out that speaking about the self effectively always entailed a relationship: "Virtually all the occasions for talking or writing involved a relationship: with God or God and one's confessor, with a patron, with a friend or a lover, or especially with one's family and lineage."[45] For her period of analysis, she is able to show that family is often the occasion for discussing and writing about the self.[46] Thus, in contrast to the findings of earlier research, it was not necessary for a writer to dissolve ties with the family to become an individual. On the contrary, an important precondition for this could also be the bond to the family or an affiliated group. It was, therefore, not individualization that was a key springboard for writing about the self, but rather the familialization of the late Middle Ages.[47] This observation is also significant for the relation between childhood and emotion. Certainly the possibility cannot be excluded that some writers used "writing for their children" as a pretext for writing about themselves and circumventing a writing ban. Before endorsing such speculative interpretations, however, the relation to the addressees that is formulated in the text should be taken seriously. It was not only women, as often supposed, but also men who emphasized in their autobiographical writings that they were writing for their children. This particular motivation to write is most frequently mentioned in house and family registers. The duty of recording the family history usually fell to the *paterfamilias*. If he was no longer living, the mother in charge of the household could also take on the responsibility. In autobiographical texts that are not strictly counted as house registers, references can also frequently be found to the fact that the authors are writing for their children. Writing for one's children signified a way of taking care of them and one's self. Niklas Muffel hoped that, when recalling his life, his children and grandchildren would recognize the grace of God. With his narrative, he also wanted to honour the esteemed personalities mentioned in his memorial book in the expectation that they would treat his descendants with particular deference and care.[48]

The act of telling one's children about one's life – of providing an example for them, equipping them with useful knowledge about their ancestry and their friends, instructing them to live in an upright manner and do good works – is an expression of the emotional relationships within the family circle that also extend beyond the life stage of childhood. It justifies a permanent and careful inclusion of children into a generation-spanning family group and thus establishes identity, if one prefers to use the term. Occasionally, the writing that is for one's children is based expressly on personal affection. At the beginning of his chronicle, Konrad Pellikan (1468–1556) explains that it is with "fatherly devotion" (*in vätterlicher Zuneigung*) that he wishes his son Samuel to be God-fearing more than anything else because it is "the beginning of all saving wisdom" (*der Anfang aller heilsamen weisheit*).[49] He defends his writing by asserting that he wants it to provide an example for his descendants: "This is my desire: that you should learn yourself from my failures: the history of your ancestors, their lineage, their pursuits, their residences, their fortunes, and, if heaven should provide us with descendants who, as I hope, are pious people who cultivate the welfare of their kin and pay tribute to God, let it also be for their instruction, their warning, their example and their benefit" (*Dies ist mein Begehr: was mir versagt blieb, sollst du kennen lernen: die Geschichte deiner Altvorderen, ihr Geschlecht, ihre Beschäftigungen, Wohnorte, Schicksale, dir selbst und wenn uns der Himmel Nachkommen schenkt, wie ich sie wünsche, fromme Leute, die des Nächsten Wohlfahrt fördern und Gottes Ehre, auch ihnen zur Belehrung, zur Warnung, zum Vorbild und zum Guten*).[50] His writing was not intended for publication, but only for his son's use.

The Alsatian tinsmith Augustin Güntzer maintains in his autobiography that he did not write because of a thirst for fame, but rather for the sake of his heirs: "I didn't write it for glory or in the vain hope that many people would read it, but rather only for the heirs that I leave behind, so that they can see how I led my poor, sinful life on earth in fear and privation" (*Ich habe es nicht geschrieben zum Pracht oder aus Fihrwitz, dass viel leit lesen sollen, sonder nur allein die meinigen hinderlaßen Erben, damit sie sehen, wie ich mein armes sindliches Leben mit Angst und [Not] zugebracht hab auf erden*).[51]

When he wrote his life story, he was an impoverished labourer without his own household. Due to his tenuous material situation, he was dependent on his daughter and his son-in-law. He no longer supported himself as a labourer, but as an itinerant merchant. He felt the need to justify himself for having lost his entire inheritance. The only thing that Augustin Güntzer could leave to his children was his life story and he made every effort to find time to record it.

The assertion is also frequently made in regard to texts from women, the volume of which increased from the late seventeenth century, that they were written for their children. I would like to mention just a few of these texts, without a fuller discussion.

Certainly, the most famous autobiography is that of Glikl bas Judah Leib.[52] She states that she wrote her life story for her children in order to sketch a portrait of her family that would be suited to establishing and stabilizing a generation-spanning familial group: "My dear children, I write so that if today or tomorrow your dear children or grandchildren do not know about their family, I have recorded here briefly who their people are."[53] In her text, Glikl also wrote a great deal about her children, tears, living in mortal fear and joy and pride. She undoubtedly also wrote for herself – or better out of concern for herself – to cope with her grief over the death of her husband. Nevertheless, her writing was tied to her care for her children to whom she wanted to transmit her knowledge and her values.

Additional examples that cannot be explored here in more detail include the memoirs of the Countess von Schwerin, which have been passed down to us in transcription from the year 1731.[54] The title alone, *Historie de la Vie de madame la comtesse de Scheverin, écrite par elle-même à ses enfants*, indicates that she recorded her life story for her children.[55] The commentaries of Countess Leonora Christina Ulfeldt (1621–1698), the daughter of Denmark's King Christian IV, were written while she was in detention. They begin with a long address to her children, who were already adults by this time.[56] Texts like this one also sometimes have dialogical passages in which the author speaks directly to her or his children.[57]

My knowledge of these texts, unfortunately, does not permit me to determine whether there was a shift in the intended addressees over the course of the Early Modern Period. Similarly, I cannot say whether women tended to write for their children in the eighteenth century, whereas in the sixteenth and seventeenth centuries it may have been largely men. What is more, the prefaces of the texts of individual self-narratives are rarely accessible. Even less research has been conducted on the writing situations, which would make it possible to contextualize the dedications. Interestingly, however, a new group of life stories emerged at the end of the eighteenth century that was written for children. They were not written for one's own children, but instead served larger pedagogical aims.[58] Friedrich Christian Laukhard (1757–1822), for instance, saw his reflections on his life as "a contribution to practical pedagogy".[59]

Conclusion

In conclusion, I have attempted to understand self-narratives in terms of the writing situations. Writing is a practice that involves the body and the mind. Moreover, it is emotionally charged: in the eighteenth century, one spoke of writing pleasure, writing bliss and writing addiction.[60] Some authors, such as Ulrich Bräker, described the intensity of their writing pleasure. In the introduction to his diary for the year 1779, he wrote: "It satisfies something so great inside of me, and this something is the driving force." He was true to the motto "pleasure and love for a thing make all work and struggle trifling" (*lust u. lieb zu einem ding macht alle müh und arbeit ring*).[61] Elsewhere he wrote: "Shouldn't I write, Creator – of course, you know the pleasure of your creation – which you haven't denied me" (*Sol ich nicht schreiben – schöpfer – nein, du kennst die lust deines geschöpfs – hast mir diese ia nicht verboten*).[62]

From this perspective, writing for children appears to have been emotionally charged in two ways. It served to gratify an urge, thus giving pleasure, and to meet the need to care for one's children and their future. This does not exclude the possibility that writing often had an apologetic character. Nor does it mean that addressing the children did not offer an opportunity for self-fashioning. It nonetheless opens up a dimension of writing that has often been overlooked in autobiographical research, with its focus on the question of individuality *vis-à-vis* autonomy and self-referentiality. Concern for the self, which has received all too little attention in the research, had considerable importance in the canon of values in the Early Modern Period.

Michel Foucault provides us with a significant clue about this in his later work.[63] In his reflections on the technologies of the self, he stressed that the subject emerges in those practices in which it cares for itself. It is not the Delphic "know your self", but Plato's "look after your self" that is the point of departure for the development of a self-technology that was critical in Christian Europe until the eighteenth century. The invocation of these maxims can be found both in the Greek-Roman philosophy of the first and second centuries of the Roman Empire, as well as in the rules of monastic life in Christian spirituality as they took shape in the fourth and fifth centuries. Although Foucault outlined their history in regard to monastic life, it is hard to imagine that they remained limited to this sphere alone.

It is precisely the perspective of a history of emotions that seems to lend itself to including such a self-concept more fully in reflections and to interpreting within this scope the care for children. In order to further clarify this point, I would like to return once again to the memorializations of death mentioned at the outset. In the late Middle Ages, the concern of human beings for themselves and their families not only related to the living, but also to the deceased family members. In self-narratives, above all in home and family registers, this concern found expression in the endowment rolls for donations for the soul that were tied to announcements about the deaths of wives and children. As already mentioned, the memorialization of death changed in the sixteenth century, at least under Protestantism. The plea for divine mercy, which was no longer thought to be subject to human influence, was replaced by the hope of a reunion in the afterlife: "The intercession was no longer a prayer for the soul of the deceased, but a prayer for the resurrection of all family members." Consequently, not only did the rituals of mourning change, but also the process of grieving and the way of talking about it.[64]

Even if this communication frequently drew on literary models, was oriented towards conventions of writing or was done in passing, it is nevertheless possible to observe that the concern for oneself and for others was an essential motivation of early modern (male and female) autobiographies. By setting aside the assumption that the formulation of this concern was merely a common sign of humility to justify one's own egocentric writing, taking the authors' statements seriously, self-narratives may be recognized as an outstanding source for understanding the history of childhood and emotion. Many authors spent a great many hours recording their lives for their children and in this way tried to show them how to lead fulfilling lives themselves. They also passed on to us an excellent starting point for investigating the history of emotions.

Notes

1 This chapter was written within the scope of the DFG Research Unit "Selbstzeugnisse in transkultureller Perspektive" and for the conference "Childhood and Emotion" in 2010. Only minor revisions have been made. For an overview of recent contributions in the self-narrative research, see C. Ulbrich, H. Medick and A. Schaser (eds) *Selbstzeugnis und Person: Transkulturelle Perspektiven* (Cologne, 2012); F.-J. Ruggiu (ed) *The Uses of First Person Writings/Les usages des écrits du for privé* (Bern, 2013).
2 B. von Krusenstjern, "Die Tränen des Jungen über ein vertrunkenes Pferd. Ausdrucksformen von Emotionalität in Selbstzeugnissen des späten 16. und des 17. Jahrhunderts", in K. von Greyerz, H. Medick and P. Veit (eds) *Von der dargestellten Person zum erinnerten Ich: Europäische Selbstzeugnisse als historische Quellen (1500–1850)* (Cologne, 2001), pp157–168.
3 W. Mahrholz, *Deutsche Selbstbekenntnisse. Ein Beitrag zur Geschichte der Selbstbiographie von der Mystik bis zum Pietismus* (Berlin, 1919).
4 J. Peters (ed) *Ein Söldnerleben im Dreißigjährigen Krieg. Eine Quelle zur Sozialgeschichte* (Berlin, 1993); new edition: idem (ed) *Peter Hagendorf – Tagebuch eines Söldners aus dem Dreißigjährigen Krieg* (Göttingen, 2012).

5 B. von Krusenstjern, "Die Tränen", p168.
6 G. Jancke and C. Ulbrich, "Einleitung", in Jancke and Ulbrich (eds) *Vom Individuum zur Person. Neue Konzepte im Spannungsfeld von Autobiographietheorie und Selbstzeugnisforschung* (Göttingen, 2005), pp7–27, esp. p26.
7 G. Jancke, "Autobiographische Texte – Handlungen in einem Beziehungsnetz. Überlegungen zu Gattungsfragen und Machtaspekten im deutschen Sprachraum von 1400 bis 1620", in W. Schulze (ed) *Ego-Dokumente. Annäherung an den Menschen in der Geschichte* (Berlin, 1996), pp73–106, esp. p76.
8 See also L. Heiligensetzer, "' … wie wol ich von natur schamhafft und forchtsam geweßen bin'. Zur Darstellung von Gefühlen in Pfarrer-Autobiographien des 17. Jahrhunderts", in K. von Greyerz, H. Medick and P. Veit (eds) *Von der dargestellten Person zum erinnerten Ich. Europäische Selbstzeugnisse als historische Quellen (1500–1850)* (Cologne, 2001), pp169–182, esp. 170f.
9 A. Keller, *Frühe Neuzeit. Das rhetorische Zeitalter* (Berlin, 2008), pp71–72; I. Bernheiden, *Individualität im 17. Jahrhundert. Studien zum autobiographischen Schrifttum* (Frankfurt/Main, 1988), p240.
10 L. Heiligensetzer, " … wie wol", p171.
11 A. Kammeier-Nebel, "Der Wandel des Totengedächtnisses in privaten Aufzeichnungen unter dem Einfluss der Reformation", in K. Arnold, S. Schmolinsky and U. M. Zahnd (eds) *Das dargestellte Ich. Studien zu Selbstzeugnissen des späten Mittelalters und der frühen Neuzeit*, vol 1 (Bochum, 1999), pp93–117.
12 Ibid, p102.
13 K. Pellikan, *Die Hauschronik Konrad Pellikans von Rufach. Ein Lebensbild aus der Reformation*, T. Vulpinus (ed) (Straßburg, 1892), p136, according to Kammerer-Nebel, p106.
14 Ibid, p111; "Brief von Luther an Nikolaus Hausmann vom 5. August 1528 und an Justus Jonas v. 23. September 1542", in *D. Martin Luthers Werke*, Kritische Gesamtausgabe, Briefwechsel Bd. 4 (Weimar, 1933), unveränderte Neudruck Graz 1969, Nr. 1303 und Bd. 10 (Weimar, 1947), Nr. 3794.
15 Ibid, p114.
16 Ibid, p109.
17 K. von Greyerz, "Erfahrung und Konstruktion. Selbstrepräsentation in autobiographischen Texten des 16. und 17. Jahrhunderts", in S. Burghartz, M. Christadler and D. Nolde (eds) *Berichten, Erzählen, Beherrschen. Wahrnehmung und Repräsentation in der frühen Kolonialgeschichte Europas* (Frankfurt/Main, 2003), pp220–239; G. Piller, *Private Körper: Spuren des Leibes in Selbstzeugnissen des 18. Jahrhunderts* (Cologne, 2007), pp7–13.
18 When historical developments are argued on the basis of self-narratives, this occurs via an assumption of large historical theories, such as the history of individualism or, as in the example provided by A. Kammeier-Nebel, of privatization. That is to say, historians attempt to local, specific presumed changes in the texts of the self-narratives.
19 C. Jarzebowski, "Loss and Emotion in Funeral Works on Children in Seventeenth Century Germany", in L. Tatlock (ed) *Enduring Loss in Early Modern Germany* (Leiden, 2010), pp187–213, esp. p188.
20 G. Jancke, "Autobiographische Texte", p73.
21 C. Ulbrich, "Schreibsucht? Zu den Leidenschaften eines gelehrten Bauern", in A. Lüdtke and R. Prass (eds) *Gelehrtenleben. Wissenschaftspraxis in der Neuzeit* (Cologne, 2008), pp103–112.
22 J. S. Amelang, "The Dilemmas of Popular Autobiography", in K. von Greyerz, H. Medick and P. Veit (eds) *Von der dargestellten Person zum erinnerten Ich. Europäische Selbstzeugnisse als historische Quellen (1500–1850)* (Cologne, 2001), pp431–438, esp. p434.
23 J. E. Petersen, *Petersen, Johanna Eleonora, geb. von und zu Merlau: Leben, von ihr selbst mit eigener Hand aufgesetzet:Autobiographie*, Prisca Guglielmetti (ed) (Leipzig, 2003).
24 Regarding Petersen, see E. Kormann, *Ich, Welt und Gott. Autobiographik im 17. Jahrhundert* (Cologne, 2004).
25 P. Guglielmetti, "Nachwort", in J. E. Petersen, p103.

26 K. von Greyerz, "Erfahrung und Konstruktion", 220ff.

27 F. Brändle, K. von Greyerz, L. Heiligensetzer, S. Leutert and G. Piller, "Texte zwischen Erfahrung und Diskurs. Probleme der Selbstzeugnisforschung", in: K. von Greyerz, H. Medick and P. Veit (eds) *Von der dargestellten Person zum erinnerten Ich. Europäische Selbstzeugnisse als historische Quellen (1500–1850)* (Cologne, 2001), pp3–34.

28 *Heinrich Bosshard von Rümikon, eines schweizerischen Landmannes Lebensgeschichte*, D. Schmid (ed) (Elsau, 2005), pp53–55.

29 J. S. Amelang, *The Flight of Icarus: Artisan Autobiography in Early Modern Europe* (Stanford, CA, 1998), p169.

30 T. M. Safley (ed) *Die Aufzeichnung des Matheus Miller. Das Leben eines Augsburger Kaufmanns im 17. Jahrhundert* (Augsburg, 2003), p52; idem, *Matheus Miller's Memoir: A Merchant's Life in the Seventeenth Century* (Basingstoke, UK, 2000).

31 Kaspar von Greyerz offers a thoroughgoing analysis with regard to the representation of birth, education and rearing on the basis of self-narratives. See K. von Greyerz, *Passagen und Stationen. Lebensstufen zwischen Mittelalter und Moderne* (Göttingen, 2010). Dwight Reynolds suggested a systematization through the integration of a concept of misfortune. See D. F. Reynolds, "Childhood in One Thousand Years of Arabic Autobiography", in *Edebiyât: Journal of Near Eastern Literatures*, Special issue: Arabic Autobiography, vol 7, no 2 (1996): pp379–392.

32 A. Güntzer, *Augustin Güntzer, Kleines Biechlin von meinem gantzen Leben: Die Autobiographie eines Elsässischen Kannengießers aus dem 17. Jahrhundert*, F. Brändle and D. Sieber (eds) (Cologne, 2002).

33 A. Güntzer, *Augustin Güntzer*, p93.

34 H. Medick and D. W. Sabean (eds) *Interest and Emotion: Essays on the Study of Family and Kinship* (Cambridge, UK, 1984).

35 L. Heiligensetzer, *Getreue Kirchendiener – gefährdete Pfarrherren. Deutschschweizer Prädikanten des 17. Jahrhunderts in ihren Lebensbeschreibungen*, (Cologne, 2006), pp56–59; idem, " … wie wol", pp174–176.

36 J. H. Hummel, Dekan zu Bern. (1611 – 1674): ein Lebens- und Charakterbild aus dem 17. Jahrhundert (Bern, 1856), http://www.mdz-nbn-resolving.de/urn/resolver.pl?urn=urn:nbn:de:bvb:12-bsb10480084–1.

37 L. Heiligensetzer, *Getreue Kirchendiener*, pp104–105.

38 J. H. Hummel, p19.

39 L. Heiligensetzer, " … wie wol", p182.

40 For further details, see K. von Greyerz, *Passagen und Stationen*, pp71–140.

41 N. Muffel, "Gedenkbuch von Nicolaus Muffel, 1468," in K. Hegel (ed) *Die Chroniken der fränkischen Städte*, Nürnberg, Bd. 5 (= *Die Chroniken der dt Städte v 14. bis ins 16. Jahrhundert*, Bd. 11) (Leipzig, 1874), pp735–751, 746.

42 Ibid, p749. For information on the person and text, see G. Jancke, "Selbstzeugnisse im deutschsprachigen Raum (Autobiographien, Tagebücher und andere autobiographische Schriften), 1400–1620", Eine Quellenkunde, together with M. Jarzebowski, K. Krönert and Y. Aßmann (13 August 2008), http://www.geschkult.fu-berlin.de/e/jancke-quellenkunde, Eintrag Nikolaus III. Muffel.

43 F. Brändle et al, "Texte zwischen Erfahrung und Diskurs", p10.

44 G. Jancke, "Autobiographische Texte", p73.

45 N. Z. Davis, "Boundaries and the Sense of Self in 16th-Century France", in T. C. Heller and C. Brooke-Rose (eds) *Reconstructing Individualism: Autonomy, Individuality, and the Self in Western Thought* (Stanford, CA, 1986), pp53–63, esp. p53.

46 Ibid, 56ff.

47 C. Ulbrich, "Libri di casa e di famiglia in area tedesci: un bilancio storiografico", in G. Ciappelli (ed) *Memoria, famiglia, identità fra Italia ed Europa nell' età moderna* (Bologna, 2009), pp39–61, esp. p60.

48 B. Schmid, *Schreiben für Status und Herrschaft. Deutsche Autobiographie in Spätmittelalter und Früher Neuzeit* (Zürich, 2006), p73.

49 K. Pellikan, *Das Chronikon des Konrad Pellikan. Zur vierten Säkularfeier der Universität Tübingen*, B. Riggenbach (ed) (Basel, 1877), p1 ("qui initium sit sapientiae salutaris").

50 K. Pellikan, p1 ("Quandoquidem cupio te consequi, quod mihi dolet fuisse ademptum, historiam tuorum Majorum, genus, studia, loca, fata, ad tuam et posterorum nostrorum, si dare dignabitur dominus, quod opto, pios et utiles ad proximorum salutem et Dei gloriam, institutionem, praemonitionem et ad exemplum in bonis").

51 A. Güntzer, *Augustin Güntzer*, p80.

52 G. bas Judah Leib, *Memoires 1691–1719*, edited and translated from the Yiddish by Chava Turniansky (Jerusalem, 2006); English edition *The Life of Glückel of Hameln (1646–1724): Written by Herself*, translated from the original Yiddish and edited by Beth-Zion Abrahams (London, 1962, reprinted New York, 1963). For the following, see N. Z. Davis, "Arguing with God: Glikl bas Judah Leib", in idem, *Women on the Margins: Three Seventeenth-Century Lives* (Cambridge, UK, 1995), pp5–62, n. 220–259.

53 N. Z. Davis, "Arguing with God", 20.

54 *Mémoires de la comtesse de Schwerin: Une conversion au XVIIIe siècle*, M. Daumas and C. Ulbrich, with S. Kühn, N. Mönich and I. Peper (eds) (Bordeaux, 2013).

55 Ibid, p76. The children are also mentioned as addresses in the preamble.

56 *Denkwürdigkeiten der Gräfin Leonora Christina Ulfeldt*, translated by H. Grössel (Munich, 1968), pp9–19; English edition *Memoirs of Leonora Christina, Daughter of Christian IV of Denmark: Written during her Imprisonment in the Blue Tower at Copenhagen, 1663–1685* (London, 1872)

57 See, for example, *Mémoires de la comtesse de Schwerin*, p86; *Jammers Minde*, p246.

58 Regarding children in the "pedagogical era", see A. Baggerman and R. Dekker, *Child of the Enlightenment: Revolutionary Europe Reflected in a Boyhood Diary*, translated by D. Webb (Leiden, 2009).

59 *Friedrich Christian Laukhard, Leben und Schicksal von ihm selbst beschrieben*, K. W. Becker (ed) (Leipzig, 1989), p8.

60 C. Ulbrich, "Schreibsucht?", p105.

61 Bräker, *Sämtliche Schriften*, A. Bürgi, H. Graber, Chr. Holliger, C. Holliger-Wiesmann, A. Messerli and A. Stadler (eds) 4 vol, (Munich, 1998–2000), vol II, p4.

62 Ibid, p40.

63 M. Foucault, R. Martin et al, *Technologien des Selbst*, L. H. Martin, H. Gutman and P. H. Hutton (eds) (Frankfurt/Main, 1993). See also M. Ruoff, *Foucault-Lexikon: Entwicklung, Kernbegriffe, Zusammenhänge* (Stuttgart, 2009), pp205–216.

64 A. Kammeier-Nebel, "Der Wandel", p102.

5

EMOTIONAL SOCIALIZATION IN EARLY MODERN GERMANY

Otto Ulbricht

The theory of emotion has little to say about emotions and childhood since it takes adults as its model. As in other discourses, "children are frequently excluded from being 'present'".[1] Some historians of emotion writing syntheses use a stereotype of childhood for historiographical purposes: children are seen as emotional, wild, and as vacillating between the extremes of tender and cruel. They take this stereotype to characterize certain periods in history as the "childhood" of humankind. Alternatively, the emotional side of the history of children is "hidden" as a part of the history of the family.[2] From the perspective of culture there can hardly be any doubt that there is a relationship between emotion and childhood. As the anthropologists Lutz and White wrote in 1986: "Cultural views of emotion and cultural views of the child overlap in crucial ways, giving meaning and motivation to the relations between children and adults."[3] Historians may feel obliged to add two things: first, these cultural views are embedded in overarching frameworks; second, they change over time. For an example of the importance of keeping an eye on the understanding of the world at a certain time, we need only look at the sixteenth century. When Jacob Andreae, still an infant in the cradle, filled the house with his crying day and night, his artisan parents believed that he was plagued by "demons".[4] Modern psychologists would probably interpret Andreae's behaviour as a sign of distress, an emotional expression.[5] Thus the focus has shifted from the outside world to the psyche of the child, from a religious and magical explanation to a secular and psychological one.

Although a discussion of the Early Modern Period's cultural views of emotion and children and their changes is not the subject of this chapter, a few comments should nonetheless be made. It is clear that both views changed during the Early Modern Period. In academic discourse "passions" became "emotions". Whereas it is easy to find out what great philosophers, from Aquinas to Descartes and Spinoza, thought about the *passiones*, there is hardly any research on the popular understanding of them. It may have been more influenced by the Bible, the age-old theory of the temperaments and the concept of the seven deadly sins which includes some emotions. As for the concept of childhood, the Ariès thesis of the rise of a concept of childhood in the seventeenth century cannot be maintained, as a phased concept of childhood had been in existence long before. Nor is the "dark legend"[6] of childhood as a time of horror and sorrow tenable anymore.

There were a number of variables that played a role in emotional socialization, the most general being the prevailing "emotional regime". The term "emotional regime" is borrowed from William Reddy who deals with modern states that rely on certain emotional regimes to make their rule last.[7] For the Early Modern Period, a slightly different understanding of the term seems appropriate: the emotional regime is created not by a political system, but first of all by the church and the state. Religion and order in society formed the overarching framework for the emotional regime of the Early Modern Period. Consequently, piety and obedience (or discipline) can be said to have had the most influence on emotions during that time. Within the Christian framework some emotions were considered as positive – the love of God, for example; others negative – anger and even grief, if excessive. In a society based on inequality and hierarchy, obedience is of foremost importance. It frequently required the suppression of emotions.

The findings of an investigation limited to this general level cannot be more than a first step, however. The concept of emotional regime is too generalized once one turns to a society which had distinct "class" differences. The ideal of sensibility, for example, which favours spontaneous expression of cultivated emotions was clearly an ideal of the upper middle class in the second half of the eighteenth century. But such ideals were not followed by the other classes – that is, by the majority of the population. Another important factor is gender – that is, gender stereotypes and gender roles. There can hardly be any doubt that there was a difference not only between the emotions ascribed to women and those ascribed to men, but also in their actual emotional behaviour.

Within this general framework, the concept of "emotional socialization" may permit a closer look at the topic of childhood and emotions. Socialization, the process of adjustment to society's rules and norms, has been discussed ever since Durkheim; its application to past periods is more recent. The psychological concept of emotional socialization, however, is new.[8] Apparently there has not been a historical study of it.[9] So this chapter can be considered a first attempt to tackle this problem.

In the process of the socialization of emotions many agents became involved besides parents. These included other relatives, particularly those living in the household of the parents, peers, tutors and teachers. This chapter will concentrate on parents. In this respect, emotional socialization asks "how parents ... may affect children's understanding, experience, and expression of emotion".[10] Successful emotional socialization is believed to play an important role in social competence and is considered an important factor for success in later life. It can work as direct verbal or non-verbal intervention (through instructions or warnings, rewards or punishments) or in an indirect way – that is, through observation.

Psychological research on the parents suggests a number of topics for study, ranging from the child's family experience of emotions, parental expression of emotion concerning the child, the parent's reaction to the child's emotions, and the parents' discussion of emotion to the child's understanding, experience and expression of emotion.[11] A short look at the topics is sufficient to reveal that some can be made good use of in a historical study, whereas others cannot. As there have been quite a number of studies of the parent–child relationship in the past, parents' reaction may well be a field that can be investigated. The parents' discussion of emotion, however, which relies on methods and sources not available to the historian, such as close observation or self-reports, is almost completely barred for the Early Modern Period. Another approach that is closed to historians involves the children's understanding of emotion, which is based on interviews.

Autobiographies seem a good choice for studying emotional socialization in practice.[12] This chapter uses more than 60 of them from the German-speaking countries, covering the period from about 1500 to 1800. In principle, such a study would profit from the inclusion of diaries and letters. Apart from the fact that this is outside the scope of this chapter, diaries were often written while traveling or during times of war, and their focus on family life differed from that of autobiographies. Private letters, particularly family letters, would be useful, but they have been grossly neglected by research (in this respect, Chapter 9 in this volume by Valentina Sebastiani marks an important departure).[13]

Autobiographies offer detailed information on childhood, as numerous similar projects have demonstrated. There is no reason to be overcautious as to the quality of the information. Of course, any childhood is presented from a certain perspective, but as long as factual statements about it cannot be proven wrong, are plausible and cannot be found in other sources, it does not seem wise to exclude them.[14] It is to the advantage of the subject that emotion-related events are much better remembered. As suitable as autobiographies are, there are, nevertheless, some drawbacks. First, quite a number of them attach no importance to childhood; the authors write only that they were born, baptized and sent to school. This is not what has been called "childhood amnesia": the lack of memories of the first three or four years.[15] Childhood simply is not relevant to these authors. If childhood is given some space, it is accidents and illnesses that are recalled. At the end of the eighteenth century, autobiographers begin to include pranks and anecdotes. As most autobiographies concentrate on such important, even dramatic events of childhood, "the ephemeral nothings of domestic life"[16] are left out. The day-to-day, parent–child conversations about emotional events, which are so important, remain, therefore, sadly missing. So the common reaction to "normal" crying or to other emotional moments can rarely be found. One rarely finds passages where the authors describe what their parents (or they as parents) did to calm down a child after it had "nearly explode(d) with laughter and delight".[17] Accounts of the battles of wills that often start when a child can walk and its parents have to tell it what to do and what not to do are rare as well. Such a rare example is the following passage from Veit Konrad Schwarz, who at two years old had a favourite cushion:

If I was carried, it was not all right with me, if I was led by the hand or if something good was done to me, I would not have it. So they let me push the cushion around and tumble about.[18]

Another reason for the elusiveness of the subject is that most autobiographies of this time concentrate on the outward life of a person, a tendency that continues well into the nineteenth century. It comes as no surprise, therefore, that emotions are hardly ever discussed; in most cases they are only mentioned in the description of an event.[19] If dramatic, emotion-evoking actions are reported, they generally do not reveal how the parents reacted to them. If parental actions are noted, the accounts usually still lack the words – the explanation, praise or blame – that may have accompanied them.

There is, however, a subset of sixteenth-century autobiographies that is to some degree open to the discussion of emotion. These are autobiographies that are influenced by the Renaissance idea of life-writing with its emphasis on the importance of education. The same is true of autobiographies from the eighteenth century that were influenced by the Enlightenment and its belief in the omnipotence of education. These authors devoted more space to their childhoods and youths and, so, the chances of finding something relevant to the subject increase. One has to keep in mind, however, that an air of nostalgia soon starts to hang over childhood memories, now considered the golden time[20] of life, a result of the rapid change of that time.

The available information remains limited, however, as most autobiographies were written by men. Such sources by women are grossly under-represented for most of the Early Modern Period. Moreover, of those written by women, quite a number come from the quills of nuns or religious zealots. This is unfortunate, since it was mainly women who were in charge of rearing the children. Fathers took control of formal education, teaching their children the alphabet and to read. Writing about their children, they offer few details, registering the materially important events, such as births, apprenticeships and marriages. Having to rely mainly on autobiographies by men means that the evidence is gender specific because the socialization of girls and boys differed significantly. For these reasons this chapter concentrates on boys. The boys turned authors come mainly from the educated classes – that is, mainly from the urban upper class; there are also a few noble autobiographers. From the 1770s onwards, members of the labouring classes too wrote their lives.

It is well known that emotions (and their understanding) develop in stages:

> Socialization plays an increasing role in determining what situation elicit[s] what emotions, as well as how these are expressed. One might think of development of emotional life as requiring an ever increasing socialization influence.[21]

Therefore it would make sense to proceed by age groups. There is not, however, sufficient evidence to allow us to study the different phases of childhood. The question of when childhood ends has often been discussed. In this chapter the end of

Latin school attendance or of trade apprenticeship will be taken to mark the end of childhood, for it is when boys move to university or undertake their travels as journeymen that a new period definitely begins.

The first question to be answered is what effect did the emotional regime have on emotional socialization? As argued above, piety and discipline were of foremost importance in early modern society. Education aimed primarily at shaping a good Christian who obeyed the dictates of church and state.

The emotional socialization of children was framed and interpreted in religious terms because emotion is fundamental for religion.[22] Often children were taught the basic teachings of Christianity at home. There they learned prayers, psalms and sayings before being given some formal religious instruction at school and church. Parents made use of Christian knowledge in order to help the child cope with his emotions or to interpret emotionally disturbing events. So a lot of emotional socialization was intimately connected to a religious moral universe.

When nine years old, Augustin Güntzer had a dream in which he experienced "great fear": he was forced to fight with the devil. He told his father, who said: "That is indeed a bad dream, may God help."[23] The consolation held out to the boy was that God who had helped the boy in the dream would also help in the future. In the eighteenth century another boy dreamed that he was chased by the devil: he managed to escape, but woke up afraid. His father said: "How fine is everybody when they enjoy God's mercy and his protection as well as his love. For then Satan, be he as powerful and cunning as he is, cannot harm us."[24] Trust in God was fundamental to coping with fear. Children on their own could turn only to God in dangerous situations in order to withstand the emotions they experienced. In one account a young shepherd boy had to stay on his own with the lambs and the dogs overnight. Being afraid of the wolves, he was instructed as to what he had to do should they turn up, but it was a terrible thunderstorm that brought "cruel terror" to him, the roar of thunder, the bright lightning, the hail, the howling of dogs and the crying of lambs. To pray to God as well as he could was all he could do.[25]

Johannes Fabricius Montanus was given a much wordier explanation after he fell into a well. His mother told him over and over again that his survival was a sign of God's providence. God's protection comforted the boy in the end, but the author goes on to say that the mother interpreted the event as a sign of great things God had in store for her son, which one might well take as a retrospective interpretation.[26] In another case of a child's fall, the father and a government official ran to him to inspect his body. Johann Gerhard Ramsler was then promised the roasted liver of a stag if he would jump about – obviously a means of finding out whether he had suffered any internal injuries. The boy could indeed jump, to the great joy of the administrator and the father who thanked God and his angels for saving him.[27] So the boy was made to forget his terror by enjoying a delicacy which was prepared for him on the spot; at the same time he learned that God was the cause of the adults' joy and gratitude. In yet another case of a fall, in the 1790s, Martin Hudtwalker was punished with a few slaps to the face.[28] That is all the author tells us. One could easily argue that, by then, all reference to God would have disappeared until one takes into consideration that the man who beat the boy was a country vicar. This example illustrates the problems of interpretation which arise because the sources report the actions, but rarely the words that accompanied them.

Sometimes the religious comfort offered disregarded the age of the child. Some boys were too young to understand the Christian interpretation of an emotional event. Ulrich Bräker, when four years old, slipped down a slope and almost fell into a dangerous river. When visiting the spot, his father praised God's wonderful helping hand and explained the danger to the boy. The boy turned author recalled that he did not understand any of it, only his fear and the danger remained in his mind.[29] In yet another case, Hermann von Weinsberg grew impatient while suffering from the German measles at age four. When his parents or other adults tried to comfort him by saying that God sometimes tests those whom he loves, such Christian wisdom did not meet the religious understanding of the toddler. He cried out, "he does not love me, he is an evil man."[30]

Karl Phlipp Moritz received religious books and songs from his Quietist father to help him cope whenever a wish was not fulfilled or something sad was in store for him.[31] The gifts were probably intended to console by teaching that suffering is a Christian's lot, but they also inculcated discipline and deepened faith:

> One day after he had recovered from the smallpox, Oswald was impatient because, where he was sitting, the sun shone into his eyes [he had been unable to see for nine days]. His mother asked him who it was who made the sun shine and whom did he now have to thank that he could see her again. Oswald was ashamed and became quiet.[32]

In contrast to this instrumental use, children also learned Christian virtues with a strong emotional quality. Of course, they learned charity when they saw their fathers putting money in the box for the poor in the church;[33] but they also learned sympathy through the actual practice of charity. As a little boy, Schad himself gave alms to the poor who came to the door. The more often he performed such acts, the greater the joy they caused him; as he puts it, a kind of enthusiasm began to grow within him.[34] From a slightly different point of view one might say that he took pride in being a good Christian. Schad was a Catholic, but the same attitude of sympathy for the poor can be found among Protestants. As a child, Lucas Geizkofler gave food to his poor classmates and their tutor.[35] After the father of the poet Schubart, a man of rather modest means, had given money to a poor widow, he addressed his son: "Christian, if you give to the poor, you have a treasure in heaven."[36] The author claims that this was the only advice of his father that he had always followed. An exceptional case of giving is reported by a mother whose six-year-old son made his will on his deathbed and distributed his savings, of his own will, as she says.[37]

Discipline, which often meant obedience, was the other pillar of early modern society, inculcated, if it met with any resistance, by corporal punishment. Physical punishment was acceptable (though nevertheless feared) for children when deserved and moderate – that is, when parental anger was under control.

Obedience to parents, then, was fundamental. During the sixteenth century, Hieronymus Wolf set his mind on becoming a scholar, but his father ordered him home from Latin school. Overcome by rage, he responded that if his father intended to make a tailor or shoemaker out of him, he would have to obey. Aware of the implicit defiance, the father shot back that were it not for the second part of the sentence, he would indeed make a tailor or shoemaker out of him. To mend his son's stubborn ways, the father devised a special method of emotional socialization: he sent him to serve as a scribe in a nearby court of law where he would have to control his emotions. The mockeries and insults of the knights and the young noblemen would moderate his son's melancholic temper. And, indeed, the remedy seemed to work.[38]

The change of surroundings was also used in another case. A number of authors describe themselves as "wild" in their childhoods. This may have been a gendered stereotype, but in some cases it was definitely a problem. Because of his wildness as a boy, Büsching was sent away to live with his uncle. When the uncle went for a walk, he set the boy a lesson to learn, locked the door and left, with the boy watching him from the window. At night, when they slept in one bed, the boy sometimes fell out of bed because of the tossing and turning of his uncle, whom he feared to awaken, when he tried to climb back in. One early morning he finally ran home, imploring his parents not to send him back again.[39]

Attending school was intimately connected with obedience because quite a few boys did not like it. The fear and punishment made attending school hard. In consequence, some of them played truant. Eberhard Werner Happel, who often did so, was punished for his ignorance and made to wear a fool's cap, which was tied to his hat. Shame overcame him on his way home, so he hid the fool's cap. When he returned to school and the cap could not be found, he had to confess what he had done. His father, a pastor, wrote a few lines in his defence and his mother accompanied him to school, determined to fight for him. Even though he ran away again, she managed to prevent him from being beaten.[40] Most parents thought that the fear of the rod was as necessary as the shaming methods. They objected, however, to excessive beating and humiliation. One mother, whose son was undressed, bound to a pillar and beaten excessively for playing truant, even managed to have the teacher dismissed.[41]

Apprenticeship was also an emotionally difficult time for young boys, particularly when they had to suffer the moods of their master[42] and his household. When Andreas Ryff was an apprentice in Strasbourg, the mistress of the house and her daughters poured scorn upon him: they regarded him as a poor, ignorant Swiss, which must have hurt more than he admitted because there was some truth in it. Ryff felt so ashamed that he wrote to his father several times, begging to come home. But his father told him in a letter to withstand the mockery of the women and to concentrate on his job. He and other parents wanted their children to learn endurance, which meant suppressing negative emotions.[43] During the eighteenth century, a master worried about the melancholy state of his new apprentice named Johann Christoph Pickert and asked him and his colleague what the reason for it was.[44] Neither told him – again, one can perceive the suppression of emotions. In this case, it would have been embarrassing for the boy to confess that he was sad over having lost his first love through the separation and, moreover, that his self-confidence had gone, too, after leaving home in tears.

The impact of disobedience sometimes led to very painful memories, as one autobiographer tells his readers. He wanted to partake in the night-time celebrations of the youth at the time of the wine harvest and secretly left the house though his mother had forbidden him to do so. His mother came to look for him; he could hear her wailing and begging for her son. "And I could resist!" he writes. Of all his pranks, this was the one he could least forgive himself, he writes, and it remained one of the most bitter memories of his life.[45] Permanent feelings of guilt were the result of disobedience in this case.

Before launching into particular fields, we have to look at two things that had an impact upon emotional socialization. First, differences caused by class in parental standards of emotional socialization played an important role for their understanding of the child's reactions. Second, the gender-specific emotional styles of fathers and mothers must be considered. The different standards can best be compared for the second half of the eighteenth century, which saw the rise of autobiographies from the labouring classes. Peter Prosch, son of a poor widow from the rural lower class, tells us that by playing a trick on his mother, his brother received the severe beating Prosch had deserved. It seems possible that a parent of the educated classes would have instructed him on the unfairness of his behaviour and then, perhaps, punished the child. But Prosch's mother just laughed.[46] There are indications that parents of the educated classes sometimes had the same impulse to laugh but tried to suppress it in order to maintain their principle.[47] Or they laughed first and punished afterwards. Young Christoph zu Dohna made an applicant for the position of his tutor crawl to his father on all fours. His father burst into loud laughter, but the boy ran away immediately, knowing what was in store for him.[48] Bronner, when still a toddler, fought with a gander over a nutshell. His lower-class mother did not run to protect the little boy; she clapped her hands and encouraged him to keep on fighting.[49] Even harsher was the attitude of Thomas Platter's mother, a widow from the labouring classes, in the sixteenth century. After he had eaten frozen grapes while helping her, he experienced such pain that he rolled on the ground in anguish. She just laughed and said, "If you want to burst, burst. Why did you eat them?"[50] When he was a schoolboy attending a convent school, Bronner escaped from a room he had been put in because of his alleged misbehaviour. The mistress of the school complained to his father, who worked in a brickyard. He could not suppress a smile when his son told him what had happened. Instead of the usual beating, he was only severely reprimanded.[51] Another author from this class maintains that the only time his parents showed pity towards him was when one of his feet was going to be amputated.[52] Although this autobiographer shows a tendency to self-pity, it seems, on the one hand, that a certain kind of harshness often was an element of emotional socialization in the lower classes. But one must keep in mind, first, that autobiographies do not lend themselves to accurate description of everyday moments of love and tenderness, often not expressed verbally in this class; and, second, that the authors who had risen from their origins probably concentrated on the darker sides of their childhood. On the other hand, these parents recognized the funny element of some situations and were then not as strict as they were expected to be. Parents from the educated classes as they appear in these sources seem high principled and more protective. Apart from those strict adherents to principles, they showed more empathy, as will become clear.

Class was also a variable in parents' understanding of a child's emotion. Ulrich Bräker's father, a saltpetre worker, had to spend long spells away from home. When he returned, the toddler was afraid of the strange man and ran away from him. His father wanted to punish him, interpreting such behaviour as disobedience. He obviously lacked the empathy to understand his son's quite normal reaction.[53] If one compares his understanding to that of the Nuremberg humanist Scheurl, who headed a patrician household in the sixteenth century, there is a striking difference. He understood clearly that an infant or a toddler often had closer emotional ties to his mother or wet-nurse. About his one-year-old son Georg, he wrote: "He loves his wet-nurse as she loves him"[54] and five years later made this entry: "He begins to love his father more than three years ago."[55] Such an aptitude was far from atypical of urban upper classes at that time, as a study of childhood based on letters has shown.[56]

Due to the gender-related differences between the mother's and the father's emotional behaviour, children in early modern society were confronted with two distinct emotional styles. Throughout the period, urban upper-class mothers, in general, showed more affection and were more protective of their sons. There are examples of mothers contradicting the fathers' decision to send the boy far away;[57] or, when the son went off to a school in a distant town, it was often she who accompanied him part of the way.[58] They often stopped fathers when beatings appeared too severe or out of control.[59] Even in cases when disobedience endangered the life of the child – as, for example, when Wilhelm Traugott Krug took the horse of a visitor for a ride and fell off – the mother protected the child from the father who in his anger wanted to punish him as severely as possible.[60] They themselves beat their children not as often as fathers did. It was their gentler, loving ways the boys remembered. It is not before the end of the eighteenth century, however, that evidence appears that the gentleness of mothers had some effect. One author reports that when his mother was about to punish him physically for the first time, she dropped the birch and started crying. He thought that she was crying over his misbehaviour and never did it again.[61] Two others write that their consciousness of motherly care hurt them each time they made their mothers angry.[62]

In contrast to the gentler emotional attitudes of mothers, anger was characteristic of fathers. Some incidents bespeak excessive, uncontrolled anger. In such a passage, in Bartholomäus Sastrow's sixteenth-century autobiography, the author comments on the way in which his father raised him and his siblings: "My father was a little too quick in his reactions, in particular when his choleric temperament got the better of him."[63] In the preceding paragraph he had reported the following incident from his childhood:

> I was standing in the door to the stable, while he was inside it. He got angry at me, grabbed a pitchfork and hurled it at me. I managed to step aside. He hurled it so hard that it got stuck in a beam and was difficult to pull out.[64]

Felix Platter's father, intent on making him a doctor of medicine, regularly beat him in school – he was his schoolteacher – and even threatened to flog him and to kick him with his feet for things that could be regarded as trifles. By mistake, he once hit him in the face with a rod, causing bleeding and swelling. The boy had to be treated by a physician.[65] Psychologists have found that such intense expressions are one factor which determines what emotional behaviours are regarded as appropriate.[66] Indeed, both Sastrow and Platter knew as children that their fathers had over-reacted emotionally. The type and intensity of the reaction of other people involved support such a view. Moreover, it is obvious that such experiences affected Sastrow's and Platter's own emotional attitude, or, more broadly speaking, they are particularly relevant for the formation of children's self- and world schema.

Yet, there were thoughtful fathers in the urban upper and middle classes as well. As children often do, little Hermann von Weinsberg ran from his mother to his father, complaining about the beating he had received from her. His father asked: "Shall we make your mother leave the house for good or shall she live from now on downstairs and we upstairs?"[67] This teasing way of making a child think is reminiscent of the way in which the Inuit present their children with "emotionally powerful problems" by asking them questions such as: "Your mother's going to die – look she's cut her finger – do you want to come live with me?"[68] The conclusion which little Weinsberg reached pleased his father: he opted for separation by stories. As Weinsberg himself remarks, he had shown some moral sense for what was more important.[69]

It is necessary to consider the reactions of parents to particular emotions of their children. The response to the crying of a child in distress or pain is a good starting point. Early modern sources discuss crying only in the context of illnesses.[70] We can detect various parental reactions when the pain of illness made children cry. Herman von Weinsberg did not himself remember what happened when he suffered from smallpox, but reports what he learned from his parents – namely, that his father sat up at night, while the little boy cried with all his might, playing the cymbals and whistling in order to soothe him.[71] At the end of the eighteenth century, Pickert's step-father, a soldier and roofer, threatened to beat him if he did not stop crying when the boy was suffering from a kind of dysentery.[72]

As has been shown in these autobiographical sources, there was a difference between the emotional attitude of fathers and mothers towards their children. This is also reflected in an extraordinary incident told by Johann Peter Frank. As a nine-month-old baby, he was crying, which annoyed his father, who told his mother to suckle him and leave the room, which she refused to do. When she insisted on staying in the room after a second command, he grabbed the infant in a fit of rage and threw it some distance out the open door.[73] The author maintains that he suffered for nine months from bodily pain, but it seems likely that his psyche also suffered.

The sixteenth-century Swiss physician and autobiographer Felix Platter offers another glance at parents' reactions to the crying of an infant. In Platter's unusual case, we hear of their reaction to a distinct emotion. He tells us that as an infant, so his parents told him, he started crying whenever he saw his nurse's mutilated finger and even refused to eat the porridge she tried to feed him. Platter showed clear signs of disgust. When his parents found out what had caused his crying, the nurse was dismissed.[74] This must be interpreted not so much as a measure of the parents' relief, but rather as a supportive action in contrast to an attitude which interprets the infant's crying as tyrannical disobedience.[75]

Using public shaming to make children adopt certain norms characterized the Early Modern Period.[76] To inculcate respect for another's property – a fundamental social, religious and legal norm – or, in other words, to prevent theft, public shaming was used to create fear of shame. The anticipation of shame would prevent a boy from actually breaking the norm. The social construction of the so-called self-conscious emotion of shame, which most psychologists say can be found from two years onwards, can be observed in the sources.[77]

Parents reacted rigidly to minor violations of this fundamental norm by their off-spring. In his earliest childhood memories, Friedrich Paulsen says that he sees himself "reluctantly walking at his mother's hand to a neighboring woman, a bunch of flowers in his hands; white daffodils they were. But they were not meant as a present, they were stolen flowers which my mother made me return. ... my mother soon found out the origin of the flowers, and she at once forced me to take that walk of shame, ... she took the matter very seriously."[78]

Although this is admittedly an example from the middle of the nineteenth century, instances of this way of teaching children through public shaming can also be found for the eighteenth century and probably much earlier. Franz Xaver Bronner reports that as a little boy he stole a small clay figure he coveted. His mother found out its origin and, following him at a distance, made him walk to the shopkeeper to return the figure and ask for pardon. Franz Xaver was so ashamed that he devised a trick to return the figure without asking for forgiveness. To inculcate the norm his mother said that stealing the small figure "was the beginning of a godless, unhappy life that usually leads to the gallows, the sword or the wheel".[79] Much harder to bear was the mockery and derision another boy had to experience. Sent to glean the crop, he found three ownerless bundles of ears and took them home. After the boy to whom they belonged had told his father, a publican and baker, the father of the thief made his son call all the young people in the village to his house. He then made his son, at the head of the crowd, carry the bundles through the village, back to the owner's home.[80] Shame in the Early Modern Period was thus often constructed in a ritualis-tic, public way.[81] Bronner's father worked in a brickyard, Feder's was a Protestant preacher. After young Feder had uttered a religious curse, his father beat him. When the next Sunday school lesson came, his father told the boys that vileness can be found even at a very young age – and made his son step forward as an example. Feder described that he felt more numbed than morally touched, but nevertheless presumed that the impression the scene left on him may have been beneficial.[82] Thus, autobiographical sources reveal no class difference when it comes to inculcating shame in response to the violation of fundamental norms. When an apprenticed boy took money out of the cash box of his master, the result dramatically changed his life: having to face his mother and his aunt, who both had sacrificed so much for him, seemed like "a clap of thunder" and, full of guilt, he ran away for good.[83]

Parental expression of emotion directed at the child is another important factor in emotional socialization. It may affect children's expression of emotion in many ways; the most important ones are probably the processes of imitation and contagion. The two examples of direct expression presented here differ substantially, although they both concern fatherly emotional expression. When one boy said goodbye to his family, about to leave for the life of a travelling student, his father burst into tears, looked at him a long time in great pity and hugged him with all his might and kissed him, and could not speak anymore because of his tears. At that moment, the boy who had been looking forward to leaving because he thought the grass would be greener on the other side, began to feel the sadness of leaving.[84] So his self-centred joy became coloured by the social feeling of mournfulness. Although this scene appears somewhat dramatized, boys at that age can distinguish mixed feelings.[85]

Johann Dietz tells his readers how he reacted to being shunned by his family. Of the seven children of the Dietz family, Johann was the only one who had white hair, whereas the others had black. His father claimed he was not his son, and the other children despised him, called him names and pushed him around. He reacted by preferring to be on his own, painting and writing.[86] This example points at a constellation that must have been frequent; parents did not have the same emotional relationship with all of their children and step-children.

Sometimes parents did not show enough empathy and, therefore, could give no support when children suffered from shame or embarrassment. This happened when they were made to play roles – in particular, gender roles – that made them feel inferior and ignorant. Von Hippel, for example, when still in his early childhood, was made to play the bridegroom of adult women in a nearby noble household. The princess laughed at his childish answers and the embarrassment it caused him. As his mother, too, tended to present him with brides, there was only his father left to turn to. Yet, von Hippel dared not tell him of these feelings because his father did not take part in such jokes and, according to Hippel, might have thought them trivial.[87]

In another case, an older boy, already an apprentice, came to realize that he was playing a certain role in the eyes of others without even noticing it: he had to accompany his master's wife on her business in the countryside and to carry her baby in a basket.[88] When he asked her why people were looking at them in a strange way, she told him smiling: "You stupid boy, they think we are husband and wife."[89] As she kept on joking about it, he left her. He felt ashamed, he says, but probably he also felt humiliated for not understanding the situation and uneasy in the gender role ascribed to him. Parents and others may not have recognized that the boys had already developed a gendered sense of self that caused shame and embarrassment at such role-playing.

Things are somewhat different in the case of Felix Platter, also caught up in a role-playing situation. Once he was to dress as a shepherd and to recite Vergilian verses in the house of a famous humanist printer. He was too embarrassed to do so and pretended to be sick. Looking back, he thought that he had been too young and, therefore, not courageous enough to present himself in torn clothes in front of strangers. Being the son of a headmaster, he might also have felt that the role of a shepherd was humiliating for him.[90]

Parents (and siblings) sometimes showed little empathy when talking about dramatic events in the world. After he had been told about the comet of 1680 and listened to all the dramatic interpretations connected with it, little Adam Bernd, not yet four years old, was put to bed with all the terrible imaginings in his head. During the siege of Vienna three years later, the singing of a certain religious song in school, the talk of the adults and the transport of all valuables for safe-keeping in the town frightened him and led him to strange thoughts. In later life, whenever he heard the song they had sung in school during that dangerous time, the same "dark fear" which he had felt then arose in him again.[91] But one has to keep in mind, of course, that children show great temperamental differences and that this boy was very fearful.

Considering the characteristics of the sources, it seems impossible to find evidence for a child's experience of an emotion and its interpretation. Surprisingly, however, there is an example in which the interpretation is conveyed in a metaphorical way and in another there is at least an intuitive, though not verbalized, understanding. When Hermann von Weinsberg, following the example of other students, played truant for the first time, he was so afraid that every cobblestone seemed to stare at him while he was strolling along the Rhine.[92] The cobblestones seem to stand for the internalized norm of school attendance and thus caused a feeling of guilt and fear in him because he was breaking it. He reports the effect of this experience: he never played truant again. This seems to indicate an intuitive understanding, and it is only remembered, one must assume, because of the sudden shock it had caused. The other instance is from the end of the eighteenth century. Children had gathered at the coffin of the author's step-brother, when the author, Wilhem Harnisch, was some-how led to pull another boy's plait. "Whenever I remembered this scene, I was ashamed of myself",[93] he writes. The author does not explain why, but it is obvious that by pulling the plait he was violating a fundamental religious and emotional norm. To express it in modern terms, although he had not yet learned to manage his emotions, which required him to show some kind of sadness, he knew that he should have refrained from pranks at such a moment. His emotional socialization in this particular field had failed. There is another related case that illustrates the difficulty of this kind of management for school children. Eberhard Werner Happel was to inform his mother that her mother was seriously ill; in fact, she had already died. He enjoyed the run to the village, however, and hoping to be freed from school attendance for a few days, played with his mates whom he met on the way and told them carelessly that his grandmother had died. His failure to manage his emotions resulted in his mother learning the bad news before he delivered it.[94]

Emotional socialization in the past is a difficult subject to research. The impact of the emotional regime of early modern Germany, characterized by religion and dis-cipline, can be observed in the religious interpretation of highly emotional events and in the use of fear to enforce emotional discipline. Throughout the period, class made a great difference in the understanding of and reaction to boys' emotions. The gen-dered roles of mothers and fathers also influenced it. On the one hand, the strategy of public shaming makes it clear how different emotional socialization was then. On the other hand, attitudes found in the urban upper classes during the sixteenth century and in the middle classes at the end of the eighteenth century are not completely different from ways of socializing the emotions of children today.

Notes

1 H. Hendrick, "The Evolution of Childhood in Western Europe, c. 1400 – c. 1750", in *The Palgrave Handbook of Childhood Studies*, J. Qvortrup, A. Corsaro and M.-S. Honig (eds) (Basingstoke, UK, 2009), p99.

2 B. H. Rosenwein, "Worrying about Emotions in History", *American Historical Review*, vol 107 (2002): pp829–830; R. van Daalen, "The Emotions", in P. Stearns (ed) *Encyclopedia of European Social History*, vol 1 (New York, 2001), pp355–390.

3 C. Lutz and G. M. White, "The Anthropology of Emotions", *Annual Review of Anthropology*, vol 15 (1986): p426.

4 In German "Unholde", *Leben des Jakob Andreae, Doktor der Theologie, von ihm, selbst mit großer Treue und Aufrichtigkeit beschrieben, bis auf das Jahr 1562*, H. Ehmer (ed) (Stuttgart, 1991), pp20, 21.

5 L. A. Comras, "Human Development", in D. Levison, J. J. Ponzetti, Jr. and P. F. Jorgensen (eds) *Encyclopedia of Human Emotions*, vol 1 (New York, 1999), p369.

6 H. Hendrick, "The Evolution of Childhood", p101.

7 W. M. Reddy, *The Navigation of Feeling: A Framework for the Study of Emotions* (Cambridge, UK, 2001), 124f.

8 N. Eisenberg, A. Cumberland and T. L. Spinrad, "Parental Socialization of Emotion", in *Psychology of Emotions*, vol V, A. S. R. Manstead (ed) (Los Angeles, CA, 2008), p157. See also the short paragraph by G. Peterson, "Cultural Theory and Emotions", in *Handbook of the Sociology of Emotions*, J. E. Stets and J. H. Turner (eds) (New York, 2007), pp123–124.

9 W. Ruberg, "Epistolary and Emotional Education: The Letters of an Irish Father to his Daughter, 1747–52", *Paedagogica historica*, vol 44 (2008): 207–218. This chapter comes close to it, but does not use the concept.

10 N. Eisenberg et al, "Parental Socialization", p157.

11 Ibid, passim.

12 It does not seem necessary to discuss the age-old question of the value of autobiographies as historical sources. See L. A. Pollock, *Forgotten Children. Parent–Child Relations from 1500 to 1900* (Cambridge, UK, 1988), pp65–67.

13 M. Beer, "Private Correspondence in Germany in the Reformation Era: A Forgotten Source for the History of the Burgher Family", *Sixteenth Century Journal*, vol 32 (2001): pp948–951.

14 Brändle and others say autobiographies can only be used for the judgements and views of the writer. This argument is as weak as the one that maintains that you cannot find out anything about crime by studying trial records and that only the view of the court is accessible. See F. Brändle, K. von Greyerz, L. Heiligensetzer, S. Leutert and G. Piller, "Texte zwischen Erfahrung und Diskurs. Probleme der Selbstzeugnisforschung", in K. von Greyerz, H. Medick and P. Veit (eds) *Von der dargestellten Person zum erinnerten Ich* (Cologne, 2001), p9. It is necessary to be careful when using autobiographies after 1770, first because they became a literary genre from then on, and second because the rapid change from then on made childhood seem to belong to a world that was lost. Moreover, the perspective of the passages on childhood is that of the parents in some cases.

15 R. Pohl, "Was ist Gedächtnis/Erinnerung?", in C. Gudehus, A. Eichenberg and H. Welzer (eds) *Gedächtnis und Erinnerung* (Stuttgart, 2010), pp80–81.

16 P. Auster, "Introduction", in N. Hawthorne, *Twenty Days with Julian and Little Bunny by Papa* (New York, 2003), pxxvi.

17 N. Hawthorne, *Twenty Days*, p10.

18 A. Fink, *Die Schwarzschen Trachtenbücher* (Berlin, 1963), p192. This and all other translations are the author's. Born 1541 (I shall give the date of the birth of the authors so the

reader can place the passage or quotation in time). For an interpretation of putting the child on the cushion as punishment, see R. Frenken, *Kindheit und Autobiographie vom 14. bis 17. Jahrhundert*, vol 2 (Kiel, 1999), pp550–551.

19 A qualification has to be made for highly dramatic events in life (e.g., death of a spouse or a child) when grief is shown.

20 J. Nettelbeck, *Eine Lebensbeschreibung, von ihm selbst aufgezeichnet*, vol 1 (Berlin s.d., circa 1885), p15; J. B. Schad, *Lebens- und Klostergeschichte, von ihm selbst beschrieben* (Erfurt, 1803), p135. Born 1758.

21 M. Lewis, "The Self-Conscious Emotions", in *Encyclopedia on Early Childhood Development*, www.childhood-encyclopedia.com (2011), p4.

22 J. Corrigan, "Introduction: The Study of Religion and Emotion", in *The Oxford Handbook of Religion and Emotion*, J. Corrigan (ed) (Oxford, UK, 2008), p7.

23 A. Güntzer, *Kleines Biechlein von meinem ganzen Leben. Die Autobiographie eines Elsässer Kannengießers aus dem 17. Jahrhundert*, F. Brändle and D. Sieber (eds) (Cologne, 2002), pp94, 95. Born 1596. In another case of a religious nightmare, in which the cross with Christ on it fell on the dreaming boy, we read only that the mother was worried and the father spoke of him as a fool. H. L. Nehrlich, *Erlebnisse eines frommen Handwerkers im späten 17. Jahrhundert*, R. Lächle (ed) (Tübingen, 1997), p28. Born 1653.

24 J. C. Müller, *Meines Lebens Vorfälle und Neben-Umstände*, K. Löffler und N. Sobirai (eds) (Leipzig, 2007), p14. Born 1720.

25 H. L. Nehrlich, *Erlebnisse*, p23.

26 *Der lateinische Dichter Johannes Fabricius Montanus (von Bergheim im Ober-Elsass) 1527–1566* (Straßburg, 1894), p7. Born 1527.

27 *Lebens- und Leidensweg des M. Johann Gerhard Ramsler, Specials zu Freudenstadt. Die Lebenserinnerungen eines württembergischen Landpfarrers (1635–1705)* (Stuttgart, 1993), p23. Born 1635. After Wilhelm Traugott Krug, who was clinging to stairs that had broken under him, had been saved by jumping on this teacher's shoulders, he was reprimanded and immediately made to kneel down and say the Paternoster. Urceus [i.e., Wilhelm Traugott Krug], *Meine Lebensreise. In sechs Stazionen* (Leipzig, 1825), pp19–20.

28 M. H. Hudtwalker, *Ein halbes Jahrhundert aus meiner Lebensgeschichte* (Hamburg, 1862), p11. Hudtwalker calls himself Oswald in his autobiography. Born 1787.

29 U. Bräker, *Lebensgeschichte und Natürliche Ebentheuer des Armen Mannes im Tockenburg*, H. H. Füßli (ed) *Sämtliche Schriften*, vol 4, C. Holliger-Wiemann, A. Bürgi, A. Messerli and H. Graber (eds) (München, 2000), pp366, 367. Born 1735.

30 "Das gedenkboich der jaren meines liebens, darin von mir samt den meinen soll vermellt werden mit gottes gnaden, durch mich Herman von Weinsberch licentiaten angefangen zu schriben", http://www.weinsberg.uni.bonn.de/Edition/Liber_Iuventutis/LI1.HTM, p, 14; also *Das Buch Weinsberg*, J. J. Häßlin (ed) (Cologne, 1990), pp38–39. Born 1518.

31 K. P. Moritz, *Anton Reiser. Ein psychologischer Roman*, W. Martens (ed) (Stuttgart, 1995), p22. Born 1756. On the views of this author on the importance of childhood memories, see J. Schlumbohm, "Constructing Individuality: Childhood Memories in Late Eighteenth-Century 'Empirical Psychology' and Autobiography", *German History*, vol 16 (1998): pp31–33.

32 M. H. Hudtwalker, *Ein halbes Jahrhundert*, p3.

33 As a child, Paul Anton watched his father; see "Achte Historie/Hn D. Pauli Antonii ... von ihm selbst beschrieben", in J. H. Reitz, *Geschichte der Wieder-Gebohrnen*, vol 4, H.-J. Schrader (ed) (repr. Tübingen 1982), p234.

34 J. B. Schad, *Lebens- und Klostergeschichte*, pp99, 103. Born 1758.

35 A. Wolf, *Lucas Geizkofler und seine Selbstbiographie* (Vienna, 1873), pp24–25. Born 1550.

36 Ch. F. D. Schubart, *Leben und Gesinnungen. Von ihm selbst, im Kerker aufgesezt*, Part 1 (Stuttgart, 1791), p7.

37 *Das Hausbüchl der Stampferin* (Klagenfurt, 1982), p35.

38 H. Zäh, *Hieronymus Wolf, Commentariolus de vita sua* (PhD thesis, Universität Augsburg, 1988), p35 f/35★ f. Born 1516.

39 A. F. Büsching, *Eigene Lebensgeschichte in drei Stücken* (Halle, 1789), 35f.
40 *Lebensbeschreibung des Eberhard Werner Happel (1647–1690)*. From his novel *Der Teutsche Carl*, G. Könnecke (ed) (Kirchhain, 1990), 15f.
41 J. Butzbach, *Odeporicon. Zweisprachige Ausgabe*, A. Beriger (ed) (Weinheim, 1991), pp148 (Latin), 149 (German).
42 As Ramsler states for his son Samuel Friederich, see *Lebens- und Leidensweg*, p76. Cf. fn 27.
43 "Selbstbiographie des Andreas Ryff (bis 1574)", W. Vischer (ed) *Beiträge zur vaterländischen Geschichte*, vol 9 (1870): pp64–65. Born 1550.
44 Pickert, *Lebens = Geschichte*, p27. As apprentices were integrated within the households of their masters, and he and his wife acted in the place of parents, it seems justified to include such examples.
45 J. G. H. Feder, *Leben, Natur und Grundsätze* (Leipzig, 1825), 30f.
46 *Leben und Ereignisse des Peter Prosch, eines Tyrolers von Ried im Zillerthal, oder Das wunderbare Schicksal. Geschrieben in den Zeiten der Aufklärung*, K. Pörnbacher (ed) (München, 1964), pp13–15. Born 1744.
47 J. G. Seume, "Mein Leben", in J. G. Seume, *Werke*, vol 1, J. Drews (ed) (Frankfurt am Main, 1993), p15. Born 1763.
48 *Die Denkwürdigkeiten des Burggrafen und Grafen Christoph zu Dohna (1665–1733)*, R. Grieser (ed) (Göttingen, 1974), p33. Born 1665.
49 F. X. Bronner, *Ein Mönchsleben aus der empfindsamen Zeit. Von ihm selbst erzählt*, vol 1, O. Lang (ed) (Stuttgart s.d.), p37. Born 1758.
50 T. Platter, *Lebensbeschreibung*, A. Hartmann (ed) (Basel, 1999), p58. Ralph Frenken thinks this may have been a case of oral envy by the mother. See R. Frenken, *Kindheit und Autobiographie*, vol 1, (Kiel, 1999), p407.
51 F. X. Bronner, *Mönchsleben*, pp50–52.
52 K. P. Moritz, *Anton Reiser*, p17.
53 U. Bräker, *Lebensgeschichte*, p14.
54 H. Heerwagen, "Bilder aus dem Kinderleben in den dreissiger Jahren des sechzehnten Jahrhunderts", *Mitteilungen aus dem Germanischen Nationalmuseum* (1906): p105.
55 Ibid, p113.
56 M. Beer, *Eltern und Kinder des späten Mittelalters in ihren Briefen* (Nürnberg, 1990).
57 J. Butzbach, *Odeporicon. Zweisprachige Ausgabe*, A. Beriger (ed) (Weinheim, 1991), p157; *Des Schlesischen Ritters Hans von Schweinichen eigene Lebensbeschreibung*, E. von Wolzogen (ed) (Berlin, 1908), p9.
58 J. Butzbach, *Odeporicon*, p157; "Das Leben Johann Conrad Kranolds", J. Moser (ed) *Zeitschrift des Harz-Vereins*, vol 28 (1895): p666; F. X. Bronner, *Mönchsleben*, p91.
59 J. G. Seume, "Mein Leben", p19; F. X. Bronner, *Mönchsleben*, p46; W. Harnisch, *Mein Lebensmorgen. Nachgelassene Schrift zur Geschichte der Jahre 1787–1822*, H. E. Schmieder (ed) (Berlin 1865), p26.
60 Urceus, *Meine Lebensreise*, p15.
61 J. F. Reichardt, *Der lustige Passagier. Erinnerungen eines Musikers und Literaten* (Berlin, 2003), 23f.
62 *Aus dem Tagebuch des Bremer Kaufmanns Franz Böving (1773–1849)*, K. H. Schwebel (ed) (Bremen, 1974), p19; J. O. Thieß, *Geschichte seines Lebens und seiner Schriften aus und mit Aktenstükken*, vol 1 (Hamburg, 1801), p10. Today such feelings would be considered as indicative of "a warm, mutually responsive parent–child relationship" (of temperamentally fearless children). K. H. Lagatutta and R. A. Thompson, "The Development of Self-Conscious Emotions", in J. L. Tracy, R. W. Robins and J. Price Tangney (eds) *The Self-Conscious Emotions* (New York, 2007), p99.
63 *Bartholomäi Sastrowen Herkommen, Geburt, vnd Lauff seines gantzen Lebens*, G. Mohnike (ed) (Greifswald, 1823), p77.
64 Ibid. Mentioned under the heading of "accidents in childhood" by K. Arnold, "Familie, Kindheit und Jugend in pommerschen Selbstzeugnissen der Frühen Neuzeit" in W. Buchholz (ed) *Kindheit und Jugend in der Neuzeit 1500 – 1900* (Stuttgart, 2000), p24.

65 Felix Platter, *Tagebuch (Lebensbeschreibung) 1536–1567*, V. Lötscher (ed) (Basel, 1976), 80f. Born 1536.
66 N. Eisenberg et al, "Parental Socialization", p186.
67 Das gedenkboich der jaren meines liebens, http://www.weinsberg.uni.bonn.de/Edition/Liber_Iuventutis/LI1.HTM, p18.
68 J. L. Briggs, *Inuit Morality Play: The Emotional Education of a Three-Year-Old* (New Haven, CT, 1998), p5.
69 "Das gedenkboich der jaren meines liebens", http://www.weinsberg.uni.bonn.de/Edition/Liber_Iuventutis/LI1.HTM, p18. Cf, fn 30.
70 There is only one exception: the case of a girl aged three or less in the artisan world. The father gives a summary description of his wife's inconsistent emotional education of their daughter: "When she wanted something, she did not get it, but was whipped. But when she was most angry, her mother gave her something to drink." *Meister Johann Dietz des Großen Kurfürsten Feldscher Mein Lebenslauf* (Munich s.d.), p198.
71 "Das gedenkboich der jaren meines liebens", http://www.weinsberg.uni.bonn.de/Edition/Liber_Iuventutis/LI1.HTM, p7. Weinsberg was not yet two years old.
72 J. C. Pickert, *Lebens = Geschichte des Unterofficier Pickert*, G. Frühsorge and C. Schreckenberg (eds) (Göttingen s.d), p23.
73 J. P. Frank, *Seine Selbstbiographie*, E. Lesky (ed) (Bern, 1969), p31. Born 1745.
74 F. Platter, *Tagebuch*, p54.
75 We do not know how his parents reacted to his disgust when he was older because throughout his childhood and youth, Platter would run away whenever he came upon a person who lacked a limb.
76 A similar statement can be found for Puritan New England; see J. Demos, "Shame and Guilt in Early New England", in R. Harré and W. Gerrod Parrott (eds) *The Emotions: Social, Cultural and Biological Dimensions* (London, 2000), p83.
77 L. A. Comras, "Human Development", p377.
78 F. Paulsen, *Aus meinem Leben. Jugenderinnerungen* (Jena, 1910), p20. This incident is dealt with from the perspective of class by S. Ungermann, *Kindheit und Schulzeit von 1750–1850. Eine vergleichende Analyse anhand ausgewählter Autobiographien von Bauern, Bürgern und Aristokraten* (Frankfurt am Main, 1997), p302.
79 J. B. Schad, *Ein Mönchsleben*, 44f. The same line of argument can be found in J. G. Seume, *Mein Leben*, pp20–21.
80 J. B. Schad, *Ein Mönchsleben*, p124.
81 Authors always note when they were punished or blamed in front of a third person or in the open street. See, for example, J. G. H. Feder, *Leben*, p23; Hudtwalker, *Ein halbes Jahrhundert*, p11. On the importance of the audience, see P. S. Harris, *Children and Emotion: The Development of Psychological Understanding* (Oxford, 1989), pp94–96.
82 J. G. H. Feder, *Leben*, p8.
83 J. C. Brandes, *Meine Lebensgeschichte*, vol 1(Berlin, 1799), p44.
84 J. Butzbach, *Odeporicon*, p151. Butzbach was about 11 years old.
85 P. S. Harris, *Children*, p186.
86 Dietz, *Lebenslauf*, pp14–16.
87 T. G. Von Hippel, *Selbstbiographie*, in *Hippel's sämmtliche Werke*, vol 12 (Berlin, 1978), 36f. Born 1741.
88 Ibid.
89 J. C. Pickert, *Lebensgeschichte*, p29.
90 F. Platter, *Tagebuch*, p94.
91 A. Bernd, *Eigene Lebensbeschreibung*, V. Hoffmann (ed) (Munich, 1973), p25.
92 "Das gedenkboich der jaren meines liebens", http://www,weinsberg.uni.bonn.de/Edition/Liber_Iuventutis/LI1.HTM, p39.
93 W. Harnisch, *Mein Lebensmorgen*, p28.
94 Happel, *Lebensbeschreibung*, pp20–21.

6

PURITAN CHILDREN AND THE EMOTIONS OF CONVERSION

Paola Baseotto

A history of childhood and emotion must, of necessity, include a discussion of views held by the puritans over an extended period of time, the sixteenth and seventeenth centuries, in England and America. My claim has two mainstays: one is a historical fact; the other is the argument I put forward in this chapter. Regarding the first, puritans' remarkable attention to the child's intellectual and spiritual condition, their production of the majority of early modern child-rearing advice literature in English, as well as of the first books specifically for infant leisure reading have received such vast treatment by so many historians dealing with various aspects of the puritan experience that no more than passing mention is needed here. The second rationale behind my contention about the puritans' title to consideration by historians of childhood and emotion is my view of the unprecedented and distinctive spiritual, ecclesiological, social and political relevance of the emotional practices of children in puritan England and America. What I hope to show is that infant "emotionology" was the catalyst of a collective, deliberate and systematic educational effort, the object of scrutiny and orientation by parents who received specific instruction from ministers to this end.[1] In this regard, my findings confirm the theories advanced by ethnographers, such as Catherine Lutz, in relation to the prevalent role of culture and social interplay over biology or genetics in the formation and expression of emotions.[2]

In an article on the role of emotions in the puritan paradigm of salvation, I have recently claimed that by reason of shared, distinct emotional norms and practices, deriving from specific theological focuses, the heterogeneous group of zealous Protestants (Presbyterians, Independents, Congregationalists and non-conformist preachers, among others) who defined themselves as "godly" and were collectively defined by contemporaries as "puritans" may be seen as a coherent cultural community.[3] My main argument in this chapter is that because of the puritan accent on the doctrine of divine grace and on sanctification (that is, on the inner working of grace entailing emotional transformation), central to the educational endeavours of puritan parents was their teaching by precepts, example and practice from their own spiritually useful emotionology. Their foremost responsibility, as described in a vast corpus of instructional and autobiographical literature, was to prepare children for inclusion in the puritan emotional community by teaching them the devotional style, articulated in a distinctive emotional practice, conducive to conversion.[4] A crucial mission, indeed, since children's practice of the prescribed emotional style signalled their awakening, a vital event for the survival of the puritan movement and for the eternal destination of parents, which depended in large measure on fulfilling their calling as the spiritual guides of their children. The child's religious arousal that ran parallel (indeed, identified with and was expressed by gradual acquisition of competence as an emotional subject) was central to the dynamics of puritan family life. This process entailed a redefinition of the affective mode of the parent–child relation, which appears of great relevance for studies of family history, in particular, and the history of emotions, more generally.

All leading historians of early modern England lay stress on the abundant documentary evidence regarding common perceptions of the moral and material welfare of the nation as proceeding from the integrity and prosperity of the family.[5] Views of the focal role of the family are even more distinct in the case of the puritans, whose life in general and religious practice, in particular, pivoted on the household and on aggregations of households.[6] Each widely read puritan text published from the sixteenth century to the first decades of the eighteenth in old and New England emphasizes the spiritual, ecclesiological and political centrality of the family, "the Mother Hive, out of which both those swarms of State and Church, issued forth".[7] Authoritative works, such as Baxter's *Christian Directory*, specify the consequences of exemplary or evil family government on church and nation: because "A holy well-governed family is the preparative to a holy and well-governed Church", Baxter argues, "from the wickedness of *families* doth National wickedness arise."[8]

If many popular texts emphasize the close interdependence of the integrity of church, state and family, they are even more vocal regarding the fact that the eternal destination of individuals is entirely determined within domestic walls, as suggested by these nautical metaphors: "An ungoverned ungodly family is a powerful means to the damnation of all the members of it: It is the common Boat or Ship that hurrieth souls to Hell"; a holy, well-governed family is like a "Ship which is bound for Heaven, and where Christ is the Pilot".[9] In his interesting discussion of the puritan family as a "theocracy" based on the Bible, Schücking rightly argues that the ultimate purpose of marriage or parenting was mutual help and guidance towards sanctification and very aptly describes members of puritan families as "travelling companions on the road to the next world".[10] Indeed, "Christian Families are called Churches", Baxter explains, "because they consist of holy persons, that worship God, and learn, and love, and obey his word".[11]

Given the key role of the family in the puritan spiritual and social project, the synergic effort to awaken children (that is, to teach them the emotional style instrumental in their conversion) hinged on the household, while school and pulpit played auxiliary roles. Whereas schoolteachers were mainly required to implement children's memorization of their catechism and relevant passages from sermons, ministers' foremost responsibility was the instruction of parents in the art of awakening their children.

Protestantism, especially the Calvinist and Zwinglian streams at the base of the puritan pattern of religious experience, had extended the concept of calling from the strict ecclesiastical sphere to all human activities. In the light of the puritan emphasis on family, particular stress was laid on one's calling as husband or wife and especially as father or mother.[12] Growing awareness of the impracticability of thorough reform of church and state through political action, from Queen Elizabeth's early dashing of such hopes to the 1662 Act of Uniformity, which wiped away all illusion of a puritan commonwealth, is documented by the multiplication in miscellaneous writings of appreciative remarks on the saints' calling as parents of godly children, the only hope of group survival. Far from being ignored or unwanted as some historians have maintained, children were the nucleus of families, the cells which composed the puritan body.[13] Unsurprisingly, the puritan educational energy and focus soon out-stripped the mainstream Anglican established tradition of parental contribution to the spiritual fashioning of children.[14]

All puritan spiritual authorities concur that "the chief part of Family-Care and Government consisteth in the right Education of Children".[15] This marked sensitivity to parental duties, as Leverenz points out, is shown by the fact that:

> ... most of the family-advice books were written by Puritans. Anglican treatises on the family are much less frequent. Moreover, where Anglican treatises tend to mention children only in passing, urging conventional hierarchic discipline, Puritans emphasized parental as well as marital duties.[16]

All literary sources, whether prescriptive or autobiographical, agree in identifying the "right Education" of children with their religious education. Parents were reminded that children "have an everlasting inheritance of happiness to attain: and it is that which you must bring them up for".[17] Many texts advance the view that religious education is the most perfect expression of parental love, the cement of family bonds. While Baxter accounts the undertaking of religious education as a sure sign of parents' affection, "if you Love them, shew it in those things on which their everlasting welfare doth depend". In his advice to parents, the non-conformist minister Thomas Cobbet suggests that "the bond of love is doubled, when natural Fathers, by Gods blessing upon their instructions and admonitions, become spirituall Fathers of their Children".[18] This connection between parental love and spiritual instruction also emerges from autobiographical recollections; with reference to his mother, Heywood uses a felicitous metaphor of childbirth to suggest the pre-eminence and more intense painfulness of spiritual parenthood over the physical: "She travelled in birth again for us til Christ was formed in us, and the latter travel was mostly sharper."[19]

Because children "are not borne but made Christians", the aim of puritan parental care was nothing short of their children's new birth.[20] Instrumental to this spiritual refashioning was a distinctive piety and it was the primary duty of parents to instruct their children in it. Teaching children piety, my sources agree, equalled teaching them the emotional style required for transformation of their heart into "*a New Heart, and a Clean Heart, and a Soft Heart*".[21] Heywood offers a graphic description of the great responsibility of parents who receive "Children from God unpolish, without any form" and must "return them back to him with his Son Christs Image on them".[22] Heywood's analogy characterizes parents as God's delegates in perfecting his creation, a challenging role, indeed, especially in view of the puritan endorsement of Calvin's emphasis on original sin and utter inborn corruption. Unpolished and formless as in Heywood's depiction, children were nevertheless no clean *tabulae rasae* on which to draw Christ's image with ease. On the contrary, they were seen as "the Children of Death, and the Children of Hell, and the Children of Wrath, by Nature".[23] The small *tabulae rasae* clearly needed thorough cleaning before Christ's image could be carved on them.

Puritan devotional and instructional works are replete with variations on Calvin's conception of the child as a "seed-bed of sin". The influential *Looking Glass for Children*, for example, characteristically stresses children's "undone estate by nature" accounting for "the powerful prevalency of Satan to sin and disobedience".[24] References to innate sinfulness are a cliché of puritan conversion narratives and autobiographical recollections in general. The Salem minister Joseph Green confesses how as a very small child his "enmity to God" deriving from the inborn corruption of his heart "did plainly discover itself".[25] By way of a metaphor evocative of an early modern larder, the minister Kilby dates the open manifestation of his inner depravity from the utterance of his first words:

> The Devil had leisure to take full possession of my heart. Who deeply seasoned me with sin, that I have continued sinful ever since.[26]

Anne Bradstreet offers a poetic version of appropriate awareness of inherent sinfulness: "Stained from birth with Adams sinfull fact/Thence I began to sin as soon as act."[27] The pithy report of the London artisan Nehemiah Wallington testifies, "May the 12, 1598, at five o'clock in the morning was I born in sin and came forth polluted into this wicked world", which is a prosier, but no less powerful expression of the prescribed sense of inborn corruption.[28] Clearly, influential catechisms which bombarded children with addresses of this kind, "Thou mightst justly have been cast into hell before thou didst breath in this open world," did their persuasive trick.[29]

Beyond its theological import as one of the crucial focuses of Calvinistic belief, emphasis on children's congenital sinfulness was also the pivot of ministers' pressure on parents to engage to their utmost capacity and energy in the religious education of their children. Parents were constantly reminded of their responsibility as transmitters of original sin either through matter-of-fact statements, such as "Thou euen by breeding thy children hast helped them into corruption", or, more frequently and certainly more convincingly, by way of grisly addresses such as Cotton Mather's "thy Children are dying of an horrid poison in their Bowels; and it was thou that poison'd 'em".[30] This view of infant sinfulness is the spring of puritan anxiety about the need for exceptional re-formational efforts. Religious conversion, not baptism, puritans believed, was the winning weapon against Satan. Given the inherent corruption of their children and in consideration of the very high rate of infant mortality, parents were urged to throw themselves wholeheartedly into their duty to facilitate the earliest new birth. As widely read authors, such as James Janeway, tirelessly reminded parents, children "are not too little to die; they are not too little to go to hell".[31] Small voices of young saints from the large collection of instructional biographies so popular with both young and adult readers depicted grim images illustrative of the fatal consequences of delayed religious education: "how many poor Children lately may have been carried Christless thither, and like sheep layd into the grave (whose Parents thought it time enough perhaps to teach them soul-concernments at leisure)".[32] In this light, the likes of Cotton Mather reassured parents that pressure on their little ones could never be untimely: "You can't begin with them Too soon."[33]

Religious precocity is presented as utterly desirable in a wide variety of texts. Insistence by prominent theologians that children be exposed to religious instruction as soon as possible refracts in all popular collections of biographies of pious children, typically depicted as absorbed in prayer and meditation on scriptural texts. Janeway's *Token* includes stories about real champions of precocity: "a child that was admirably affected with the things of God when he was between two and three years old", a Charles Bridgman who "had no sooner learned to speak, but he betook himself to prayer".[34] Regarding the "Lovely Child", Joanna Reynell, whose early conversion and exemplary behaviour in her fatal illness he proposes for imitation, Edward Reynell reports how she began "to suck in the milk of Gods words (as it were) with the milk of her Nurse".[35] About the frequent mention of very early religious instruction in diaries, it is difficult to establish whether what is documented is an actual practice produced by warnings such as Kilby's reference to a competition with Satan ("Take good heed, least the Devil get the first possession of your Children") or an indication of the author's desire to characterize themselves or their children as exemplary.[36] Lucy Hutchinson, for example, reports her habit of repeating the sermons she heard in 1620 as a young churchgoer of just four and in his commonplace book Joseph Green recalls that when he was between four and five years old his father urged him to pray to God "to pardon [his] sins and save [his] soul from hell".[37] A very interesting instance of deliberate transmission of educational styles is found in a 1688 *Advice of a Father*: "if thou art a father […] let him suck pious and prudent Principles with his Milk".[38]

Judging from the frequency and quality of references in autobiographical and prescriptive texts, coercive measures by "selectmen", such as the policing of parental performance of their duties to impart religious education and the removal of children in case of negligence, were less persuasive than pressures exploiting parental love and threats of eternal punishment, thus capitalizing on the emotions of tenderness and fear.[39] The eye of God was felt as more searching than the eye of neighbours or authorities. Parents were required to be aware that God kept their educational efforts constantly under scrutiny. Not surprisingly, the yardstick by which they were judged was their children's spiritual condition. Hence, parents were told by the authors of child-rearing manuals and by clergy in church sermons to expect eternal rewards or punishments according to their proficiency as inciters and supervisors of their children's emotional responses to God's summons. On both shores of the ocean and over a wide span of time, puritan spiritual authorities employed a rich repertoire of rhetorical devices to sound a persuasive note. Strategies varied considerably as some authors inflected the theme of parental protective instincts, while others likened negligent parents to cruel beasts or exploited their anxiety regarding the possibility of their unregenerate children's early death and damnation.

One way of convincing parents to engage vigorously in religious child rearing was to appeal to their tenderness, as does Cotton Mather through images of children as little birds in the nest, crying for spiritual food:

> How *deaf* art thou, that thou dost not hear a loud cry from the *Souls* of thy Children in thine Ears, *O my Father, my Mother, Look after me!* [...] Are you sollicitous that their *Bodies* may be *Fed*? You should be more sollicitous that their *Souls* may not be *Starved*, or go without the *Bread of Life*.[40]

Further on, Mather appeals to parents' instinct of protection towards their little ones when he evokes a vision of children at nightfall, in the hands of evil creatures: "Can thy Heart Endure that thy Children should be Banished from the Lord Jesus Christ, and Languishing under the Torments of Sin among Devils, in outer Darkness throughout Eternal Ages?"[41] While Mather's outpourings inflect the motif of instinctive tenderness and care, other texts suggest the dehumanizing effect of negligence in matters of spiritual instruction. Gouge describes parents who suffer their children to die in an unregenerate state as "more cruell then the Ostrich and Dragon", a view that Baxter confirms by defining such parents "Monsters [...] of inhumanity".[42] Also turning the theme of cruelty and insensitivity to account and using language and imagery that are reminiscent of the Donne of the Holy Sonnets, Mather denounces the "Adamantine Hardness of that Bloody Heart" of negligent parents whose "Heart-strings [...] are Sinewes of Iron".[43]

A favourite field of inspiration for ministerial advice was that of divine justice; all popular instructional writings include one or more references to heavenly tribunals. Gouge appropriates scriptural solemnity to warn parents that if children "liue and die in impietie through their parents negligence, their bloud shall be required at their parents hands".[44] Janeway elaborates on divine severity to rouse parents from their putative laziness and unfaithfulness: "in the name of the living God, as you will answer it shortly at his bar, I command you to be faithful in instructing and cate-chising your young ones".[45] This lesson was dutifully learned by parents and was often repeated in their diaries. The English noblewoman and medical practitioner Grace Mildmay reflects that "parents have much to answer for before God, who neglect theyr duty in bringing up their children".[46]

The most persuasive strategy to pressure parents regarding their children's spiritual reformation, to judge by the frequency and intensity of its use, depicted scenes from the Day of Judgement with damned children cursing their negligent parents. Richard

Mather stages one such scene in which children throw their condition back at their parents. "All this that we here suffer is through you: You should have taught us the things of God, and did not, [...] and now we are damned for it."[47] Bunyan imagines that when children "drop down into hell, and find themselves in irrecoverable misery, then they cry [...] But ye ungodly fathers, how are your ungodly children roaring now in hell!"[48] Visions of hell had at times an unintended comic colour as in this lively sketch of an infernal chase with children following their parents "up and down in the ever burning Lake, crying out, Woe to us, that ever we were born of such Parents that had no grace to teach us the wayes of God".[49]

Ministers' energies, however, were only partially spent on minatory comments on parents' responsibility and accountability concerning their children's salvation. They were more often employed instead in communication to parents of the theoretical and practical skills required of facilitators of new birth. Heywood, a minister and a father, hence an interesting figure at the intersection of this chain of transmission of competences, openly refers to the function of ministers as instructors of parents: "Have you not many helps, the Bible, Catechismes, good Books, Ministers to Move, Admonish and instruct you in training up your Children?"[50] Authors of widely read manuals were clear about the purpose of their texts, such as Cotton Mather, who presents his *Family Well-Ordered* as a practical guide to "the Duties to be done by Pious Parents, for the promoting of Piety in their Children" and in his diary articulates a particularly acute sense of ministerial calling "to do some special Thing, for the exciting and assisting of Parents, unto their Duty, about the Salvation of their Children from the Fire of the Wrath of God".[51] A survey of the voluminous child-rearing advice literature clearly shows that central to the "matter of instruction" entrusted to parents was the teaching of the emotional practices conducive to spiritual regeneration. Parents were expected to play in the household – the generative nucleus of puritan worship – the role played by ministers in the community. As I argued in an article that identifies a specific emotionology as the mainstay of puritan piety, one of the chief responsibilities of ministers was management and manipulation of emotional responses to further conversion.[52] Like spiritual midwives, they had to provoke and heighten "those violent passions, and pangs in [...] new-birth".[53] Godly parents were urged to guide their children along the same saving path marked by a progressive intensification of emotional states along which they themselves had toiled. Regarding this deliberate and systematized transmission from ministers to parents of the ability to rouse and orientate emotions, many texts offered specific instruction to parents on how to stimulate, monitor and manipulate the emotional responses appropriate to puritan piety. In this regard, catechisms played a crucial role.

As aides to the optimal discharge of their duty to catechize their children, parents could rely on a wide variety of graded texts in dialogic form to suit all ages and learning abilities. Some of them were compiled by authors in their dual capacities as fathers and theologians, such as Thomas Becon's *Catechism*, which offers a didactic pattern in its recording of Becon's invitations to his little son to memorize the essential facts of faith, salvation and damnation. The most popular and authoritative manuals of family instruction, including the works by Gouge, Baxter and Cotton

Mather, which are often cited in this chapter, contain sections devoted to practical advice on how to use catechisms to awaken children. Abbot's very widely used *Milk for Babes or, a Mothers Catechism* is structured as a real script for mothers as overseers of their children's paradigm of salvation, their "Generation, Degeneration, Regeneration, and Glorification", as Abbot describes it with unequalled succinctness.[54] Mothers are required to rouse the sequence of emotions characterizing the typical puritan *ordo salutis*. Abbot's good mother at first stimulates her child's painful awareness of innate depravity ("thou hast a principle of wickednesse in thee, which makes thee as ready to break the Commandements as Cain"), then urges it to "feare, and tremble under this burthen". After due discussion of the "doctrine of curses", she urges it to confess his sins "from lesse sins to greater, till thou shake thy heart, and cover thy face with confusion". Abbot teaches mothers how to monitor their children's new birth by assessing their emotional progress through specific questions whose suggested answers proposed for children's memorization instruct them regarding spiritually useful emotions. Following a preliminary urging to self-examination, Abbot's mother asks these questions: "art thou full of *indignation* against thy sins, and thy self for sin?; [...] art thou full of fear of offending God? [...]; art thou full of *desire*, to walk with thy God? [...]; art thou full of *zeal* to run the way of Gods commandements?" Correct instruction aims at making the child aware of the emotional manifestations of spiritual states; the appropriate answer, for example, to a question like "how doest thou know thy repentance?" is "by sorrow for my sinne".[55] It is worth noticing that specific question-and-answer pairs amount to a manifesto of the puritan understanding of conversion as an emotional rather than a cognitive process. John Cotton instructs parents to ask their children: "What are you thereby the nearer to Christ?" and teach them this eloquent answer: "So I come to feele my cursed estate, and need of a Saviour."[56] This pattern, which recurs in all major puritan catechisms, points to ministers' endeavours to transmit their knowledge of the nature and operation of emotions, as well as to their ability to rouse and orientate them. It also documents ministerial and parental will to forward children's awareness and mastery of themselves as emotional subjects.

Trust in the efficacy of catechizing was based on views of repetition and memorization as instructional techniques appropriate to children's specific learning abilities. Some authors openly propose their texts for memorization. Regarding his narrative of the short life of an *Elect Person*, Abraham Chear observes that it has been "translated into familiar Verse, for Childrens better remembrance".[57] Besides the standard material for memorization in the many primers used in England and America to teach children to read and write, other popular books were compiled with the explicit aim to appeal to children's imagination and leave permanent traces in their memory. An interesting example is John Bunyan's 1686 *Book for Boys and Girls: Or, Country Rhimes for Children*. This anthology, complete with scores for its songs, includes a description by a little child of the emotional steps characterizing new birth. "The awakened Childs Lamentation" articulates a paradigmatic *ordo salutis* as the child recalls that his "Soul and Spirit shaked" upon his gaining awareness of his being innately "with filth bespaked", his heart was "wounded" upon realization of sins committed, then was filled with fear of God's rejection and despair of salvation.[58]

Bunyan makes complex theological tenets intelligible even to very little children; regarding the necessity of new birth, he composes a rhyme with a proverbial tone and a familiar subject: "The Egg's no Chick by falling from the Hen;/Nor man a Christian, till he's born agen." He refers to a universal experience when he likens the impossibility of perfect assurance of salvation to the difficulty of telling night from day at dawn: "Thus 'tis with such, who Grace but now possest,/They know not yet, if they are curst or blest." Interestingly, in his address to the reader, Bunyan states that his book is suitable for "Children on the Knees", thus confirming the puritan view of the desirability of very early religious education.[59]

A rich repertoire of rhymes offered for repetition and clearly designed to induce in children the sense of self-loathing and helplessness that puritans saw as a prerequisite for conversion is found in *Looking Glass*, in which the young prodigy of piety, Caleb Vernon, recites: "By nature in my first estate/A wretched babe was I/In open field deserving hate/In bloud and filth did lie"; and Abraham Chear urges his friend's child to sing this song: "Lord what a worm am I?/[…]/Shall God through Grace, himself abase/So vile a Wretch to save?"[60] These children are portrayed as diligent learners of dialogic lessons found in catechisms: "Q. What is your corrupt nature? Answ. My corrupt nature is empty of Grace, bent unto sinne, and onely unto sinne, and that continually."[61]

Among the main emotions of new birth that parents were to rouse in their children were fear of God, terror of premature death, and judgement and guilt for the suffering of parents. Arousal of fear of God requires no discussion here, as this strategy was commonly used with both adults and children who had to be brought to conversion through "Feare and Trembling."[62] Specifically devised for children's awakening and hence more interesting for my present analysis was the strategy pivoting on the prospect of early death and damnation. To judge by their recurrence in miscellaneous texts aimed at children's rebirth, references to these themes were seen as excellent means of persuasion. Playing the detached demographer, Cotton Mather remarks: "Tis now upon computation found, that more than half the children of men dy before they come to be seventeen years of age." In doubt perhaps about the efficacy of abstract data, the minister urges children to visit the local graveyard: "Children, go unto the burying-place; there you will see many a grave shorter than your selves."[63] Mather's exhortation is reminiscent of the image evoked by the child narrator in the immensely influential *New England Primer*: the sight of "Graves shorter" than himself suggesting his reflection that "[…] young Children too may die." The didactic aim of this image is made explicit: "My God, may such an awful Sight/Awakening be to me!"[64] As an appropriate introduction of his rich gallery of portraits of infant saints at death's door, Janeway rouses his little readers from their natural reluctance to consider the option of a premature death: "Did you never hear of a little child that died? and if other children die, why may not you be sick and die?"[65] Repetition throughout instructional works of allusions to the possibility, indeed, the probability of early death was clearly meant to expedite the process of conversion. In his *Advice* to his little daughter, Heywood urges her to "take heed that you do not defer your Repentance, or adjourn it to another day: It's very dangerous so to do."[66] Authors of well-thumbed biographies of exemplary children, such as the *Bracteola Aurea*, often exploit to the full the persuasive potential of the macabre: "how often [alas!] do we deferre the welfare and happiness of our Soul, until [...] our Sinews shrink, our blood congeals. [...] this being but a bad time, to provide for the great Birth day of Eternity".[67] Cotton Mather and John Norris, among others, articulate their views in the form of proposed behavioural examples or instructions to parents regarding the need to accustom children to the idea of death, in general, and their own death, in particular. In his diary, Mather refers to his conversation with his daughter Katy about his imminent death and in his *Father's Advice to his Children* Norris invites them:

> [...]to be much in the Contemplation of the shortness and uncertainty of life, [...] Place yourselves frequently upon your Death-beds, in your Coffins, and in your Graves. Act over frequently in your Minds, the Solemnity of your own Funerals.[68]

As disturbing as they might ring to modern ears, Norris's words express an urgency shared by all puritan parents who have left written testimonies. The puritan emphasis on damnation generated deep parental anxiety regarding children's spiritual condition and stimulated their employ of strategies – rhetorical or otherwise – aimed at rousing useful emotions.

Painful recognition of the possibility of an early death was to be accompanied by fear of God's judgement. Edward Lawrence advises parents to make their children aware that "death and judgment, and heaven or hell are at the door of young children". At any time God can "summon them to appear before his Bar".[69] In this light, Cotton Mather instructs parents on how to accustom children to search their conscience and assess their spiritual condition in the prospect of early death: "Charge them to Consider, [...] if they should immediately go out of the World, what will become of them throughout Eternal Ages."[70] Children were constantly reminded that whereas for young saints, premature death equals early enjoyment of eternal bliss, it delivers the ungodly to hell's fire. Bunyan's repertoire of fundamental concepts for children's memorization includes this chilling rhyme: "Death's a cold Comforter to Girls and Boys/Who wedded are unto their Childish Toys."[71] Very few authors endeavour to instil fear of death in young readers by stimulating anxiety about desecration of their bodies, as does Kirkwood who declares that children who ignore their parents' teachings "shall die a shameful death, and remain unburied, and shall be exposed to the Birds and Beasts of prey, to be eaten of them."[72] Much more often, it is "the Carnivorous Fowls of Heaven" ready to devour the "Carcases" of unconverted children that instructional literature presents as frightening.[73]Appropriately, well-read authors provide instruction on how to avoid damnation as the main aim of their writing. Robert Russell advertises his *Little Book for Children*'s offer of "nine Directions, thou shalt do to escape Hell and go to Heaven".[74] We have autobiographical testimonies of children's emotional responses to passages about damnation. John Brock, an English puritan who emigrated to New England, recalls how as a child "By Reading through admonitions of Parents in a Book called *The Practice of Piety* I found some Description, of the Misery of Men in Hell & of Happiness of the Godly which somewhat stirred me."[75]

A strategy, which has left numerous and important written traces, combines fear of damnation with fear of separation from parents. As Stannard notices with reference to the recurrent visions of judgement, puritan writings focus with particular intensity on threats of separation from parents, which, according to modern psychologists, is a primary source of fear of death in young children.[76] Authors vie with each other to depict vivid scenes of children in despair at the simultaneous and irrevocable loss of divine and parental love; some texts emphasize children's sense of desolation, others inflect parental harshness. As usual, Cotton Mather offers representative examples of forceful addresses to children:

> Thy Pious Parents themselves will not own thee, in the Day when God shall Curse thee [...]. And all the Grief which thy Pious Parents here Endured for thee, and from thee, will but be Oyl to the Everlasting Flames of that Grief, which thou shalt Endure in the Place of Dragons.[77]

Cotton Mather even casts parents in the role of accusers of their children, a role which contrasts painfully with filial expectations of protection: "Your godly Parents will testifie against you before the Son of God at that day."[78] As expected, puritan personal writings include many passages about childhood responses of dismay and terror at the idea of a lonely eternity in hell.[79]

Space only permits a quick reference to another strategy often employed, though not mentioned as often as premature death, to stimulate intense emotional response in children: arousal of a sense of guilt with respect to parents. Visions exploiting filial love are evoked for the benefit of unconverted children who are likened to "so many Dogs and Lyons" tearing "in pieces the hearts and bowels of their tender parents"; these, in turn, are depicted "weeping many a time over you, and for you before God", desperately trying to "rescue you from the bottomless pit, into which they fear you are hasting".[80] Another emotion that texts propose as appropriate to further children's new birth is anxiety or, better, sense of guilt regarding the consequences of failure to convert on family, local communities and the whole puritan experience. Given children's focal role, their spiritual shortcomings appear ruinous: "God made you his Trustees, and so did Ancestours and Parents make you their spirituall Trustees, under God, to hold up Religion, Truth, the Worship, Waies, and Government of Christ." Unregenerate children, Cobbet argues, "break and ruin posterity, and the succession of Churches".[81] Shower is even more absolute: should children "cast off God, here is an intercision of the line, and an end of the relation between God and us".[82]

Besides catechizing and arousing fear and guilt, behavioural example was also deemed very effective for the purpose of children's spiritual reformation. Confirming the puritans' attention to the specific learning styles of children and their endeavour to devise effective educational techniques, numerous instructional texts propose behavioural examples as a successful means of transmitting a saving emotionology.

Dod and Cleaver, for example, urge parents to exploit children's natural propensity to "apish" imitation of behavioural patterns.[83] Cotton Mather explains the technique step by step and exalts its efficacy:

> Carry the Child with you, into your Secret Chambers; make the Child kneel down by you, while you present it unto the Lord, [...]. Let the Child hear the Groans, & see the Tears, and be a witness of the Agonies, wherewith you are Travailing for the Salvation of it. The Children will never Forget what you do; It will have a marvellous Force upon them.[84]

The New England *Token* tells the story of a father pouring out "Floods of Tears" before his child, and autobiographical sketches of family life often include recollections of childhood observation of highly emotional parental behaviour. Thomas Shepard describes his mother as "a woman much afflicted in conscience sometimes even unto distraction of mind".[85] Besides offering their own behaviour for imitation, many parents also left written instructions regarding appropriate emotional and behavioural norms.

Another source of behavioural instruction was the vast collection of biographies of pious children, rich in detailed descriptions of their emotional practices. These collections are among the most frequently reprinted texts of the day and the number of editions suggests a wide market. Almost all authors indicate the didactic function of their writings and specify that the child behaviour they depict is proposed for imitation. A very interesting reflection on the efficacy of the genre is found in the "Epistle to the Reader" of the *Bracteola Aurea*, which tells the story of little Joanna: "We have more need of Patterns then Precepts: and is observable in Children, [...] to imitate their like."[86] Janeway addresses parents in his typical vehement tone: "put them, I beseech you, upon imitating these sweet children".[87] In the title page of the popular *Token for the Children of New England*, Cotton Mather declares that the biographies he presents are "Preserved and Published, for the ENCOURAGEMENT of PIETY in other CHILDREN" and warns that, should unconverted children fail to imitate young saints, the "exemplary Children", about whom he writes, "will Rise up against them for their Condemnation".[88] The patterns offered for emulation are basically the same in all collections: young saints are invariably portrayed as they very quickly and very intensely experience the spiritual transformation leading to new birth before their premature death. The emotional manifestations of their *ordo salutis* receive special emphasis, and complacent descriptions of peaks of despair and exaltation marked by very visible and audible displays of inner turmoil – floods of tears and loud cries – are central in all narratives. Authors like Janeway urge parents to scrutinize children's response to accounts of highly emotionalized conversion: "let them read this book over a hundred times, and observe how they are affected".[89] Many parents have left written testimony of their practice in this sense. Some texts are particularly interesting as they describe examination of children for emotional responses which are clearly identified as signs of conversion: Heywood interprets his son's tears as the "beginning of god's work upon his heart".[90] Parents were instructed to identify "Affliction" and

"Amazement" with indexes of God's opening of children's heart.[91] Some auto-biographical writings signal mixed feelings as satisfaction for the optimal discharge of the duty to awaken children, and joy at detecting marks of new birth are expressed alongside concern and grief for the suffering caused. An often quoted example is that of Judge Sewall's reaction to the deep distress of his eight-year-old daughter, Elizabeth: "Sympathy with her draw Tears from me also."[92]

Contrary to theories of neglect or mistreatment of children, the painful attention of parents to children's spiritual condition attests to their love, if also certainly to their anxiety regarding the survival of the entire puritan project and divine judgement of their own proficiency as spiritual guides. It is possible to infer that taking one's children to the verge of the abyss of despair and teaching them that God "sends men to heauen by the gates and suburbes of hell" or that "a broken heart is an *House* wherein *God* dwels" must have been a distressing task.[93] What is clear is that puritan parents' memoirs and the impressive body of ministerial instruction attest to a distinctive attention to the emotional development of children and to a view of the relevance of early personality shaping that had an impact upon later psychological and pedagogical approaches to childhood and parent–child relations.

Notes

1 I use the term "emotionology" coined by Peter and Carol Stearns to describe the "attitudes or standards that a society, or a definable group within a society, maintains toward basic emotions and their appropriate expression". P. N. Stearns and C. Z. Stearns, "'Emotionology': Clarifying the History of Emotions and Emotional Standards", *American Historical Review*, vol 90 (1985): pp813–836, esp. p813.

2 See Lutz's seminal study, C. Lutz, "Emotion, Thought, and Estrangement: Emotion as a Cultural Category", *Cultural Anthropology*, vol 1 (1986): pp287–309. Major streams of research on childhood and emotion are analysed in C. Lutz and G. M. White, "The Anthropology of Emotions", *Annual Review of Anthropology*, vol 15 (1986): pp405–436.

3 P. Baseotto, "Theology and Interiority: Emotions as Evidence of the Working of Grace in Elizabethan and Stuart Conversion Narratives", in J. Liliequist (ed) *A History of Emotions, 1200–1800* (London, 2012), pp65–77.

4 My notion of "emotional community" follows B. H. Rosenwein's definition in *Emotional Communities in the Early Middle Ages* (Ithaca, NY, 2006), p2: "group[s] in which people adhere to the same norms of emotional expression and value – or devalue – the same or related emotions".

5 Regarding sources, I have read very widely from different types of texts – autobiography, diary, spiritual relation, instructional and devotional literature, biography – from the sixteenth century to the beginning of the eighteenth, by both old and New England puritans. My quotations from authors of various religious temperaments and geographical contexts may seem the product of lack of method and consideration of changing historical and social backgrounds. In fact, while texts bear traces of the specific circumstances of their authors, a notable consistency of themes and opinions with respect to family instruction and infant emotion is clearly detectable. This is not surprising given that the linchpin of the distinct emotionology at the base of puritan views of child rearing was an unchanged emphasis on specific aspects of Protestant theology. The final part of this prefatory notice concerns my selection of citations: though I have examined hundreds of texts by a large number of authors (endeavouring to consider the whole of each and not looking for passages which could easily confirm my thesis), my quotations are taken from a restricted group of individuals. This is due partly to authors' influence,

as in the case of William Gouge, Richard Baxter and Robert Abbot whose works were very popular on both sides of the Atlantic and were reprinted over very long periods of time, and partly to the superior rhetorical gifts of some of them like Cotton Mather, whose utterances, however, I use only when they express current and typical puritan views also found in a score of less impressive and vivid writings.

6 As D. Leverenz, *The Language of Puritan Feeling: An Exploration in Literature, Psychology, and Social History* (New Brunswick, NJ, 1980), p109. As he notes: "Puritanism was a family experience. People worked in families, emigrated as families, took notes on sermons for later family discussion."

7 T. Cobbet, *A Fruitfull and Usefull Discourse Touching the Honour due from Children to Parents, and the duty of Parents towards their Children* (London, 1656), sig. A3^v.

8 R. Baxter, *A Christian Directory: Or, A Summ of Practical theologie, and Cases of Conscience* (London, 1673), pp513, 515. In this and all subsequent quotations, spelling and punctuation conform exactly to the originals, unless otherwise specifically noted.

9 R. Baxter, *Christian Directory*, pp512, 514.

10 L. L. Schücking, *The Puritan Family: A Social Study from the Literary Sources* (London, 1969), pp66, 91.

11 R. Baxter, *Christian Directory*, p514.

12 Luther's views of vocation were also very influential. On the high value placed on parents' divine calling, see J. E. Strohl, "The Child in Luther's Theology: 'For What Purpose Do We Older Folks Exist, Other Than to Care for … the Young?'", in M. J. Bunge (ed) *The Child in Christian Thought* (Grand Rapids, MI, 2001), pp134–159.

13 See L. A. Pollock, *Forgotten Children: Parent–Child Relations from 1500 to 1900* (Cambridge, UK, 1983), pp1–67. For an excellent survey and critical discussion of the most influential theories of childhood, see H. Cunningham, *Children and Childhood in Western Society since 1500* (London, 1995), pp3–17.

14 For a useful description of and comparison between mainstream Anglican and puritan educational theories and practices, see C. J. Sommerville, "The Distinction between Indoctrination and Education in England, 1549–1719", *Journal of the History of Ideas*, vol 44 (1983): pp387–406.

15 R. Baxter, *Christian Directory*, p515. While, as integral components of the household, servants and apprentices were also entrusted to the spiritual care of puritan spouses, the primary objects of parental responsibility and efforts were children and the vast majority of family advice literature is devoted to the parent–child relation.

16 D. Leverenz, *The Language of Puritan Feeling*, p70.

17 R. Baxter, *Christian Directory*, p515.

18 R. Baxter, *Christian Directory*, p516; T. Cobbet, *A Fruitfull and Usefull Discourse*, p87. Regarding Cobbet's and other authors' references to fathers, my survey of Puritan texts confirms Leverenz's observation that although "role divisions were encouraged, […] in talking of child care after infancy Puritans almost always say 'parents', not 'fathers,' even when the Bible's language is explicitly male. Many explications of Proverbs apply fatherhood to mothers as well, or simply say that 'father' signifies 'parents'." Moreover, I think that male authors, almost all themselves fathers, quite naturally spoke from their own perspective.

19 O. Heywood, *Diaries*, in *The Rev. Oliver Heywood, B.A., 1630–1702: His Autobiography, Diaries, Anecdote and Event Books*, J. H. Turner (ed), 4 vols (Brighouse, 1881–1885), vol 4, p50.

20 W. Gouge, *Of Domesticall Duties. Eight Treatises* (London, 1622), p537.

21 C. Mather, *A Family Well-Ordered, Or, An Essay to Render Parents and Children Happy in one another* (Boston, MA, 1699), p33.

22 O. Heywood, *Advice to an Only Child: Or, Excellent Council to all Young Persons* (London, 1693), p84. In my quotation above (see note 19), Heywood depicts his own mother as a successful performer of this daunting task.

23 C. Mather, *A Family Well-Ordered*, p10.

24 J. Calvin, *Institutes of the Christian Religion*, translated by H. Beveridge, 2 vols (Edinburgh, 1845), vol II, p293; H. P., *A Looking-Glass for Children* (London, 1673), sigs A2, A2^v. On

Calvin's view of children, see B. Pitkin, "'The Heritage of the Lord': Children in the Theology of John Calvin", in M. J. Bunge (ed) *The Child in Christian Thought*, pp160–193.

25 J. Green, *His Book; Anno Domini 1696*, A. B. Forbes (ed) (Boston, MA, 1943), vol 34, pp191–253, esp. p236.

26 R. Kilby, *The Burden of a Loaden Conscience: Or the Penitent Confession of a Clergy-Man* (London, 1699), sig. B4^v.

27 A. Bradstreet, *The Works of Anne Bradstreet in Prose and Verse*, J. H. Ellis (ed) (Charlestown, MA, 1867), p151.

28 P. S. Seaver (ed) *Wallington's World: A Puritan Artisan in Seventeenth-Century London* (London, 1985), p14.

29 R. Abbot, *Milk for Babes; Or, A Mothers Catechism for Her Children* (London, 1646), p85.

30 J. Dod and R. Cleaver, *A Godly Forme of Houshold Gouernment, For the Ordering of Priuate Families, According to the Direction of Gods Word* (London, 1630), sig. C7^v; C. Mather, *A Family Well-Ordered*, p11.

31 J. Janeway, *A Token for Children* (New York, 1811), piv. For a more general discussion of child mortality in the period, see M. J. Dobson, *Contours of Death and Disease in Early Modern England* (Cambridge, UK, 1997), p216, which concludes on the basis of a survey of parish registers that "about half of all burials were of children under the age of five years"; B. A. Hanawalt, "The Child in the Middle Ages and the Renaissance", in W. Koops and M. Zuckerman (eds) *Beyond the Century of the Child* (Philadelphia, PA, 2003), p33, which confirms Dobson's observation; E. A. Wrigley and R. S. Schofield, *The Population History of England, 1541–1871: A Reconstruction* (Cambridge, UK, 1981), which offers a wealth of data regarding infant mortality rates in the sixteenth and seventeenth centuries.

32 J. Vernon, *The Compleat Scholler; Or, A Relation of the Life, and Latter End especially, of Caleb Vernon* (London, 1666), sig. A7^v.

33 C. Mather, *Small Offers towards the Service of the Tabernacle in the Wilderness* (Boston, MA, 1689), p59.

34 J. Janeway, *Token*, pp32, 48. Janeway felt the need to reassure readers regarding the credibility of his reports, hence his listing of his sources: himself, "godly ministers", Christians of "unspotted reputation", young paragons themselves whose words were "taken verbatim, in writing, from their dying lips", pvi.

35 E. Reynell, *Bracteola Aurea; Or, Filings of Gold* (London, 1663), title page, sig. B.

36 R. Kilby, *The Burden of a Loaden Conscience*, sig. C. It should be noticed that because of very low life expectancy, early participation in all adult activities was deemed desirable. Given the centrality of religion in puritan life, however, it is hardly surprising that authors harped on religious precocity.

37 L. Hutchinson, "The Life of Mrs. Lucy Hutchinson, Written by Herself", in *Memoirs of the Life of Colonel Hutchinson* (London, 1848), p17; J. Green, *His Book*, p236.

38 *The Advice of a Father: Or, Counsel to a Child* (London, 1688), p36.

39 *Charters and General Laws of the Colony and Province of Massachusetts Bay* (Boston, MA, 1814), pp73–74.

40 C. Mather, *A Family Well-Ordered*, pp10, 9.

41 C. Mather, *A Family Well-Ordered*, p12.

42 W. Gouge, *Of Domesticall Duties*, p538; R. Baxter, *Christian Directory*, p516.

43 C. Mather, *A Family Well-Ordered*, p13. See Donne's use of "Adamant" and "iron heart" in Holy Sonnet 1, *The Collected Poems of John Donne*, R. Booth (ed) (Ware, 1994), p247.

44 W. Gouge, *Of Domesticall Duties*, p537.

45 J. Janeway, *Token*, piv.

46 G. Mildmay, "The Journal of Lady Mildmay", *The Quarterly Review*, vol 215 (1911): pp119–138, esp. p128.

47 R. Mather, *A Farewel Exhortation to the Church and People of Dorchester in New England* (Cambridge, MA, 1657), p10.

48 J. Bunyan, *Sighs from Hell; or, The Groans of a Damned Soul*, in: *The Works of that Eminent Servant of Christ, John Bunyan*, 2 vols (Philadelphia, PA, 1836), vol 2, p178.

49 I. Mather, *A Call from Heaven To the Present and Succeeding Generations* (Boston, MA, 1679), p21.
50 O. Heywood, *Advice to an Only Child*, sig. A5.
51 C. Mather, *A Family Well-Ordered*, title page; *Diary*, W. C. Ford (ed), 2 vols (Boston, MA, 1912–1913), vol 1, p295.
52 P. Baseotto, "Theology and Interiority".
53 R. Bolton, *Instructions for a Right Comforting Afflicted Consciences* (London, 1640), p468.
54 R. Abbot, *Milk for Babes*, pA2.
55 R. Abbot, *Milk for Babes*, pp38, 76, 84, 85, 159, 167, 171.
56 J. Cotton, *Spirituall Milk for Boston Babes in either England* (London, 1657), p7.
57 H. P., *A Looking-Glass for Children*, p54.
58 J. Bunyan, *A Book for Boys and Girls: Or, Country Rhimes for Children* (London, 1686), p2.
59 J. Bunyan, *A Book for Boys and Girls*, sig. A, pp7, 9.
60 H. P., *A Looking-Glass for Children*, pp83, 29.
61 J. Cotton, *Spirituall Milk*, p2.
62 R. Williams, *Experiments of Spiritual Life & Health, and their Preservatives* (London, 1652), pA5.
63 C. Mather, "An Essay upon the Good Education of Children (1708)", in *American Educational Thought: Essays from 1640–1940*, A. J. Milson et al (eds) (Charlotte, NC, 2010), pp15–31, esp. p28.
64 *The New England Primer: A Reprint of the Earliest Known Edition*, P. L. Ford (ed) (New York, 1899), p22. Combining school-book and catechism, the *Primer* was the New England version of the *English Protestant Tutor*. First published between 1687 and 1690, the *New England Primer* was used by all puritan children and was still in print in the nineteenth century.
65 J. Janeway, *Token*, xiii.
66 O. Heywood, *Advice to an Only Child*, p42.
67 E. Reynell, *Bracteola Aurea*, p4.
68 C. Mather, *Diary*, p239; J. Norris, *Spiritual Counsel: Or, the Father's Advice to His Children* (London, 1694), p76. Cf. Norris's statement with this verse from *The New England Primer*: "At Night lye down prepar'd to have/Thy sleep, thy death, thy bed, thy grave", p23.
69 E. Lawrence, *Parents Groans over their Wicked Children* (London, 1681), p70; J. Shower, *A Sermon Occasion'd by the Late Repentance and Funeral of A Young Man* (London, 1681), p2.
70 C. Mather, *A Family Well-Ordered*, p27.
71 J. Bunyan, *A Book for Boys and Girls*, p62.
72 J. Kirkwood, *Advice to Children* (London, 1693), p8.
73 C. Mather, *A Family Well-Ordered*, p50.
74 R. Russel, *A Little Book for Children and Youth* (London, 1693?), p4.
75 *The Autobiographical Memoranda of John Brock, 1636–1659*, C. K. Shipton (ed) in *Puritan Personal Writings: Autobiographies and Other Writings* (New York, 1983), pp96–105, esp. p97.
76 D. E. Stannard, "Death and the Puritan Child", *American Quarterly*, vol 26, no 5 (1974): pp456–476, esp. pp471–472.
77 C. Mather, *A Family Well-Ordered*, p79.
78 I. Mather, *Pray for the Rising Generation* (Boston, MA, 1679), p28.
79 See, for example, Judge Sewall's report of his daughter's terrors: Elizabeth "said she was afraid she should goe to Hell, her sins were not pardon'd", S. Sewall, *Diary* (1674–1729), Collections of the Massachusetts Historical Society, series 5, V (Boston, MA, 1878), p419.
80 E. Lawrence, *Parents Groans*, p11; T. Cobbet, *A Fruitfull and Usefull Discourse*, pp187–188.
81 T. Cobbet, *A Fruitfull and Usefull Discourse*, pp197–198.
82 J. Shower, *A Sermon*, sig. A8.
83 J. Dod and R. Cleaver, *A Godly Forme of Houshold Gouernment*, sig. T6.
84 C. Mather, *A Family Well-Ordered*, pp35–36.

85 C. Mather, *A Token, for the Children of New-England. Or, Some Examples of Children, In Whom the Fear of GOD was Remarkably Budding, Before They Dyed* (Boston, MA, 1700), p28; N. Adams, *The Autobiography of Thomas Shepard* (Boston, MA, 1832), p16.

86 E. Reynell, *Bracteola Aurea*, pA2^v.

87 J. Janeway, *Token*, pvi.

88 C. Mather, *A Token*, title page, sig. A2^v. Mather describes his book as a "Supplement, unto the Excellent JANEWAYES *Token for Children*. Upon the *Re-printing* of it, in this Countrey", title page.

89 J. Janeway, *Token*, pvi.

90 O. Heywood, *Diaries*, p233.

91 C. Mather, *Small Offers*, p62.

92 S. Sewall, *Diary*, p308.

93 W. Perkins, *Whole Treatise of the Cases of Conscience* (London, 1619), p68; R. Williams, *Experiments of Spiritual Life & Health*, sig. D6^v.

7

THE INFINITE UNIVERSE OF EIGHTEENTH-CENTURY CHILDREN'S LITERATURE

Arianne Baggerman

> The selection of books for children is one of the most important details of an educa-
> tion. All parents and educators should be very careful in this important matter, since
> the souls of children are susceptible to both bad and good impressions, and reading
> books, no less than listening to conversation, makes a very deep impression on chil-
> dren. … Friends of mankind, allow me to ask you: do all of you know the writings
> that your children so assiduously peruse? Are you confident that no poison of any kind
> is disseminated therein, that they contain nothing evil or excessive that could spoil the
> imagination or hearts of your children?[1]

This warning is to be found in a 1789 Dutch journal that bore the optimistic title
Bijdragen tot het Menschelyk Geluk (*Contributions to Human Happiness*). This example
could easily be extended by including similar exhortations from English, German and
French parental advice books published during the same period.[2] Never before in
European history were books regarded as so important and, at the same time, seen as
so dangerous, especially for children. Reading by children had become a dreadful
moral dilemma for parents: on the one hand, they should encourage their children to
read, but at the same time their children's reading had to be checked carefully.

This concern was a logical consequence of the new pedagogical insights that
human beings are formed by their environment – Locke's *tabula rasa* – and Rousseau's idea that they are by nature good. Rousseau believed that children should
develop in freedom, according to their own inborn nature, and should stay away as
much as possible from culture. He did not believe in knowledge from books, therefore, and stated that they should be kept away from children: "Reading is the plague
of childhood."[3] Rousseau's Emile was educated in the countryside with nature as his
most important tutor, far away from cities, which Rousseau called "the abyss of the
human species".[4] Emile's first confrontation with culture only takes place after he had
built up enough resistance, around his twelfth year. From that moment on, he is

encouraged to read books that will, "in a pleasant way, introduce him to the study of sophisticated thinking". Writing in the years before real children's books were published, Rousseau approved of Greek and Roman authors, because of their simplicity, and of historical works, but only with moderation and only if well supervised. In addition to developing resistance against worse forms of printed matter, Emile had to get a brief taste of, in Rousseau's words: "anthologies, newspapers, translations and dictionaries". One glance at this inferior printed material should be enough for Emile to never wish to take it up again.[5]

Rousseau preferred empirical knowledge above book learning, but he was not fundamentally against reading by children. His most important objection was the lack of reading matter appropriate to young readers. Parents who gave children their own literature – for instance, the *Fables* of De la Fontaine – were reprimanded by Rousseau. To demonstrate that such reading is not compatible with the mental *outillage* of children and only makes them develop the wrong attitude to life, he analysed Fontaine's fables extensively from a children's point of view:

> The sentence "Sans mentir, si votre ramage" has the phrase "without lying". "Without lying?" a child will ask. "So lying sometimes takes place?" What will your child think if you explain to him that the fox says that he is not lying just *because* he is lying?[6]

Rousseau made only one exception to his verdict on books: Daniel Defoe's *Robinson Crusoe*. That book fit the child's realm of experience. Rousseau saw it not as a novel, but as a true story and, as such, it was much better than fiction. Moreover, it contained directly applicable knowledge and correct morals. Defoe recounts the vicissitudes of a shipwrecked sailor stranded on a desert island who survives by learning from nature. Robinson even manages to lead a pleasant life – cultivating grain, domesticating goats, building a little house – and records this learning process in a journal, made possible by the miraculous recovery of paper, pen and ink from the wreckage of his ship. The account of this castaway must have been a source of inspiration for Emile, who, like Robinson Crusoe, had to tend his own goat and grow his own vegetables.[7]

Emile was published in 1762 at just the right moment. This was a period during which traditional educational methods were discussed everywhere. More pedagogical studies appeared in the 1760s than in the entire century before. Following Rousseau, authors of the period saw reading by children as a problem because of the lack of books suitable to their age. None of these pedagogues went as far as Rousseau, who completely rejected reading by children under the age of 12. Instead, they wrote that parents should carefully select a list of suitable books and closely control their children's reading of them.[8]

The problem was solved in the 1770s. After 1780 there was a boom in "sound and sensible" children's books, many of them written by the same educators who had turned children's reading into a pedagogical problem. This did not mean, however, that the discussion about reading by children fell silent. On the contrary, the boom in the new genre of children's literature was accompanied by a sharp increase in the number of parental advice books, which cast reading by children as a problem and which attempted to adapt Rousseau's contradictory inheritance to the daily practice of education.[9]

In just about all pedagogical writings from the years around 1780, the advice to parents is that they need to ensure that the reading diet of their children is carefully composed. In most cases this is elaborated by addressing the genres that are the most appropriate for children: national history, classical history, natural philosophy and stories which were written especially for children. Others go even further by recommending a number of specific titles. Obviously, the preferences differ according to country, especially regarding national history. In The Netherlands, one could not exclude *Wagenaars Vaderlandsche historie* (*The History of the Dutch Republic* by Jan Wagenaar); in England Gilbert Burnet's *History of My Own Time* was unavoidable. While English parents were advised to inaugurate their children into natural philosophy using Pope's *Essay on Man*, Dutch parents were recommended *Natuurlijke historie* (*Natural History*) by Dutch Minister Martinet.[10] Certain titles were highly regarded by French, English, Dutch and German pedagogics. Rollin's *Histoire romaine* is praised by the German pedagogue Basedow as well as by the Scottish author Catherine Macauly and the Dutch author Betje Wolff.[11] The books by Madame de Genlis and the children's magazine *L'Ami des enfants* (*Children's Friend*) were published in different languages in various countries, and obviously crossed several national borders.

The careful selection of suitable reading matter for children did not guarantee a correct reception by them. Pedagogues therefore emphasized the importance of giving exactly the right fragment of a book to children at exactly the right moment. Many pedagogical tracts advocated a system in which book recommendations were accompanied by an indication of the appropriate age category. Other authors advised parents to include consideration of the specific characters of their children in their choice of the right books for them:

> Be guided in the choice of books which you give your children to read, by their individual characters. Seek therefore, dear parents, to learn thoroughly the specific passions of your children, and let your choice of reading matter for them be guided thereby.[12]

Parents should not only inspect their children's reading in advance. Supervision *during* reading was also prescribed in order to be able to control and rectify its reception if needed. In, for example, *Zedekundig Huisboek voor jonge lieden* (*Moral Household Book for Young People*) by C. M. Doll-Egges (1830), parents are encouraged to make "young people read out loud and in their presence".[13] When, in the foreword to her *Avondtijdkortingen* (*Tales from the Castle*), the French children's author Madame de Genlis states that she has attempted to make her notes as "informative and important as possible (for children, to be sure)", she likewise anticipates a collective reading practice of parents and their children.[14] In a prospectus from 1785 for the boarding school of the German pedagogue Salzmann, we learn that collective reading and discussion of what has been read are the spearheads of this modern educational institute.[15] In Salzmann's children's book on morals *Moralische Elementarbuch*, which had appeared during that same year, he instructed parents that they should read this book to their children, but not allow them to read it themselves.[16]

Supervision during reading could be substituted or supplemented, by retrospective inspection of a reading diary kept by children themselves. The advice that children should read with a pen in their hand became standard during this period. It is a recurring issue in the advisory literature.[17] One author wrote: "Follow the example of Plinius the Elder, who never read without a pen in his hand."[18] We also encounter this in the children's literature itself, in which characters figure who actually follow this advice. In *Lettergeschenk voor Nederlandsche jeugd* (*Literary Gift for Dutch Youth*) of 1790, Nicolaas is, in many ways, exemplary. He reads the books that are handed to him by the local minister and faithfully registers from them the "useful details" in a separate notebook that was probably also provided to him by the local minister.[19]

The propaganda for good books in children's literature was always combined with the remark that children should be encouraged to read. There is no greater joy in children's book-land than a fresh supply of books. Not surprisingly, the family friend, Philoteknus, in *De Vriend der Kinderen* would not dream of showing up empty handed when visiting the children. As soon as he arrives, he tells them that he has been to the fair, where he searched the book stalls for "the latest novelties", from which he selected a book for each of them:

> "Well? Did you get something nice for me? – and for me? – and me too?" they cried out, each trying to make himself heard above the others while feeling the man's pockets. Philoteknus then turned out his pockets and said to them, "Yes, of course, for all of you. Something for everyone, and very beautiful things they are, too."[20]

The gifts are presented on the condition that each child "will be so good as to tell the others the contents of his or her particular book". Frederik is naturally overjoyed to receive Raff's *Geographie voor kinderen* (*Geography for Children*); Lotje is equally ecstatic about Trembley's *Onderwijs van een vader aan zijne kinderen* (*A Father's Lessons to His Children*); Karel gratefully accepts Ebert's *Onderwijs in de natuurlijke historie voor de jeugd* (*Instruction in Natural History for the Young*). Likewise, Lijsje *De Kindervriend* (*The Children's Friend*) by the philanthropinist Rochow:

> "The Children's Friend! The Children's Friend!" she cried. "Oh, I've already got it!" "You've already got it, you say? No, Lijsje, not this one. *The Children's Friend* you have in your hand is possibly a brother of the one you already own: at least they are completely equal in your affections."[21]

In De Genlis's *Tales from the Castle*, one of the children is presented with the other *Kindervriend*, that of the French philanthropist Arnaud Berquin:

Delphine listened, attentively and with astonishment, to Henriëtte. "How much you know!" said Delphine. "I," resumed Henriëtte, "I know nothing. I have only a very shallow and muddled knowledge of everything, but I have the most fervent desire to learn, and I love to read. Shall I lend you some books?" "Gladly," said Delphine, "since my doll has not yet arrived from Paris." "Well then, I'll lend you the *Conversations of Emily* and *The Children's Friend*."[22]

I discovered this network of mutual references – and mutual admiration – when I was, so to speak, reading over the shoulder of an actual young reader from the eighteenth century: the Dutch boy Otto van Eck. In 1790, at the age of ten, he began a diary in which his reading played an important role. Most of the books mentioned above can be found on Otto's reading programme. It included, among others, D'Epinay's *Conversations of Emily*, De Genlis's *Tales from the Castle*, Martinet's *Natural History*, Pluche's *Histoire Naturelle*, Wagenaar's *History of the Dutch Republic*, Rollin's *Histoire Romaine*, Basedow's *Manuel Elementaire* and the inevitable *The Children's Friend*.[23]

Reading of a real-life reader in the company of fictional friends

Otto's books provided him with fictional friends his own age, all of whom possess an infectious enthusiasm for reading, and fictional parents who supervise their little readers along with their story-book children. Otto's reading included many stories within a story, in which fictional children and their educators form the outermost narrative frame. The children in these books have all kinds of experiences themselves, but at the same time they read books together or have stories told to them. These stories are the heart of such books, but in a way they become interactive because the fictional children continually interrupt the inner narrative to comment or express feelings of horror, grief, pity or enthusiasm. These feelings are taken up, in turn, by the fictional educators and commented upon, encouraged or steered in another direction, if they are considered inappropriate.

The children in *De Vriend der Kinderen* read on their own a book of which we are told little at first, except that it had moved the children to tears.[24] Their father therefore decides to have his daughter Lotje read aloud the most poignant passages. The story is about the profound love between a father and his son, both seriously wounded in battle and each more worried about the welfare of the other than about his own injuries. The narrative is regularly interrupted by the children's tears or fits of weeping that last so long the father has to take over the task of reading aloud:

> "I simply cannot go on reading, dear Papa," Lotje stammered. "Then give it here," I said, "and I shall do it – but should I read it to myself, or out loud? How do you feel about it? Do you really want to hear this mournful story a second time?" "No, Papa, no!" cried the children, "Don't read it to yourself! Read it out loud if you will, out loud!" So I continued reading.[25]

The son in the story gets better, but suffers a setback when he hears that his father has died. Only when he is told that there was a misunderstanding, and that his father is recovering, is the son able to accept his own death: "'Thank God! Why on earth did they tell me that? Now I'm at ease. Now I'm ready to die!' Whereupon speech becomes difficult for him, and his throat ever more constricted, and he grew short of breath."[26] The listeners are so choked with emotion that they also have lumps in their throats, and a hush falls over the narrative. After a moment of suitable silence, the father takes the floor to point out the lessons to be learned from the story.

That children should take such lessons very seriously is made clear to them in another story, in which children who ignore the moral of a story told by their father pay for this mistake with their lives. Their father has just finished telling them that cruel acts will bring earthly retribution upon the perpetrator, when the eldest boy steals all the young birds from a nest and divides them up among his younger brothers and sisters. Unlike the two sisters, who take loving care of their birds, the boys indulge in all kinds of animal abuse:

> The lad who had found the nest tied a rope to the leg of his bird and dragged it along behind him. The second boy stuck a needle into his bird's eye, and took pleasure in watching the creature bleed.[27]

These brothers are first punished by their father, who treats them to the same cruelties they had inflicted on their victims, and then they are dealt with by God: "It pleased God that six or seven months later the eldest son, who had actually masterminded the evil deed, fell ill and died." Nature then sends vengeful birds to complete the punishment: "Many people say that, when he was buried, they saw ravens, magpies, vultures and other birds of prey fall screeching upon his grave ... and that after a great deal of effort, when they had finally got him under the ground, the birds dug him up again and devoured him." The girls came to a good end, at least in the author's opinion. The youngest dies a year after her brother, but is buried in a well-tended grave, "for the birds pulled out the weeds, and God let all kinds of beautifully coloured wildflowers grow on it." The moral of the story is so convincing in itself that the father decides to make an exception and keep his conclusions to himself: "We understood his meaning very well, and it had a wonderful effect."

The same structure is seen in another book Otto read, *Avondtijdkortingen van het kasteel* (*Tales from the Castle*). The main characters find themselves in a draughty old castle far from Paris, where they gradually learn to appreciate country life, despite their initial aversion to it. This transformation is the result not only of their pleasant experiences in the countryside, but also of the stories their mother tells to liven up the evenings. It is no coincidence that the mother – Madame de Genlis, *alias* Mrs de Clemire – chooses the story "Delphine or the fortunate recovery" as the first in a long series of stories told in the tradition of *Tales from a Thousand and One Nights*. Delphine, a city girl, is rich and conceited, though she has a good heart. She has been ruined by unhealthy city life, and her "vehement emotions" and "unbridled passions" have made her "the unhappiest child in all of Paris". After various physicians examine her and pronounce her incurable, her desperate mother consults "a renowned German doctor named Steinhausse". His methodical observation of the child leads him to diagnose a potentially fatal condition and to prescribe a remedy that he will administer personally, if the mother agrees to entrust her child to him for eight months. Delphine is to be taken to the countryside, where she will live in a cowshed, in the dung, which, according to De Genlis' footnote, is an effective remedy for chest complaints. The girl, still ignorant of her fate, suffers such fits of despair and rage that she has to be led away by force.

This prompts one of the listeners – Pulcherie – to remark, with tears in her eyes, that she can understand the girl's reaction. She is immediately reprimanded, however, by her story-telling mother: Delphine's reaction to what happened was exaggerated, "Religion and reason must always keep us from despair."[28] This argument not only convinces the fictional reader, Pulcherie, but also the real reader of this story, Otto van Eck. In his diary he wrote that he read this book, and that he learned from it "that one can become accustomed to anything, which during my own illness I have also experienced myself".[29] This conclusion was obviously intended by Madame de Genlis, and confirmed by his own experience. Otto's reaction was clearly based on his own experience: in this period he suffered from a serious skin complaint that required treatment with evil-smelling ointments composed of tar and sheep's fat, which he had to rub on his whole body, including his face.[30]

The way in which both fictional and real-life readers are manipulated in children's literature is completely in keeping with the approach suggested by Joachim Campe in his *Beknopte zielkunde voor kinderen* (*Concise Handbook of Psychology for Children*). The self-contained world in which Rousseau experiments with his protégé Emile is here replaced by an artificial universe, safer than the natural surroundings in which Emile was expected to rough it, but also safer than the real world. Martinet is very explicit about this compromise in his *Huisboek*. Children, he maintains, should be allowed to gain "knowledge of the world" not in the world itself but in books: "We, and they, must never become similar to the world! ... Oh, that we may hand them over to society, and to the nation, as pure and uncontaminated by the world as possible!"[31]

As I mentioned earlier, the genre of children's literature began to flower after Rousseau had published *Emile*. This may seem a paradox at first sight. Rousseau wanted to keep children away from books as long as possible. Emile had to learn by experience while moving freely in a natural environment, although carefully guided by an omnipresent tutor, with whom Emile is in permanent dialogue. This ideal pedagogical setting was, as Rousseau admitted, impossible to realize for real parents. The children's books that appeared in the decades after *Emile* offered an alternative. The closed world far from modern civilization, in which Emile grew up, was in the children's literature of the late-eighteenth century replaced by a paper universe in which Rousseau's advices are simulated.

These books are populated by fictitious fathers, mothers or tutors who, walking through nature, tell their fictitious children stories about children walking through nature, and so forth. A further dimension can be added to this claustrophobia-inducing universe, where the illusion of infinity is perfected: if the recommendations found in the conduct books were truly followed up and the reception of children during their reading was actually supervised. In that case, many real children supervised by their parents read about other children who were supervised by their parents who read about still other children, and so on.

Fiction and reality

Although it sounds rather surrealistic, this pedagogical advice was, indeed, followed in reality. The diary of the aforementioned Dutch boy, Otto, shows that he hardly ever read alone, but mostly together with his parents. The reception of his books was not only controlled during the act of reading, but also afterwards. He kept a diary that was regularly read by his parents and commented upon. "Remember this now and live up to it, for it is better not to promise than not to keep your promise. Better not promise so often, but do it instead."[32] This remark in Otto's diary is written in a different hand, probably his mother's. This controlled writing practice is again fully in accordance with those depicted in Otto's children's books. Otto's fictional peers do the same, and are similarly monitored by their elders. This is true not only of the children in *De Vriend der Kinderen* and those in the little book Otto read by Feddersen, in which the youthful diary of Doddridge is held up as an example, but also of the main characters in *Adèle et Théodore*, as read by Otto. Adèle and her mother write in their diaries at the same time every day: "Every evening she gives me her written thoughts and comments, which I then correct with mine."[33] Adèle is allowed to read her mother's diary only after she has submitted her own for inspection. Adèle's attempt to destroy a few pages of her diary is thwarted by her mother, who encloses them without compunction in a letter to a friend: "You will receive it just as she wrote it."[34] In the journal *De Vriend der Jeugd* (*The Youngsters' Friend*) – not to be confused with *De Vriend der Kinderen* – Lodewijk is urged by Hermanus, his former teacher, to keep a diary as a means of perfecting his character: "In it you must write down in the evening all the feelings that have arisen in you that day, as well as all of your activities."[35] Hermanus does not ask to see the diary, but Lodewijk sends it to him anyway so that both his teacher and the journal's readers are given an idea of suitable form, appropriate content and the desired effect of such diaries:

> 6 June:
> Have I fulfilled all my duties today? Have I spent this day in such a way that I can say to myself: "Lodewijk! You have added to your understanding, bettered your heart? Let's see: let's review the day: today I studied geography very diligently – with very little joy, to be sure, but is it my fault that I'm not in good spirits today? I wish to clear myself, and yet I'm not free of guilt."[36]

If we compare the events in the fiction Otto read with those in his own small universe, we must acknowledge that the fictitious outside world, intended as preparation for real life, fits Otto like a glove. The lives of his fictional friends display a frightening similarity to his own life: not only do they read the same books he does, but they lead the same sort of lives. Like Otto, they divide their time between the city and sizeable country estates. They take walks with their goats, cultivate little gardens of their own, visit factories and workshops, care for their pet birds, go on long, edifying walks with their parents or teachers, play the piano, write poems for their parents' birthdays, keep diaries, rise early to hear the nightingale sing, and occasionally eat too many peaches:

> My father gave this peach to me
> For learning with such fervour,
> And now I eat quite happily.
> The peach has yet more flavour.[37]

That, at least, is how a boy in a poem by Van Alphen put it. The logical sequel to this incident is to be found in Otto's diary. In 1791 he wrote that in future he would be allowed to pick peaches only under supervision: "I'm still haunted by the devouring of twelve peaches in 1787."[38]

During a real-life educational walk of the kind Otto also read about, he again discussed his reading:

> Walked back with Papa while talking about the new book by Mrs Cambon, *De klijne Clarissa* [*Little Clarissa*], which we received as a gift. Like Karel in *Grandisson*, Clarissa is the heroine in whom all virtues are combined, and this book has been given to us in order to imitate them.[39]

During one of these walks, Otto was advised not to fraternise with the household servants.[40] This notion is almost identical to the advice given in *Adèle et Théodore* by a baroness who counsels a friend to stop encouraging her daughter to consider her servants "as unfortunate friends". No matter how well intended, such an attitude will lead down a slippery slope:

> We can never view people without the slightest education as our friends. I know of nothing more dangerous than a young person being intimate with servants. ... He or she will learn nothing but ridiculous expressions.[41]

The scene with the slate in Salzmann's *Stichtend en vermaeklijk handboekje* (*Edifying and Diverting Handbook*) of 1792 must also have seemed familiar to Otto. Maria is not allowed to go with the rest of the family for a walk in the woods because she has misbehaved the whole week long. When she objects to this disciplinary measure, her mother brings out the slate on which she records instances of the children's behaviour, and asks one of them to read it out loud. Maria's brothers chalk up overwhelmingly positive scores, but Maria's conduct shows a marked downward spiral: "Maria: Monday morning: diligent and peaceful; afternoon: stubborn. Tuesday morning: peevish; afternoon: peevish and quarrelsome. Wednesday: very badly at fault."[42] Otto's behaviour was tallied up in the same way, presumably also on a slate.

The list was likewise read out by his mother, and sometimes Otto was condemned to copying the whole of it on his own slate, his "private" diary. During the week of 27 February 1796, Otto even surpassed Maria by being "disobedient, contrary, short-tempered, vindictive and impudent. Truly fine virtues which in future, when I have grown older, will make me quite an amiable character."[43]

Reading and diary-writing in the company of real-life friends

In The Netherlands, other eighteenth-century supervised children's diaries have been discovered with literature and reading similar to that of Otto's.[44] For example, Theodore Baumhauer – like Otto, the son of a lawyer – began his diary in 1843 at the age of ten.[45] His diary was monitored daily by his father. When their father was away from home, Theodore's eldest brother, Marie, was responsible for reading the diaries of all the Baumhauer children. When the father returned, he heard about – and punished – all instances of disobedience, especially any deviation from the strict regimen of diary-writing.

The invisible hand in the diary that Abraham van der Hoop started in 1788, at the age of 13, only becomes clear after his tutor leaves. From that moment on the document contains corrections in another hand-writing, presumably that of his parents, who had taken over the tutor's task and were more inclined to interfere.[46] Nor do we come across any signals of an invisible parental hand in the diary of 1802 of Quirijn Verhuell, a burgomaster's son, written at the age of 15. This manuscript differs from that of Pieter Pous, which was rewritten much later and contains enough crossings-out to cast doubt on whether what we have is a fair copy.[47] Even so we know for certain that it had an educational function and that it was read afterwards by his mother, who also commented on it. This information cannot in any way be deduced from the diary, but it is contained in Verhuell's autobiography of 1839 in which he makes the following remarks about his upbringing:

> Also I had to start keeping a diary and now and then I was lucky enough to write down something or other that I had observed in a rather romantic way or else I had imitated a good style, so that I was assured of getting the approval of my mother, who usually discovered depictions of such scenes in some book or other and pointed that out to me, without in any way letting me know how far below the level of these writers I was. She didn't want to undermine my aspirations.[48]

Of Verhuell's diaries all that remains is a single year, but that is more than can be said of that of the young Johan Rudolf Thorbecke. These vanished manuscripts are symbolic, in my opinion, of a whole contingent of educational diaries, only a fraction of which has been recovered and of which an even smaller percentage is so outspoken. We know from Thorbecke's correspondence that he kept a diary from an early age. At the age of 14 he wrote to his parents: "To your question whether I still continue to keep my diary and say my prayers every day and whether I have stuck to the plan I've made, I can answer yes with a good conscience."[49] The words that follow give us a rough idea of what the content of this diary must have been: "I will apply myself to being friendly and polite here at home." Other passages also suggest a practice of keeping a diary that is comparable to that of Otto:

> My dear father, I have already promised you so often never to disobey you again and yet I have done so once more. Now, my dear father, I promise you that I will not break this promise. You won't immediately trust me in this, I know, because I have promised it so often, but this time I want to do it and so I will.[50]

In most of the children's diaries it was impossible to catch co-readers red-handed. Their existence only becomes apparent as intended readers. They show up in the diary of Anna Voet, for example, who begs her readers for absolution because she had deceived her parents and her governess. In the archive of the Rauwenhod family, I found traces of a failed project to coerce two brothers, aged six and ten, to record their behaviour themselves. This "book of behaviour" started in 1834, a year after the death of their father, and was presumably initiated by their mother. On the first page we read a few short notes, sometimes in the first person plural – "This day we behaved very well" – sometimes in the first person singular – "Both of us unbiddable." After seven pages, notes in this style of writing follow a more elaborate note in the first person singular. The I-person declares the loss of his "book of behaviour":

> I did not write in my diary for a very long time. Even haven't the faintest idea where I have left it and forgot my daily behaviour in the past but mama says that she did not see any improvement and that I gave her a lot of distress by my unbidability and pestering the small ones. William was sweet for just a few days, most of the time his behaviour was very bad.

During the following days both brothers mended their ways. At least according to Nicolas, the eldest and secretary of the two: "The 25th Both reasonable. The 26th Both reasonable, The 27th Both reasonable." The first of next month their mother lost her patience and took over the regimen: "Nicolas neglected his diary the whole month. Therefore I prefer to take it over and write about the behaviour of both boys myself in order to read it aloud to them afterwards."

My research shows supervised diary-writing by children was not a typically Dutch phenomenon.[51] I have found some examples of children who not only wrote the same sort of diaries as Otto, but also read exactly the same children's books.

Marjory Fleming, for example, a girl who lived in the area of Edinburgh, wrote a diary under supervision. Her text was controlled by what she called her "little mama", her elder niece Isabella. This supervision is present in many of Marjory's passages, but becomes very visible when – just like in the case of Otto's diary – comment in another hand-writing is added to her entries: "Marjory must write no more journal till she writes better."[52] Her reading included works by Pope, Maria Edgworth's *Moral Tales*, one of the pedagogical advisers we encountered earlier, and the *Tales of the Castle* of Madame de Genlis, which was also read and commented upon by Otto. Marjory was, as she says, "very fond" of this work. The moral of the book is summarized by her in a rather cryptical passage: "Everybody should be unassuming & not assuming – We should regard virtue but not vice for that leads us to distraction & makes us unhappy all our life."[53] De Genlis expressed her life lessons more correctly with less verbosity, but Marjory was substantially younger, younger, too, than Otto. She wrote this in 1810, at the age of eight, a year before her death.

The English sisters Wynn, Elisabeth and Eugenia were, in contrast, of the same age and generation as Otto. He started his diary in March of 1791 at the age of ten. The Wynn sisters started in August of 1789 and were, at the time, ten and nine years of age. These diaries were supervised by their tutor, Monsieur Benincasa. This co-reader, too, announces himself on one of the first pages of the diary in the guise of a woman. On 20 August, Elisabeth writes that she did not recognize her tutor and aunt in disguise when they came down the stairs. In the margin a grownup hand has written some corrections.[54] A few weeks later, his presence betrays itself in an inserted sentence by Elisabeth: "Monsieur Benincasa looked over our journals and criticized them."[55] The sisters read the *Fables of De La Fontaine*, which Rousseau and his followers reject, as well as more proper titles, some of which Otto also read: *Charles Grandisson*, the magazine *Children's Friend* and the stories by Madame de Genlis. And, as with Otto, these books were enjoyed at home, together: "I worked till supper with her whilst mamma read something from *L'Ami des Enfants* [Berquin's version of *Children's Friend*]."[56] Their diary entries with regard to their reading are less extensive than Otto's: "Passed a very dull day nothing remarquable for the journal."[57] Sometimes, however, their literature gave wings to their pens. The story *Theophilus and Olympia; or the Errours of Youth and Age* by De Genlis, for example, turned out to be a real tear-jerker:

> This evening we read Olympe and Theophile (by Mde. de G.). We all cried so much. There was not one of us that was capable of reading.[58]

This was not exactly the reaction Madame de Genlis was striving for. In this story the emotions of both fictive and real readers are cunningly manipulated to be awakened: "Oh, heavens! Pulcherie called, What will become of this unhappy girl?"[59] But these emotions have to be regulated immediately afterwards; in the end, sense has to triumph over sensibility. Jane Austen, by the way, belonged also to De Genlis's real readers, as well as, to make the circle round, some of her main characters.[60] Returning to the Wynn sisters, Elisabeth's reaction was, so to speak, over the top. Fortunately, the reaction of Elisabeth's younger sister, Eugenia, was much more suitable. Not without pride she writes in her diary: "Mesdames de Bombelles and de Regis, Mde de B., Lou Bitche and Betsie all wept; there was but me that was firm."

Reviewing eighteenth-century children's literature is like playing with Russian Matrouschka dolls. Each new piece of research reveals yet another surprise. Thus, in closing this chapter, I cannot resist sharing my last "doll": real children writing moralistic children's literature themselves. This practice by children may reveal more even about their reception of their own literature than their perfunctory diaries have done. I recently did some research into notes written by an eight-year-old Dutch boy, Willem de Clerq. De Clerq later grew up to be a famous nineteenth-century Dutch author and writer of one of the longest diaries ever written.

The first pages of this 25,000-page work consist of stories of his own making. Upon a first reading, the storyline seems familiar:

> Two little boys got their father's permission to play out in the garden on the condition that they did not go out into the woods where they might get lost. Nevertheless, after a time, one of the boys tried to persuade his brother to go out of the garden with him to take a look. "No way," said the brother, "Our father has forbidden us to do this." "You are just a coward," said the other little boy. He left the garden, got lost in the wood and was eaten by bears. Soon afterwards, the remaining boy met his father whilst walking in the garden. The father asked him where his brother was and he answered that he had gone out into the woods. The father went out in search of the boy, and found him dead. His obedient brother received a present for his obedience.[61]

Bears that eat children in the woods? This short story puts the world of eighteenth-century children's literature in a small framework, enriched with elements from fables and fairy tales, precisely the genre that conduct-books so forcefully rejected and that made Rousseau banish all books from Emile's surroundings.

Notes

1 *Bijdragen tot het Menschelijk Geluk*, vol 2 (1789), p560.
2 J. Pearson, *Women's Reading in Britain, 1750–1835, a Dangerous Recreation* (Cambridge, UK, 1999). An anthology of popular pedagogical advice books in the eighteenth century: V. Jones (ed) *Women in the Eighteenth Century: Constructions of Femininity* (London, 1990).
3 J.-J. Rousseau, *Emile, of over de opvoeding*, translated by A. Brassinga (Meppel, 1989), p128.
4 Ibid, p80.
5 Ibid, p319.
6 Ibid, p124.
7 Ibid, p176.
8 For a more detailed treatment of this subject, see A. Baggerman and R. Dekker, *Child of the Enlightenment: Revolutionary Europe Reflected in a Boyhood Diary* (Leiden, 2009), Chapter 3.
9 For an analysis of eighteenth- and nineteenth-century pedagogical advice books in the Dutch language, see A. Baggerman, "Keuzecompetentie in tijden van schaarste en overvloed. Het debat rond jeugdliteratuur voor en na Hiëronymus van Alphen (1760–1840)", in G. J. Johannes, J. de Kruif and J. Salman (eds) *Een groot verleden voor de boeg. Cultuurhistorische opstellen voor Joost Kloek* (Leiden, 2004), pp17–37. On the rise of children's literature in The Netherlands, see P. J. Buijnsters, "Nederlandse kinderboeken uit de achttiende eeuw", in H. Bekkering et al (eds) *De hele Bibelebontse berg. De geschiedenis van het Nederlandse kinderboek in Nederland en Vlaanderen van de middeleeuwen tot heden*

(Amsterdam, 1990), pp195–228. See also the *Bibliografie van Nederlandse school- en kinder-boeken 1700–1800* (Zwolle, 1996), compiled by P. J. Buijnsters and L. Buinsters-Smets. On the canonization of children's literature, see Z. Shavit, *Poetics of Children's Literature* (Athens, GA, 1986), pp133–157.

10 A. Baggerman, "The Moral of the Story: Children's Reading and the Catechism of Nature around 1800", in B. Schmidt and P. Smith (eds) *Making Knowledge in Early Modern Europe. Practice, Objects, and Texts, 1400–1800* (Chicago, IL, 2008), pp143–163.

11 J. B. Basedow, *Elementarwerk* (Dessau, 1774), p528; C. M. Graham, *Letters on Education. With Observations on Religious and Metaphysical Subjects* (London, 1790), p129; B. Wolff, *Proeve over de opvoeding* (Amsterdam, 1977).

12 *Bijdragen tot het menschelyk geluk*, vol 2 (1789), pp560–561.

13 C. M. D. E., *Zedekundig huisboek voor jonge lieden van den beschaafden stand* (Amsterdam, 1830), p34.

14 C. S. F. de Genlis, *Avondtijdkortingen van het kasteel of zedelijke verhalen ten dienste van de jeugd*, 4 vols (The Hague, 1786–1787), pXX.

15 C. G. Saltzmann, "Ankuendigung einer neuer Erziehungsanstalt", in E. Wagner (ed) *Chr. Gotth. Salzmanns paedaogische Schriften*, vol 1 (Langensalza, 1899), pp145–194, esp. p169. The first impression was published in 1785; the first Dutch translation was published in 1808.

16 C. G. Saltzmann, *Eerste onderwijs in de zedeleer voor kinderen* (Amsterdam, 1815), Foreword.

17 See A. Baggerman and R. Dekker, *Child of the Enlightenment*, 87–91. More elaborate on this subject is A. Baggerman, "Het kinderdagboek als spiegelbeeldig universum. Verlichte pedagogiek en de opkomst van kinderdagboeken rond 1800", in A. Baggerman and R. Dekker (eds) *Egodocumenten: nieuwe wegen en benaderingen* (Amsterdam, 2004), pp40–66.

18 J. Glatz, *Woldemar's nalatenschap aan zijnen zoon. Een boek voor jongelingen, ter vorming van hun verstand en veredeling van hun hart*, tranlated by J. Glatz and W. Goede (Arnhem, 1819), p40.

19 *Lettergeschenk voor de Nederlandsche jeugd* [M. Nieuwenhuyzen] (Haarlem, 1790).

20 *De Vriend der Kinderen*, vol III, p126.

21 *De Vriend der Kinderen*, vol III, pp127–131. This refers to the Swiss physicist Abraham Trembley, for a time tutor to the children of Willem Bentinck van Rhoon at Sorgvliet near The Hague. A depiction has survived of Trembley instructing the Bentinck children with the aid of a microscope. A. Trembley, *Unterricht eines Vaters für seine Kinder über die Natur und Religion. Aus dem Französisch übersetzt*, 6 vols (Leipzig, 1776–1783); idem, *Onderwyzingen van een vader aan zyne kinderen in de natuur en in den godsdienst*, 2 vols (The Hague, 1776–1777); idem, *Introduction d'un père à ses enfants* (Geneva, 1775). See also J. Trembley, *Mémoire historique sur la vie de [...] Abraham Trembley* (Neuchatel, 1787); J. Baker, *Abraham Trembley, Scientist and Philosopher* (London, 1954).

22 De Genlis, *Avondtijdkortingen van het kasteel*, vol I, p43. The publication alluded to is Arnaud Berquin, *L'ami des enfans*, which appeared from 1782 onwards.

23 More elaborate about Otto's reading diet: A. Baggerman, "Lezen tot de laatste snik. Otto van Eck en zijn dagelijkse literatuur (1780–98)", in H. Brouwer, L. Duyvendak, M. Keblusek et al (eds) *Jaarboek voor Nederlandse Boekgeschiedenis* 1 (Wageningen, 1994), 57–89; ibid, "The Cultural Universe of a Dutch Child, Otto van Eck and his Literature", *Eighteenth Century Studies*, vol 31 (1997): pp129–134; A. Baggerman and R. Dekker, *Child of the Enlightenment*, pp119–169.

24 The story is "Kapitein Spek en zoon, beiden gekwetst" ("Captain Spek and son, both wounded"), in *De Vriend der Kinderen*, vol V, pp50–59.

25 *De Vriend der Kinderen*, vol V, pp50–51.

26 *De Vriend der Kinderen*, vol V, p58.

27 *De Vriend der Kinderen*, vol V, pp170–173.

28 De Genlis, "Delphine of de gelukkige genezing", in *Avondtijdkortingen van het kasteel*, p20; the other references are to pp24, 27, 73.

29 A. Baggerman and R. Dekker (eds) *Het dagboek van Otto van Eck (1791–1797)* (Hilversum, 1998), 16 September 1792.
30 Ibid, 13 September 1792.
31 J. F. Martinet, *Huisboek voor vaderlandsche gezinnen* (Amsterdam, 1793), p193.
32 A. Baggerman and R. Dekker, *Het dagboek van Otto van Eck*, 6 May 1791.
33 De Genlis, *Adèle en Theodore*, vol II, p230.
34 De Genlis, *Adèle en Theodore*, vol II, p335.
35 *De Vriend der Jeugd*, p18.
36 *De Vriend der Jeugd*, p22.
37 Van Alphen, *Kleine gedigten* (see Chapter 1, note 52), p17.
38 A. Baggerman and R. Dekker, *Het dagboek van Otto van Eck*, 28 August 1791.
39 M. G. de Cambon-van der Werken, *De kleine Klarissa, in brieven en samenspraken, bevattende schoone characters* (The Hague, 1791).
40 A. Baggerman and R. Dekker, *Het dagboek van Otto van Eck*, 2 September 1794.
41 De Genlis, *Adèle en Theodore*, vol I, p149.
42 C. G. Salzmann, *Stichtend en vermaeklijk handboekje voor kinderen en kindervrienden* (Leiden, 1792), pp145–146.
43 A. Baggerman and R. Dekker, *Het dagboek van Otto van Eck*, 27 February 1796.
44 A. Baggerman and R. Dekker, *Child of the Enlightenment*, pp97–98.
45 Willem Theodorus von Baumhauer (1785–1849), NA II FA Von Baumhauer (2.21.205.04), pp1–44.
46 Centraal Bureau voor Genealogie, The Hague, FA Van der Hoop, 5804 fa 163/19.
47 Rijksarchief Zeeland, FA Mathias-Pous-Tak van Poortvliet, pp330–334.
48 Rijksarchief Gelderland, fa VerHuell, p54.
49 The letter is dated 3 November 1812. J. Brandt-van der Veen (ed) *Het Thorbecke-archief 1798–1872* (Utrecht, 1955) ppi, 11.
50 Ibid, p3. The quote is from an undated letter from Zwolle.
51 A. Baggerman and R. Dekker, *Child of the Enlightenment, 97–98.*
52 B. Maclean (ed) *Marjory's Book, The Complete Journals, Letters and Poems of a Young Girl* (London, 1999), p37.
53 A. Esdaille (ed) *The Journals, Letters, & Verses of Marjory Fleming in (…) Facsimile from the Original Manuscripts*, 2 vols (London, 1934), I: p10.
54 A. Fremantle (ed) *The Wynn Diaries*, 2 vols (London, 1935), I: p2.
55 Ibid, p6.
56 Ibid, p86.
57 Idem, (repro. Oxford, 1952), p24.
58 Ibid, I: p86.
59 De Genlis, *Avondtijdkortingen*, I: p176.
60 *Letters of Jane Austen, Edited with an Introduction and Critical Remarks by Edward, Lord Brabourne* (London, 1884) 7 January 1807, 8 November 1800, 13 March 1815. Emma in Austen's *Emma* read De Genlis'*Adelaide and Theodore* (Chapter 53).
61 The diary of Willem de Clercq (1803), University Library of Amsterdam, Reveil archives, FI.

8

HOW CHILDREN WERE SUPPOSED TO FEEL; HOW CHILDREN FELT

England, 1350–1530

Philippa Maddern

This chapter stems from a set of seemingly plain questions: did late-medieval English people think children were capable of feeling emotions? If so, in what forms and circumstances? If not, why not? What significance was attached either to children's emotions, or to the lack of them?

Yet, the apparent simplicity of these questions masks profound theoretical problems. Both "childhood" and "emotion" are slippery terms; "emotion", in particular, is problematic because the term did not exist in English before the late sixteenth century, when it signified not feelings, but political agitation or even simple population migration. Thus, John Shute in 1562 referred to "The great tumultes and emotiones that were in Fraunce betwene the king and the nobilitie", while Richard Knowles, compiling *The generall historie of the Turkes* in 1603, wrote of the "diuers emotions [migrations] of that people". Not until 1602 did "emotion" in the sense of mental agitation or excitement, or strong feeling, arrive in the English language.[1] Clearly, we will not find the term "emotions" handily linked to "children" in the medieval texts. How then can we set about detecting instances of childhood emotion in the medieval English past?

The problem would disappear if we could find terms synonymous with the modern "emotions" in medieval genres. Both Middle English and Medieval Latin employed words possibly cognate with "emotion" or at least "affect", plus terms apparently denoting such individual feelings as joy, anger or fear. The *Promptorium Parvulorum*, a Latin–English dictionary compiled for the use of schoolboys in circa 1440, for instance, contains the entry "Affeccion, or hertly wyllyng" for the Latin *affeccio*; while John Trevisa's early fifteenth-century English translation of Bartolomeus Anglicus's popular encyclopaedia *De Proprietatibus Rerum* described the outward signs (blushing, turning pale) of *effecciouns of herte*, including "sodeyne drede othir ioye".[2] "Passion", though most commonly used to refer to the suffering and death of Christ and his martyrs, could also refer to "strong, controlling, or overpowering emotion".

Reginald Pecock's *Donet*, compiled in circa 1445, referred to "love, hate, desijr, drede, gladnes, sorynes, reuþ, schame and oþir lijk viij passiouns". "Compassion" is likewise well demonstrated from the mid-fourteenth century onwards to mean fellow-feeling or sympathy with emotions such as sorrow or grief. "Feeling" in the sense of being emotionally affected is also attested from 1400 ("Al my passyons and felynges weren loste").[3]

Nevertheless, medieval senses of "passion", "affection" and "feeling" do not map exactly onto modern definitions of "emotions", or comprehend the same groups of phenomena. High-medieval scholars discussing the genesis of the "passions", for instance, included such items as "propensity" and "zeal" (Isaac of Stella), or classified "hope" (*spes*), "aversion" (*fuga*) or "confidence" (*audacia*) as passions, together with love, fear or sorrow (Thomas Aquinas).[4] Nor did medieval people necessarily conceptualize the phenomena of "ioy", "drede" or "wrath" in the same ways as we now conceive of happiness, fear and anger. Categorizing emotions in different ways led medieval writers to discuss them in what, to us, may be unexpected contexts and genres. Thus, emotions such as anger in some circumstances might be regarded in late-medieval England as mortal sins, and were hence analysed not primarily in terms of individual psychology or social relationships, but in devotional and didactic texts instructing the reader how to achieve salvation.[5]

Clearly, then, we cannot consistently expect to find phenomena convincingly identifiable as emotions (in our terms) in medieval texts, whether concerned with children or not; we cannot be sure that apparent emotion-terms in medieval texts actually mean what we think they do; and we must be prepared to seek even such references as we can find in unexpected sources.

But what are emotions "in our terms"? Current emotions research ranges over many disciplines – neurology, cognitive and social psychology, philosophy, anthropology and history, to name a few. Not all adopt the same definitions. Psychologists themselves over the past 150 years have used divergent criteria for identifying emotions, ranging from the notion that they comprise the individual's recognition of physiological changes following the perception of an event, to the idea that emotions are principally social – modes of relating to our environment and determining our readiness to interact with it.[6] No one has succeeded in constructing an exhaustive and authoritative list of emotions. Many (but not all) Western psychologists would accept that there are "basic" emotions – generally listed as fear, anger, happiness, sadness/ grief, disgust and sometimes surprise; but few, if any, would maintain that there are no others. Feelings such as shame, honour or pride may be subject to more highly developed cognitive development and regulation, and hence more cultural conditioning and variation, than the "basic" set, but are nevertheless experienced as emotions. There is increasing consensus that even "basic" emotions involve some cognition and social construction in their genesis, which produces cultural variance in their experience and expression.[7] There is little agreement as to what further psychological or socio-psychological states should be included in the list.[8] Globally, as William Reddy remarks, "Anthropologists' fieldwork has uncovered a fascinating array of different conceptions of emotion, different emotion lexicons, and varying emotional practices." There is no reason to suppose that the range of possible emotions would be smaller in past societies.[9] How, then, can we, as researchers of past emotions of children, be sure we are studying the same things that either other historians or other emotion researchers address?

Definitional variance is the more important because assumptions underlying each psychologist's theories of emotion affect their views as to whether, and to what extent, children are theoretically even capable of feeling emotions. Highlighting a small set of "basic" emotions, assumed to be genetically innate to humans across all cultures and times, leads to the conclusion that even neonates must feel and display emotion. Indeed, some psychologists propose that one criterion of a "basic" emotion is that "[...] it has to emerge very early in ontogenesis" (that is, in babyhood).[10] At the other extreme, those who, like Kagan, believe that true emotion generation requires reflective cognition, appraisal of the meanings of emotions stimuli, and a sense of self necessarily assert that the reactions of infants to such stimuli as cold or the appearance of a stranger cannot be termed emotions (but mere reflex-like reactions); and that even children up to age ten may be incapable of feeling some emotions (such as hopelessness) which require sophisticated assessment of risks and opportunities.[11]

Other scholars, such as Sroufe and Holodynski, argue a middle position: that neonates have a repertoire of at least five different types of emotional reactions (distress, disgust, fright, interest and pleasure),[12] and employ some appraisal of cause and sensation in producing them; but that these might be seen as precursor emotions, to be succeeded, as the child moves through a series of developmental stages, by a much greater emotional repertoire of differing qualities, expressed in different ways and eventually regulated by reference to both community and internalized, self-conscious norms.[13] Holodynski envisages a developmental process by which infants initially access interpersonal emotions (where the subject's emotional expression invokes action from another person that, in turn, regulates the original emotions, as when a hungry baby is fed) but, by toddler and pre-school stage, learn intrapersonal emotional management (where the subject acts alone, either physically or cognitively, to change their circumstances and, hence, regulate or modify their emotion). In this schema all children feel some emotions, but young babies process and use them in a way distinct from older children and adults. Holodynski cites studies suggesting that by the age of seven months, the infant's original five precursor emotions have evolved into more well-defined experiences of frustration, anger, defiance, sorrow, disgust, aversion, fear, embarrassment, interest, surprise, pleasure, joy, affection and amusement.[14] Calkins and Hill note recent developmental studies showing that children learn most emotion regulation skills as infants and toddlers, and "appear to be quite proficient in the use of ... basic skills [of emotion regulation] at a relatively early age".[15]

These studies at least allow us to posit that pre-modern children, like their modern counterparts, developed emotional categories early in their lives. But do they provide a psychological model of emotions that helps historians to establish common ground for discussion? I argue that the "componential" emotions theory on which Holodynski and his like rely provides the best hope for such a model. As Klaus Scherer, one of the main originators of this model, explains:

> ... the term is used to refer to a family of emotion theories that define emotion as a process that involves changes in several subsystems – cognitive activity, motor expression, physiological arousal, action tendencies, and subjective feeling state ... Most of these theories assume that these components ... interact during the emotion process in a recursive fashion.[16]

Thus an original event stimulates our emotion; we appraise both the event and our reactions to it (physical and mental) at a variety of cognitive levels, conscious and unconscious (using, for instance, attention, memory, motivation, reasoning and self-scrutiny); these appraisal processes act not only on the initial stimulus, but on the on-going development of the emotion; and they will almost certainly involve assessments of cultural norms (what is the socially appropriate emotional response or action to display in this situation?). The involvement of high-level cognition and acknowledgement of cultural norms in this model allows great room for cultural variance in emotions. Understandably, therefore, scholars adopting this approach "generally do not endorse the idea of a small number of [...] basic emotions [...] but rather opt for the notion of a large number of highly differentiated emotions".[17]

The advantages of this model for historians are many.[18] Because componential theories do not aim to "identify a clear set of phenomena", but to "formulate the nature of a fuzzy category",[19] they allow us (comparative) clarity about the nature of our object of research, while recognizing the futility of trying to develop exhaustive lists of all emotions possibly identifiable in the past. The concept of inter-relating components of emotion, spanning phenomena from the measurably physical, through self-reflection, to the input of cultural norms into the development and regulation of affect, licenses – indeed, necessitates – historical study of cultural norms and self-reflective practices of past emotions, without denying the physiological realities of emotions in our past subjects, which we historians cannot directly measure (though we may find them described). Importantly, because the mechanisms of cognitive appraisal and regulation, essential to emotion development in this theory, take place at a number of levels (unconscious and conscious), they must, in part, be learned and therefore can be seen to be one aspect of a child's development. This opens the way for historians to study both the expectations and the actualities of child development and socialization in the past, in relation to children's emotions.

Finally, one great advantage to historians of adopting a componential theory of emotions is that it reduces the risk of applying anachronistic definitions and categories of emotions onto our subjects. Whatever fear, sorrow, joy, anger or "passion" meant to medieval people, it is clear that medieval theorists conceptualized the generation of passions or feelings in ways surprisingly similar to those of componential emotions theorists, though they were often couched in terms of sin, virtue and spiritual experience. Simo Knuutila notes, for instance, that for Anselm of Laon and his contemporaries, a sin or passion did not consist simply in the original pleasurable response to a carnal stimulus; this constituted only a "*propassio*" (pre-passion). Only cognitively willed consent to such pleasure, leading ultimately to consent to action (action readiness in modern psychological terms?) produced full-blown sins (or passions) such as lust or anger. "*Propassio*" thus became an accepted medieval term for "the initial state of an unpremeditated desire or emotional response" – like a componential theorist's notion of the first reactions to an original stimulus/event.[20] Similarly, the many medieval scholars influenced by Avicenna accepted his postulate of an estimative mental faculty that enabled the affective appraisal of external stimuli, often based on previous experience (even a dog, thought Avicenna, might learn to fear beating at the sight of the rod). The affective evaluation performed by this "estimative" faculty (which seems to mirror the appraisal mechanisms studied by modern psychologists) in turn led either to a strong or a weak disposition to action, which might then be controlled or promoted by the controlling rational will (as the recursive cognitive effects posited by psychologists finally produce emotional action readiness). These developments might also be accompanied by physical effects. Avicenna also acutely noted that the nature of emotions such as shame or wonder, which rely on higher-order cognitive recognition of such things as social rules, or the distinction between common and rare phenomena, cannot be expected of any beings lacking higher-order cognition, such as animals.[21] If, as it appears, Avicenna and his followers could converse easily with Scherer and his adherents on emotional constitution, surely we historians can join the conversation on their terms, and have a chance of finding in our sources representations of these processes of emotion generation, even in children.

But how do we define childhood in the Middle Ages and Early Modern Period? Children can be identified in any number of ways: by legal definitions of ages of responsibility; by biological–psychological development stage; or even as participants in a relationship of care, protection and interest between parents and offspring that, far from being age limited, persists as long as both generations live. The first is difficult for historians since different cultures set differing legal age boundaries to childhood, or even to different aspects of childhood – for instance, in relation to legal ages of marriage as opposed to legal ages of inheritance. Thus, to set a universal age limit on the end of childhood may impose arbitrary cultural presuppositions on the past, blinding us to the nuances of how pre-modern people themselves defined and categorized childhood. Since this chapter investigates the development – perceived and/ or enacted – of late-medieval children's emotional capacities, the second style of definition seems the most promising; but is not without its own difficulties. No one doubts that all children go through certain physical/developmental processes (suckling, weaning, toilet training, learning to walk and talk, being educated), and most, throughout history, have done so within fairly narrow age boundaries. Just as Lyndal Roper has argued in relation to sexual difference, there is an irreducible "physiological ... reality" to childhood, of which, as historians, we need to take account.[22] Yet Roper is too sophisticated a thinker to adopt the easy conclusion that either gender/ sexuality or childhood can be understood as solely physically determined or solely culturally constructed. Instead, she argues that we need to think of subjectivities (gendered or, for our purposes, childhood) as deriving from a two-way relationship between cultural constructions and somatic bodily experience.[23]

Late-medieval English definitions of childhood (all variation notwithstanding) did involve assessments of physical, mental and emotional development. English people during 1350–1530 tended to class childhood as the first of six (or the first two of 12) Ages of "Man", lasting until the child was roughly 12 to 14 years old, yet defined not primarily by numbers of years, but by a distinctive set of physical and spiritual characteristics.[24] Under age 14, children were understood to be characterized by a certain humoral constitution, which in turn produced distinctive physical and mental behaviours. The *De Proprietatibus Rerum* ascribes to these children, especially the younger ones, the quality of "tenderness": a concept implying, apparently, both delicacy and mental and physical pliability. The fact that the child's humoral constitution was on the moist side of the spectrum meant that the new-born's flesh was "tendir, neische, quavy and vnsad". Picturing the infant's pliability in directly physical terms, Bartolomaeus noted that "for tendirnes the lymes of the childe mai esiliche and sone bowe and bende and take diuers schappis".[25] Some "tendirnes of body" outlasted infancy; children aged between 7 and 14, Bartolomaeus affirmed, "bene sone ihurt and igreued, and they mowe not wel endure harde trauaile".[26] So prevalent was this understanding that the phrase "tender age" was used in a great range of medieval texts as a synonym for childhood. The late fifteenth-century aristocratic text the *Beauchamp Pageant*, for example, recorded that Henry VI was crowned king in 1429, "beyng in his tendre age" (he was then just short of his eighth birthday); John Brown, complaining in Chancery that his master had defrauded him of his inheritance, claimed that the crime had been possible only because he was "tendr of age" at the time – that is, under 14.[27] Contemporaries did perceive a distinct developmental change at about age seven, when the child was held to begin to show powers of reason and a capacity for education.[28] But even though children aged between 7 and 14 were clearly thought to have passed the most pliant and fluid stage, they nevertheless remained on the humorally moist and physically and mentally mobile and changeable side of human nature. Thus *De Proprietatibus Rerum* characterizes children "bitwene seuen yere and fourteen" as "neisch of fleisch, lethy and pliant of body, abel and light to meuynge, witty to lerne caroles, and withoute business". Why? "For mouynge of hote humours that haue the maistrie in thaym thay mouen lightlich and ben vnstedefast and vnstable."[29]

We can fairly say, therefore, that a particular physical constitution was understood in late-medieval England to comprise a sure marker of a stage of development on the way to adulthood; and that that stage could be aligned with a distinct age group (under 14 years). For the purposes of this chapter, therefore, I shall adopt that age group as my target of study. This group is not always easy to find in the records. In particular, sources produced *by* its members are rare to the point of absence. Nevertheless, both scientific and prescriptive literatures described children at this stage; children were depicted in fictional and didactic genres, such as the medieval mystery plays, and apparently themselves acted in those plays; and descriptions of individual children's behaviour, either by outsiders, or by the individuals themselves recalling the past, do survive, though often in less widely read genres (for instance, early Chancery petitions or depositions to ecclesiastical courts in causes for annulment of marriages made under age). These very different texts can profitably be read against one another to develop a history of children's emotions in late-medieval England.

Late-medieval humoral theory acted not only to define life stage, but also to identify groups of individuals prone to (or immune from) particular emotions. An oversupply of choler, the hottest and driest humour, produced "men" "generalliche wratheful, hardy, vnmeke, light, vnstable, impetuous".[30] The phlegmatic "man", dominated by the cold and wet humour phlegm, was "lustles, heuy, and slowth" and "ferdeful of herte".[31] Blood, the best of the humours (warm, moist and life giving) bestowed both understanding, and boldness, confidence and joy on those ruled by it. Hence "he that hath clene blood and hoot and light is but litil imeued for drede"; while the sanguine humour also "maketh hem [the heart and the spirits] glad, and waketh loue".[32] Unsurprisingly, blood's direct opposite, the cold, dry humour of melancholy, "constreyneth and closith the herte", producing the "passioun" of melancholy:

> ... al that hath this passioun withouten cause beth often dredeful and sory ... And so if men asketh of suche what they drede and wherfore thei beth sory, they haueth none answere. Somme weneth that they schulen dye anon vnreso-nabliche. Somme dredith enemyte of som oon. Som loueth and desireth deth.

In extreme cases, melancholy could cause paranoid delusions and their concomitant wild emotions:

> ... somme falleth into wel euel suspicions withouten recouere, and therfore they hatith and blameth ... hire frendes and somtyme smytith and sleeth hem.[33]

Though Bartolomaeus does not explicitly say so, the combined logic of humoral emotion theories and humoral childhood theories inexorably led to the conclusion that children – dominated by warm, moist and highly mobile humours – were extremely unlikely to feel either melancholic despair or causeless fear, phlegmatic listlessness or dry choleric rage. Instead, their characteristic mood was overwhelmingly a light-hearted insouciance that reacted only fleetingly to trivial pleasures and trials. Boys between the ages of 7 and 14, we are told, "For mouynge of hete of fleisch and of humours":

> ... lede here life withoute care and busines and tellen pris onliche of merthe likynge, and dreden no perile more than betinge with a yerde.[34]

Interestingly, it appears that despite their humorally warm constitution, children were not viewed in the medical literature as capable of experiencing the true courage or deep joy of male adults. Why should this be so? Apparently, the writers were influenced by their views both of the effects of humoral balance on reason and of the role of reason in developing true emotions. As posited by the scholastics, a *passio* was distinguished from a mere *propassio* precisely in that it comprised a lasting and effectual phenomenon, developed through the use of the rational will, rather than being a mere momentary response to a stimulus. A *propassio* did not become a *passio* until the will consented to it.[35] But children, certainly until age 7 and, to some extent, until age 14, were held to lack the capacity for reason and steadfast will. Reason was enabled by a confirmed and stable humoral balance in favour not only of blood, but of blood sufficiently heated to produce wit. "[M]en with coolde blood ben ... foles, as men with hote blood ben wise and redy", wrote Bartolomaeus. But though children's humours were typically warm, they were apparently far too mobile, and not sufficiently well heated, to enable the full play of reason or to allow children to will something consistently; "children with blood that hetith nought, kannen but litil good".[36] Irrational beings – such as animals and children – could thus not be expected to experience fully formed emotions. The very instability of children's humours, and their feelings, was both a consequence of their lack of reason and higher cognition, and a cause of their emotional underdevelopment:

> When they ben preised or schamed or blamed thay sete litil therby. For mouynge of hete of fleisch and of humours they ben etheliche and sone wroothe and sone iplesed and foregeuen sone.[37]

The belief that children's feelings were so fleeting, cognitively undeveloped and inconsequential as to be irrelevant to any developed emotional system was voiced not only in encyclopaedias, but in a range of literary and advisory texts. The author of the late fifteenth-century didactic Scottish text *Ratis Raving*, for instance, actually categorizes the stages of childhood partly by the child's emotional development, or lack of it. In the first three years of life, the author asserts:

> Rycht as a best, child can no mare
> bot lauch ore gret for Joy & care.

At most – again like an animal – it has "feilinge", instinctive response to stimuli, but no true emotion.[38] From three to seven years old, the child, wholly occupied in restless imaginative play, was still governed by nature, not reason; he or she:

> ... growis vp as gers or tree,
> And *as a best* may feil & see [emphasis mine].[39]

Between 7 and 15 years "springis the rutis of resone" in the child; though the author thought that not until age 30 did "resone and discreccione" achieve perfection.[40] John Lydgate's fifteenth-century didactic work for boys, *Stans Puer ad Mensam*, likewise ends with a reflection on the slight and transitory nature of children's emotions:

> To childer longeth nat to be vengable,
> Sone mevyd and sone fforgeuyng; ...
> Wratthe of children sone is overgoon,
> With an appell partyes be maad at oon.

Hence, childhood feelings had no serious consequence, and their expression could be safely ignored:

In childeris werre now myrthe, now debate,
In her quarell is no greet vyolence;
Now pley, now wepyng, selde in on estate;
To her pleyntes yeve no gret credence.[41]

Theology to some extent supported this conclusion. In theological terms, some passions (wrath and envy, for instance) could be included in the list of mortal sins. But sin, like emotion, could not exist in the absence of the rational knowledge of, and consent to, evil. Reginal Pecock was at pains to assure his lay audience that ordinary passions such as "loue, hates, desiris, dredis, angris, schames, sorewes, routhis, ioies, gladnessis", though they might seem good or bad, were, in fact, morally neutral. They followed "vpon the sight and heeryng in oure vndirestonding or resoun", but were not willed and, therefore, could not be subjects of blame or praise. Only the choice by the will (preferably under the guidance of reason) to use them rightly or wrongly gave the passions any moral quality.[42] Wrath, he believed, was a sin and distinct from anger particularly because it was "a fre deede chosen freli bi the wil".[43] In Pecock's schema, irrational children might feel emotions at the level of bodily awareness and corporeal sense; but these emotions would have no moral significance. The dawning of the age of reason in a child was the beginning both of their awareness of moral values and of their capacity to sin. As Bartolomaeus puts it, the age between 7 and 14 can partly be defined as the stage "when [the boy] ... knoweth good and euel".[44] The Holy Innocents, so John Mirk's template sermon for their feast day explained, were so named because they had not sinned against their neighbours "by no wronge doyng ... *by no consent of synne*".[45] Logically, then, children, especially under age seven, must be immune from the fully developed sinful passions such as pride, wrath, envy, avarice (the excessive love of wealth) and lust. Furthermore, their innocence obviated any need to feel emotions such as remorse or contrition. Very young children, especially, were said to be in the condition of Adam and Eve before the Fall, without pride or shame. As Mirk put it, the Holy Innocents "lyueden here wythout schame; for they weren all wythinne too yere of age".[46]

Hence, the only emotional (or, more properly, pre-emotional) style commonly attributed to children in much late-medieval literature was an effervescent and literally inconsequent lightness or merriment, often attached to trivial sources of pleasure ("they louen an appil more than gold"[47]), and sometimes active in circumstances that make them inappropriate in adults. A late-medieval lyric in which the Virgin Mary contrasts her state after the death of Christ with that of happier mothers describes how:

Youre childer ye daunce upon youre knee,
With laghing, kissing, and mery cheer.[48]

John Bromyard's fourteenth-century *Summa Predicantium* described young children, whose parents had died, playing happily with the silk pall covering the corpse.[49]

If we took these texts as definitive of late-medieval thinking on children's emotions, we would necessarily conclude that children's feelings went almost completely unacknowledged in this period; that a child's emotion was thought to be at best a *propassio* limited to a flighty response to immediate stimuli; and that both scientific and theological writers and the general public believed children to be incapable of feeling sustained, serious, significant and sinful emotion.

Yet, in fact, prescriptive and descriptive texts are not univocal or consistent on the subject of childhood emotions. In relation to emotions that could appear as either virtues or vices, some writers thought that children could not start too early to learn to exercise virtue and repress vice. John Lydgate's version of the *danse macabre* has Death addressing even a day-old child thus:

> Litel Enfaunt/that were but late borne
> Schape yn this worlde/to haue no plesaunce ...
> Lerne of newe/to go on my daunce.

Lydgate's stated intention in writing the poem was to persuade readers to "A-mende her life/in eueri maner age." Amendment clearly included weaning one's emotional attachments from this world to the next.[50] Richard Whitford in his popular guide for household heads (1530) urged parents to begin training their children "by time in youthe as soone as they can speke" because, unlike other crafts, "vertue & vice may be lerned in eueri age". What comprised childhood virtue? According to Whitford, one primary component was "reuerende drede" both for God and their progenitors. Children should be encouraged to feel it in order to practise the "due reuerende honour to be done ... vnto the parentes".[51] It appears that some prescriptive writers thought some emotions particularly appropriate to children – among them contempt for this world's pleasures and obedient awe of one's parents.

These ways of conceptualizing childhood emotions make sense of a very different genre: that of the late-medieval mystery play cycles, which in the pageants of Abraham and Isaac contain vivid representations of children's emotions on the stage – probably enacted by boys aged about 12. The surviving Abraham and Isaac plays[52] poignantly portray the supposed emotions of a young boy facing death at the hands of a beloved father. Indeed, some seem to portray the Isaac figure as much more emotionally capable than the adult Abraham. Why would they do so if children were universally thought to be incapable of emotion?

True, there may be some backhanded adherence to the notion that children could not feel, or regulate, true emotions in the York cycle play of Abraham and Isaac, whose dramatist makes Isaac over 30 at the time of the proposed sacrifice ("of eelde to reken right", as his father tells us).[53] Yet, this Isaac's age apparently operates to repress, rather than develop, his emotions. He displays an almost unvaryingly steadfast affective control; in fact, the only emotion he allows himself to show is willing obedience to God's will. On hearing of God's command that he shall die, he immediately exclaims: "I sall noght grouche theragayne", announcing himself "bayne" (eager) to die in such a cause, and specifically enjoining Abraham "morne noght for me".[54] In this play, as in Pecock's theory of the passions, it is his "flessche", not his rational soul, that feels emotion. Anticipating that his *body* – not his reasonable soul – "for dede will be dredande", he urges the aged Abraham to bind him on the grounds that he might not otherwise be able to overcome his (Isaac's) instinctive resistance.[55]

But the Isaac figures in the other plays are clearly young – their fathers call them "my young son" or refer to them using affectionate diminutives, such as "my dear darling".[56] In the Brome play, Isaac announces himself to be still "slender".[57] In all five, ironically in view of the prescriptive literature, the Isaac figure at least matches Abraham in rendering intense, powerful (and moral) emotions, and far outstrips the York play Isaac in emotional display.

The N-town version is perhaps the most restrained. Almost like a *puer senex* – that Biblical type of the preternaturally mature boy, able to instruct his elders on the nature and will of God[58] – Isaac, told of his fate, instantly thanks God "heartily" for the chance to demonstrate his utmost obedience and urges his father:

> I pray you, father, be glad and fain
> Truly to work Gode's will.[59]

Abraham voices grief, telling Isaac: "There may no man that liveth in land/Have more sorrow than I have woe"; Isaac merely pronounces himself "All ready" to "do your bidding *as reason is*".[60] His emotions are apparently of the highest and most rational order; his obedience to his father's and God's commands, both glad and dutiful. Nevertheless, he demonstrates the capacity for emotional empathy, even while reproving his father for excessive sorrow:

> Let be, good father, your sad weeping!
> Your heavy cheer aggrieveth me sore.[61]

The Brome, Dublin, Chester and Townley versions all portray a much more overtly emotional Isaac, transforming the 13 brief verses of the Genesis original into the medieval equivalent of a three-handkerchief weepie. The emotional interchange is almost always initiated by Isaac's empathic detection of his father's trouble. In the Brome version, for instance, as father and son begin their journey to the place of sacrifice, Isaac comments on Abraham's all-too-apparent sorrow. The sight triggers his own emotions; his "heart beginneth to quake" at Abraham's drawn sword. When the dreadful truth that he must die at his father's hand is gradually revealed to him, he reacts with a rich mixture of emotions – incredulity and fear struggle with obedient love for the father who will slay him and the God who orders it. Desperately, he seeks a reason for God's judgement – what has he done wrong that deserves more than the usual punishment?

> If I have trespassed against you ought
> With a yard you may make me full mild
> And with your sharp sword kill me not.

A long-drawn crescendo of love and grief ensues, reciprocally created by both characters; as Abraham exclaims, the child's innocent questioning "breaketh my heart in two".[62] The text drips pathos, as Isaac displays his love and empathy for his whole family. He begs his father to take comfort in loving his remaining children, and urges him not to tell his mother of his death because "she would weep full sore". He says farewell to his "mother so sweet" in absentia. Almost overcome with fear, he pleads with Abraham: "smite me not often with your sharp sword/But hastily, that it be sped" and asks him to turn his (Isaac's) face downward, "for of your sharp sword I am ever adread".[63] At the (supposedly) final moment, he implores Abraham to end quickly the intensity of terror and suffering:

> Ah! mercy, father, why tarry you so,
> And let me lie thus long on this heath?
> Now I would to God the stroke were do.
> Father, I pray you heartily, short me of my woe,
> And let me not look thus after my death.[64]

The same themes recur in the other four plays; in the Chester cycle play, for instance, Isaac repeatedly begs Abraham for mercy, pathetically declaring all the while his own innocence ("What have I done, Father, what have I said?") and insisting "I love you ay."[65]

Furthermore, the Brome play makes Abraham, not Isaac, the character whose emotions seem to fluctuate in a manner supposedly more typical of children than adults. When the angel holds back Abraham's sword, showing him the ram provided by God in Isaac's stead, and bidding him "thou mayest be blithe", Abraham instantly cheers up, apparently forgetting the fraught sorrow of a moment ago. Isaac, not realizing, continues to say: "Ah! mercy, father, why smite you not yet?" Told of his last-minute reprieve, he continues to worry about the morality of this happy outcome – "Ah! my dear father, Abraham/Will not God be wroth that we do thus?" He is hardly reassured even when shown the sheep and ordered to light the fire to sacrifice it instead of himself –"But, father, while I stoop down low/You will not kill me with your sword, I trow?" – adding that he wishes the sword could go in the fire because seeing it "makes me full ill aghast".[66] Nor can he forget his recent terror when the pair turn homeward. Abraham, perhaps rather crassly to modern eyes, asks him: "Why! dearworthy son, wert thou adread?", thus giving Isaac the opportunity to declare honestly: "Yea, by my faith, father ... /I was never so afraid before."[67]

What was the purpose of this melodramatic welter of child–parent emotions? It is noteworthy that Isaac displays exactly those feelings which, according to theorists such as Whitford, the good child should harbour – empathizing love for parents, obedience to one's father to the point where (as Whitford suggests real-life children should do[68]) the child asks to be beaten for any supposed fault and a fear of displeasing God so strong as to overcome the natural dread of dying. (The Brome play Isaac finally thanks God that "my wit served me so well/For to dread God more than my death."[69]) Granted the likelihood that the parts were taken by young boys, it seems probable that these plays were intended to model, for a street audience certainly containing both parents and children, the correct emotional style that children were supposed to learn, sometimes from a very young age.

That the authors should have chosen to convey these lessons in a play about familial death is hardly surprising. Parents, adult caregivers and even the children themselves must have known only too surely that many children had cause to feel intense sorrow, grief or fear in their lives, particularly from the deaths of their parents and siblings, and the known likelihood of their own early demise. An analysis of 5529 Inquisitions Post Mortem from 1352 to 1497, for instance, shows that in 19.35 per cent of cases, or nearly one in five families, at least one parent died before the *heir* (generally the eldest son) was 12. The 1218 bereaved heirs[70] were distributed almost equally across all ages from birth to 12 years old, with just over half (630, or 52.2 per cent) aged six or under at their parent's demise. Death rates of late-medieval English children, though hard to calculate accurately, were certainly immense. Nicholas Orme summarizes much of the evidence. Comparable calculations from parish registers during 1540 to 1599 show that 27 per cent of each child cohort died in their first year of life, and a total of 42.5 per cent died before age ten. In the whole medieval period, approximately 96 children were born to English monarchs or future monarchs, of whom 45 died aged ten or less (46.8 per cent).[71] If nearly half of each cohort of children died before age 12, it follows that practically every surviving child must have experienced the death of a sibling or peer group member; while the high rate of early parental deaths meant that many must also have had to mourn the death of a parent. A particularly poignant example of both these trends comes from the Duffield family of Yorkshire in 1429. An Inquisition Post Mortem shows that Thomas Duffield died on 10 March. He then had two daughters, the elder, Margaret, aged six and the younger just two days old. The baby died 11 days later. Thomas's wife Elizabeth survived him by only a little over two months, dying on 23 May in the same year. At the age of six, Margaret, the sole remaining family member, had lost both her parents and her baby sister in the space of 11 weeks.[72]

Of course, it is unsound to assign feelings retrospectively to past subjects, without evidence. But in this case we need not rely solely on fictional works to suggest that real children observed and suffered real grief and anxiety at the death of parents. The words of one motherless child survive in the case of John, son of John Trenowyth of Cornwall. Around 1480 a former servant of Trenowyth the elder testified to seeing John the younger, aged four at his mother's death, holding his father's hand as his father interrogated a servant whom he had sent to inspect a possible second wife. The boy:

> ... demaunded of his ffader in this wyse ffader shall y haue a nother moder yea sone but thowe shall haue noon that shall loue the so well as thy owne moder ded Wheruppon the fader turned a syde and whept.[73]

Young John, in addition to his own anxieties about his new step-mother, certainly witnessed at close hand his father's uncontrollable grief. In such circumstances it is hardly surprising that some adults thought that a child could not commence too young to learn not to become too emotionally attached to the joys of this life; to face squarely the possibility of their own or their parents' deaths; and to develop an obedient awe of God's will that might help reconcile them to the ever-present shadow of death.

Furthermore, in a different set of genres again – ecclesiastical court cases – the sustained fears, sorrows and anxieties of children under the age of 14 could literally become the matter under examination, and the determinant of the outcome of the case. Particularly good examples arise in the context of marriages whose validity was disputed due to the allegation that they had been made when the participants were under legal age (12 for girls, 14 for boys) and where the participants had been coerced into marriage, making their vows against their will. Indeed, proof that the participants had been under age and unwilling to marry was one of the few reliable ways of obtaining an annulment of marriage in late-medieval England. Deponents in such cases willingly deposed to the intensity of emotion expressed, particularly by young girls, and judges accepted their testimony with no apparent sense of any incongruity between the age of the protagonists and the intensity and duration of their emotions. In 1345, for instance, Thomas Wenlok, a servant of the de Warde family, testified in the annulment case between Margaret de Warde and John de Neville. Margaret had been only 11 when the supposed marriage ceremony took place; and Wenlok said that "often and often, he could not say how often" he had heard her "saying and weeping for fear" that she would never consent to a marriage with de Neville. Her fear was understandable in the light of his claim that she was subject to "serious beatings" and the threat that her family would strip her of all her belongings and make her beg from door to door.[74] Their divorce, with right to remarry, was duly pronounced. Similarly, in the 1428 annulment case between John Threpeland and Joan Richardson, Nicholas Bayldon testified that Joan was only nine at the time of the marriage, and was "forced and compelled by the power and fear of William Richardson her grandfather". Joan Crosselay deposed that in many conversations with young Joan she had heard her "swear, bitterly weeping (*amare plorando*) that it was never her will to have John in marriage".[75] Not only tears, but general behaviour and manner were read by witnesses, and accepted by the courts, as true signs of a child's heartfelt and consistent fear and reluctance. Around 1413 in the case of the disputed marriage between Agnes Stowk and Robert Clopton, Thomas Thystylden testified that Robert Borehed, executor of the will of Agnes's father, had demanded of Agnes (then only about 11 years old) whether she would take Clopton for her husband. When she stood silent "as if terrified" (*quasi perterita*), Borehed ordered her to say the words of matrimony, backing up his command with a solid punch to the ribs. "As if compelled by fear" (*quasi per metu compulsa*) she did so. Agnes's uncle, Robert Stowk, described how she afterwards told him "with great sorrow at heart" (*cum magno cordis dolor*) how she had been forced to consent to the marriage.[76]

On the other hand, a steadfastly cheerful demeanour on the part of young marriage partners was sometimes represented by witnesses as signifying their consent to marriage. We do not know the exact ages of Richard Laton and Elizabeth Berker at their supposed wedding. Richard's father, evidently intending to confirm the validity of the marriage, claimed that Richard was fully 14 years old and that from Elizabeth's appearance and the accounts of her godparents and neighbours (she was apparently orphaned), she was the same age – "or thereabouts" (*vel eo circa*). Another witness ventured only that she appeared to be at least 12 years old. Since 14 and 12 were the canonical ages of valid marriage for boys and girls, respectively, and since Richard's father evidently wished to maintain the marriage, one must suspect that the children were at least no older and possibly younger. But whatever Elizabeth's age, Richard senior, asked "whether she was compelled", firmly replied that "she came to the contract with a joyful and cheerful face" (*jocundo & amicabili vultu*) and joyfully and happily without any coercion made the contract. Furthermore, her telling consistency of behaviour continued after the actual vows – she immediately "served to them, cheerfully, (*amicabiliter*) food and drink, as was then the custom of the country".[77]

It is hard to recognize, either from the plays or from these accounts, the inconstant and inconsequential sub-emotions attributed to children in the encyclopaedias and theological literature. Yet even these representations are second hand. The interests of adult dramatists and marriage managers may well have governed either their perceptions or their representations of children's emotions. Is there any evidence that children themselves acknowledged recognizable emotions?

I have yet to find a late-medieval child directly expressing emotion; but there is one case among the Early Chancery Petitions where the complainant herself reflected on her own childhood treatment and its subsequent psychological effect. In about 1450, Agnes Terry proffered a petition complaining of the behaviour of John Bicombe, formerly her guardian when she was left orphaned at a "right tender age". The gist of her complaint was that he took and spent her inheritance, and forcibly arranged her marriage, for his own ends:

> And ferthermore your seid besecher was caried and ladde away froo farendon aforeseid by the seid maister John … to his suster house and there kept in a chambre by the space of 40 wekes and more that noe man ne woman shulde speke with me ne knowe where your seid besecher was safe he and his seid suster to that entent that he wold marye me … to his entent and to haue the seid godes and catell atte his owne rule and disposicion by the whiche kepyng your seid besecher ys soe enfeblisshed in brayne that atte summe tyme shee is not alder beste disposed.[78]

Terry clearly believed that this abuse (largely psychological and emotional) had had serious and long-lasting effects on her psychological health.

What, then, are the distinctions between how children were supposed to feel and how they felt? On the one hand, a strong body of scientific, theological and prescriptive literature maintained that neither children's humoral state, nor their immature reason, would allow them even to develop a true emotion. At best they could feel only those corporeally generated and morally inconsequent emotions felt by irrational beings, such as beasts. In particular, children's under-developed moral sense would simply not allow them to feel passions that had been willed into being as fully blown sins. It may be that no one in late-medieval England thought children capable of feeling, or expressing, wrath, pride or envy.

Yet, other writers, sometimes in different genres (didactic, dramatic) evidently believed that this was not the whole story. Virtue and its concomitant emotions could, they thought, be early and successfully cultivated in the child. It may be, however, that these emotions were very specific to children – for instance, the "reverend dread" with which they were supposed to regard their parents, and the concomitant and distinctive obedient and dutiful love they were bound to display towards them. These are exactly the emotions that the mystery-play dramatists evidently thought that the boys playing Isaac should be able to act for, and even perhaps to generate in, their child audiences.

To adult managers of marriages, it was taken for granted that the child participants could feel emotions – either positive or negative – for their proposed partner and the marriage relationship. Granted the apparent willingness of the child protagonists to display these emotions to future witnesses, it is possible that they themselves recognized the potential force of their own emotions. And it was certainly the case that according to ecclesiastical law those emotions had extremely important consequences: they could literally make or break a marriage.

There is no simple story of emotions among late-medieval English children. The evidence is strong that the children felt intense and lively emotions. Some of these emotions were occasionally acknowledged, even encouraged and nurtured, by the adults who cared for them. Yet, those same adults, under the influence of strict medical theory, may have ignored, or even denied the existence of, other childhood emotions.

Notes

1 *Oxford English Dictionary Online*, http://www.oed.com, "emotion", last accessed 18 January 2013. Note, however, that "émotions" in the sense of civil unrest, uprising or riot appears to have been well established in French during the fifteenth century. Nicole Hochner, for instance, has found it as early as 1429 in *La Chronique du Bon Duc Loys de Bourbon* – the king "avoit tant a faire en son royaume, tant pour les esmotions d'aucunes ses communes appellés Jacques et Maillets, comme pour le roi de Navarre, et d'autres grandes compaignies, qui lui estoient contraires". *La Chronique du Bon Duc Loys de Bourbon*, A.-M. Chazaud (ed) (Paris, 1876), p5, cf. p88, where "l'esmotion du duc de Bretaigne" leads to a siege of Troye. I am indebted to Dr. Hochner, pers comm, for this invaluable reference.
2 A. L. Mayhew (ed) *The Promptorium Parvulorum: The First English-Latin Dictionary* (London, 1908), p6; M. Seymour (ed) *On the Properties of Things: John Trevisa's Translation of Bartholomaeus Anglicus De Proprietatibus Rerum; a Critical Text* (Oxford, 1975), p196 (my emphasis); cf. Mayhew (ed) *Promptorium Parvulorum*, pp240, 12 for the terms "Ioy" (Gaudium) and "Angyr or Wrath" (Ira).
3 *Oxford English Dictionary Online*, http://www.oed.com, "passion" (with examples from the mid-thirteenth century onwards), "compassion" and "feeling", last accessed 18 January 2013.
4 S. Knuuttila, *Emotions in Ancient and Medieval Philosophy* (Oxford, UK, 2005), ch 3, section 3.6, "Emotions in Early Thirteenth-Century Philosophy," n. 166 and section 3.8, "Aquinas on Emotions", n. 191.
5 Cf. Robert Mannyng of Brunne's discussion of anger as the second in the list of deadly sins in the popular devotional text, *Handlyng Synne*, Idelle Sullens (ed) (Binghampton, NY, 1983), pp94–99.

6 See the basic and very brief but useful summary in K. Oatley, D. Keltner and J. M. Jenkins (eds) *Understanding Emotions* (Oxford, UK, 2006), p28, Table 1.3 (running from William James (1884) to Frijda and Mesquita (1994)).

7 B. Rottger-Rossler and H. J. Markowitsch (eds) *Emotions as Bio-Cultural Processes* (New York, 2009), pp28–29, and Part 2, "Empirical Studies – Shame and Pride: Prototypical Emotions Between Biology and Culture"; see also below, notes 14, 16, 17 and 19.

8 See, for example, E.-M. Engelen, H. J. Markowitsch, C. von Scheve, B. Rottger-Rossler, A. Stephan, M. Holodynski and M. Vandekerckhove, "Emotions as Bio-cultural Processes: Disciplinary Debates and an Interdisciplinary Outlook", in: B. Rottger-Rossler and H. J. Markowitsch (eds) *Emotions as Bio-Cultural Processes*, pp25–27; W. Reddy, *The Navigation of Feeling: A Framework for the History of Emotions* (Cambridge, UK, 2004), ch. 1, "Answers from Cognitive Psychology," esp. p12; J. Kagan, *What Is Emotion? History, Measures, Meanings* (New Haven, CT, 2007), pp20–21. Kagan declares "a skeptical stance toward the existence of a small set of basic emotions", p27.

9 W. Reddy, *Navigation of Feeling*, p34. A commonly cited example is M. Rosaldo's work on the Ilongot people of the Philippines. Rosaldo found that the most salient and positive emotion for the Ilongot was *liget*, a state apparently encompassing a range of elements, including, but not limited to, the European categories of anger, energy, envy, heat and joy (see W. Reddy, *Navigation of Feeling*, pp36–37).

10 E.-M. Engelen et al, "Emotions as Bio-cultural Processes", pp26–28, quote from p27.

11 J. Kagan, *What Is Emotion?*, pp29–31.

12 Note, however, that these are not identical with the "basic" emotions as usually posited (fear, anger, happiness, sadness/grief, disgust, surprise).

13 M. Holodynski, "Milestones and Mechanisms of Emotional Development", in B. Rottger-Rossler and H. J. Markowitsch (eds) *Emotions as Bio-Cultural Processes*, pp139–163; L. A. Sroufe, *Emotional Development: the Organization of Emotional Life in the Early Years* (Cambridge, UK, 1996).

14 M. Holodynski, "Milestones and Mechanisms", esp. pp149–154.

15 S. D. Calkins and A. Hill, "Caregiver Influences on Emerging Emotion Regulation; Biological and Environmental Transactions in Early, Development", in J. J. Gross (ed) *Handbook of Emotion Regulation* (New York, 2007), p230, but see ch. 11 as a whole.

16 D. Sander and K. R. Scherer (eds) *The Oxford Companion to Emotion and the Affective Sciences* (Oxford, 2009), pp92–94, entries "componential theories" and "component process model", both written by Scherer; quote from p92. See also K. R. Scherer, "Emotion as a Process: Function, Origin, and Regulation", *Social Science Information*, vol 21 (1982): pp555–570; K. R. Scherer, "What Are Emotions? And How Can They Be Measured?", *Social Science Information*, vol 44 (2005), pp693–727; and K. R. Scherer, "Emotions Are Emergent Processes: They Require a Dynamic Computational Architecture", *Philosophical Transactions of the Royal Society*, vol 364 (2009): pp3459–3474.

17 D. Sander and K. R. Scherer (eds) *Oxford Companion to Emotion*, pp92–93.

18 Gerrod Parrott particularly praises its potential to facilitate interdisciplinary collaboration in the set of responses to Scherer's work by a group of psychologists from very varying traditions, published as "Klaus Scherer's Article on 'What Are Emotions?': Comments", *Social Science Information*, vol 46, no. 3 (2007): pp381–443, 419–423, esp. p420.

19 G. Parrott, in "Klaus Scherer's Article on 'What Are Emotions?'," p423.

20 S. Knuuttila, *Emotions in Ancient and Medieval Philosophy* (Oxford, UK, 2004), ch. 3, section 3.1.

21 Ibid, ch. 3, section 3.5.

22 L. Roper, *Oedipus and the Devil: Witchcraft, Sexuality and Religion in Early Modern Europe*, (London, 1994), p3.

23 Ibid, pp21–23.

24 See, for example, P. Maddern and S. Tarbin, "Life Cycle", in S. Cavallo and S. Evangelisti (eds) *A Cultural History of Childhood and Family in the Early Modern Age* (Oxford, UK, 2010), pp113–133, esp. pp120–130.

25 M. Seymour (ed) *On the Properties of Things*, pp298 and 299: "tender, delicate, flabby/full of moisture, soft-fleshed" (note that "vnsad" can also mean "changeable" or "inconstant"); "because of tenderness, the limbs of the child may easily and soon bow and bend and take diverse shapes".

26 M. Seymour (ed) *On the Properties of Things*, p300: "are easily hurt and injured, and they may not well endure hard labour".

27 *The Beauchamp Pageant*, edited with introduction by Alexandra Sinclair (Donington, 2003), pp142–143; The National Archives (hereinafter TNA) C1/22/67 (probably dated circa 1455).

28 P. Maddern and S. Tarbin, *Life Cycle*, pp113–117, 122–123 and 125; cf. M. Seymour (ed) *On the Properties of Things*, p300; a child becomes a "puer" (boy) when he "knoweth good and euel" and is "iput and sette to lore vndir tutours".

29 M. Seymour (ed) *On the Properties of Things*, p300: "tender of flesh, lithe and pliant of body, capable and light of movement, witty to learn carols, and without business"; "Because of moving of hot humours that have the mastery in them they move lightly, and are unsteadfast and unstable".

30 Ibid, p159: "generally wrathful [or angry towards everybody], bold, aggressive, light, unstable, impetuous".

31 Ibid, p157: "listless, heavy, sluggish"; "fearful of heart".

32 Ibid, pp149–153, quotes from pp151 and 153.

33 Ibid, pp161–162: "all [those] that have this passion, are without cause often full of dread and sorrow ... . And so if people ask them what they fear and why they are sorrowful, they have no answer. Some think unreasonably that they shall die soon. Some dread enmity of someone. Some love and desire death"; "some fall into truly evil suspicions, without recovery, and therefore they hate and blame ... their friends, and sometimes smite them and slay them".

34 Ibid, pp298–299: "lead their lives without care and business and take account only of inclinations to mirth, and fear no peril more than beating with a staff".

35 See S. Knuuttila, *Emotions in Ancient and Medieval Philosophy*, ch. 3.

36 M. Seymour (ed), *On the Properties of Things*, p292: "men with cold blood are ... fools, just as men with hot blood are wise and alert"; "children with blood that does not heat up know hardly any good".

37 Ibid, p300: "When they are praised, or shamed, or blamed, they care little for it. Because of movement of heat of flesh and of humours, they are easily and soon angry, and soon pleased, and forgive soon."

38 R. Girvan (ed) *Ratis Raving and Other Early Scots Poems on Morals* (Edinburgh, 1937 (1939)), p32: "Just as a beast, the child knows no more/Than to laugh or cry for joy and sorrow"; "As best it havis feilinge"; "As an animal it has feeling".

39 Ibid, p33; "grows up as grass or tree,/And as a beast may feel and perceive".

40 Ibid, p33.

41 H. N. MacCracken (ed) *The Minor Poems of John Lydgate*, Part II (Oxford, 1934, repr. 1961), p743: "It is not the part of children to be vengeable/[They are] soon moved, and soon forgiving ... . Wrath of children is soon over/With an apple, the parties are made at one"; "In children's war [is] now mirth, now debate/In their quarrel is no great violence/Now playing, now weeping, seldom in one state/To their grievances give no great credence."

42 E. V. Hitchcock (ed) *The Folewer to the Donet by Reginald Pecock* (London, 1924; New York, 1971), pp93–101, quote from p93.

43 Ibid, p110.

44 M. Seymour (ed) *On the Properties of Things*, p300.

45 S. Powell (ed) *John Mirk's Festial, edited from British Library MS Cotton Claudius A. II* (Oxford, UK, 2009), p35.

46 Ibid, p35. The author goes on to draw the direct parallel with Adam and Eve in Paradise, pp35–36.

47 M. Seymour (ed) *On the Properties of Things*, p300.

48 R. T. Davis (ed) *Medieval English Lyrics: A Critical Anthology* (London, 1963), p210, no. 112.

49 G. R. Owst, *Literature and Pulpit in Medieval England* (Cambridge, UK, 1933), p34, n. 2.

50 Lydgate, "The Daunce of Death", English Poetry Database Online (my emphasis).

51 R. Whitford, *A Werke for Housholders or for Them Tht Haue the Gydynge or Gouernaunce of Any Company* (London, 1530), unpaginated.

52 From the York, N-town, Coventry, and Towneley cycles, with single plays surviving from Dublin and Brome. It is extremely likely that these survivals are the tip of a much larger iceberg: see R. T. Davies (ed) *The Corpus Christi Play of the English Middle Ages* (London, 1972).

53 R. Beadle (ed) *The York Plays: A Critical Edition of the York Corpus Christi Play as Recorded in British Library Additional MS 35290* (Oxford, 2009), pp55–65, quote from p57: "of age to judge rightly".

54 R. Beadle (ed) *The York Plays*, p60.

55 R. Beadle (ed) *The York Plays*.

56 See, for example, R. T. Davies (ed) *The Corpus Christi Play*, p379 (Brome play), p106 (N-town cycle), p399 (Chester cycle).

57 Ibid, p380.

58 See J. A. Burrow, *The Ages of Man: A Study in Medieval Writing and Thought*, (Oxford, 1988), ch 3, "Ideals of Transcendence", esp. pp96–97. The typical Old Testament figures of the *puer senex* were Samuel and Daniel; Christ speaking with the elders in the temple was also held to be a prime example.

59 R. T. Davies (ed) *The Corpus Christi Play*, p105.

60 Ibid, pp104, 106.

61 Ibid, p105.

62 Ibid, pp381–382.

63 Ibid, pp383–385.

64 Ibid, p386. Almost all of these themes are repeated in the other play cycles. See, for example, the Chester cycle play, pp403–404; the Dublin play, pp413–414. The Towneley cycle play, in particular, has Isaac repeatedly beg for mercy, declaring all the while his own innocence ("What have I done, Father, what have I said?" and insisting to his father "I love you ay"; pp424–425).

65 Ibid, pp403–404 (Chester), pp413–414 (Dublin), pp424–425 (Towneley).

66 Ibid, pp387–388.

67 Ibid, p389.

68 R. Whitford, *A Werke for Housholders*.

69 R. T. Davies (ed) *The Corpus Christi Play*, p389.

70 The number of children exceeds the number of inquisitions because in some cases (where the surviving heirs were daughters, or where gavelkind pertained) more than one child heir was recorded.

71 N. Orme, *Medieval Children* (New Haven and London, 2001), p113. Note that parish registers are not available in England before 1540.

72 *Calendar of Inquisitions Post Mortem, vol xxv 16–20 Henry VI (1437–1442)*, Claire Noble (ed) (London, 2009), nos. 48–49, 24–25.

73 TNA C1 42/97: "demanded of his father in this way, 'Father, shall I have another mother?' [The father replies] 'Yea, son, but thou shall have none that shall love thee so well as thine own mother did.' Whereupon the father turned aside and wept." My thanks to Dr. Hannes Kleineke, who alerted me to this reference.

74 TNA DL/41/406: "audivit sepe & sepius & nescit dicere quociens"; "dicente ac timore flente"; "verberibus gravibus"; "eam omnibus bonis denudaret atque eam mendicantem hostiati transire faceret".

75 Borthwick Institute, Case Papers (hereinafter Borthwick CP), F. 96. Though other witnesses swore that she had consented willingly to the match: "coacta & compulsa per vim

& metu William Richerdson aui sui"; "amare plorando iurauit pro fidem suam quod nunquam fuit in voluntate sua ad habend. dictum Johannem in maritum suum".

76 Canterbury Cathedral Archives, X.1.1 Consistory Court Depositions 1410–1421, ff. 28d–30d.

77 Durham Cathedral Archives and Library Court Book of Prior's Official (Care of University Library) DCD off.bk f. 10r: "an erat coacta"; "ministrabat eis amicabiliter esculenta & poculenta ad tunc fuit morem patrie".

78 TNA C1/19/152.

PART III
Practices

9

CHILDHOOD AND EMOTION IN A PRINTING HOUSE (1497–1508)

Valentina Sebastiani

Introduction

In a 1943 review of the first volume of the correspondence of the Amerbach family, printers and lawyers in Basel during the Early Modern Period,[1] Lucien Febvre asked rhetorically:

> Who has never heard of the great dynasty of the Amerbachs of Basel? Who, with a learned interest in the intellectual and religious history of the 16th century, has never consulted the Amerbach archive in Basel, one of those treasures so often exploited but nevertheless inexhaustible?

The comment by the future father of the history of book culture to the 493 letters, transcribed and commented on by Alfred Hartmann, brought to light not just the enormous value of the Amerbach correspondence for investigating the history of book culture and its intellectual and material practices. Hartman did not underline the enormous value of the Amerbach correspondence for the history of book culture, but Febvre chose to stress the importance of the letters in order to give "a vivid picture of life inside schools and the University of Paris" at the time when Bruno and Basilius, Johannes Amerbach's eldest sons, were staying in the French capital as students. He focused his attention on the personality of Johannes Amerbach, defining him as a "hard worker", a "prudent" man and an "indefatigable maker of types" who was also capable of showing affectionate care and attention towards his sons, who he dearly wished would become "men of real culture, worthy of him and of his ideals".[2]

Significantly,[3] the brief critical evaluation by Febvre has probably been remembered only among specialists in the cultural and religious history of the sixteenth century. The main aim of this chapter is, therefore, to bring to the attention of the historians of childhood and emotions the incomparable documentation made available by this collection of letters. On the basis of some of the letters exchanged between 1497 and 1508 by Johannes Amerbach (circa 1440–1513), his wife Barbara Ortenberg (died 1513) and their children, Bruno (1484–1519), Basilius (1488–1535) and Margarete (1490–1541),[4] I will attempt to explore the relationships among childhood, emotion and printing in order to test the validity of the concept of emotional community[5] as it pertains to the social and cultural milieu of a printer.

This chapter argues that Johannes Amerbach's printing activity drew inspiration from a cultural and spiritual project aimed at the renewal of consciences and of knowledge in line with the principles of the new humanistic culture spreading north of the Alps at that time. Identifying the values and ideals that inspired the work carried out in his printing shop offers not just a new angle for the evaluation of Amerbach's book production. It also situates Amerbach in this undertaking and provides details about the emotional universe of this *humaniste imprimeur*. The relationship with his children, the type of education given to them and the dynamics of the bonds that developed within the family constitute a privileged field of investigation. This chapter aims to evaluate the ways in which Amerbach tried to pass to his children the ideals that shaped his professional life and to examine to what extent he shared values and emotions with his co-workers and associates.

The system of values of a printer in humanist Basel

Johann Amerbach contributed significantly to the production and dissemination of humanistic ideals throughout Europe.[6] He developed a publishing programme that strictly supported the intellectual and spiritual needs of humanists north of the Alps. By means of the books that he printed over 30 years, Amerbach strongly encouraged the study of *humanae litterae*, which had turned the city into a showcase of the new cultural and religious movement since the Council of Basel (1431–1449).[7] Many factors contributed to the success of Amerbach's business. He possessed sufficient capital to invest in the necessary equipment for the printing business. His business acumen did the rest. In fact, if one considers the ever-widening spread of his books, from the trading centre of Basel to the markets and fairs of Frankfurt and Leipzig, as far as Lyon, London and Paris, it is easy to see the success of his longstanding partnership with the great Nuremberg publisher and bookseller Anton Koberger (circa 1440–1513).

The association with Koberger gave Amerbach reasonable assurance of selling the books printed in his workshop. Consequently, he could use most of his revenue to keep the printing equipment in good working order and to pay the highly specialized workforce.

Amerbach's clear ability was not just limited to the commercial sector. The analysis can home in on the 100 or so titles that came off the presses of the *Haus zum Kaiserstuhl* in Kleinbasel between 1478 and 1513. In this way, the network of scholars revolving around the workshop and contributing to the publishing activity, whether as translators, proof-readers or editorial consultants, can be clearly seen. There were theologians such as Johann Heynlin (circa 1430–1496) and Wolfgang Capito (1478–1541);

law scholars such as Sebastian Brant (1457–1521); experts on Hebrew and Greek, such as Johann Reuchlin (1455–1522), Conrad Leontorius (1460–1511) and Johann Cono (circa 1463–1513); and men of letters and humanists, such as Jacob Wimpfeling (1450–1528) and Beatus Rhenanus (1485–1547). All of them contributed to the selection and publication of printing works, together with Amerbach, by means of their involvement in the various stages of the production.

Books are not just merchandise, as stated by Lucien Febvre and Henri-Jean Martin;[8] nor were early printers just shrewd entrepreneurs out for a profit. Besides being a profitable economic activity, printing reflected cultural and social practices; it captured knowledge and values that were handed down in new forms. Looking at the volumes printed by Amerbach and, in particular, at the dedications, prefaces and introductions, his cultural aims and personal ideals become clear.

The intellectual and practical work of scholars north of the Alps aimed at editing, collating, copying or printing "the books necessary and useful to the Christian faith". In fact, "books, like well-stocked cases, contain the splendid weapons of the Holy Scriptures through which the faith in God [...] is protected and defended, but also nurtured and increased and strengthened and preserved".[9] Amerbach's programme is a clear and well-structured attempt to synthesize, intellectually and materially in print, the cultural and spiritual aspirations of northern Christian Humanism for the purpose of the renewal and the advancement of knowledge and faith. To ally printing and humanism, there had to be not only good technical skills, business acumen and collaboration with a wide range of scholars, but also moral qualities which Amerbach shared with the members of his team and his associates. "God who looks into our hearts and inmost nature", wrote Amerbach, "knows that in my work I seek not so much on my own gain as his divine honor."[10] The correspondence testifies to the consideration and the respect bestowed on him by the numerous correspondents who, on many occasions, praised the integrity, honesty, probity and virtue of the printer from Basel. It is possible, however, to investigate the values, principles and ideals followed by Amerbach more deeply and to reach the "heart" and the "inmost nature" of his system of values. The letters not only permit insight into his business doings, but also reveal his private life. They expose his relationship with his children, the education he gave them and the interpersonal dynamics that developed within his family.

The children's education

On 6 June 1501, Johann Amerbach wrote to his two older children, Bruno and Basilius, aged 17 and 13, respectively, newly arrived at the University of Paris. His tone, firm but affectionate, reveals all his apprehension:

> Dearest children [...] please keep me informed [...] about your situation, your health, if you've been admitted to a school, if you like the French ways and if you have good and knowledgeable teachers [...] and if you have a guardian. I want to know all about your undertakings. [...] My beloved

children, you must focus on your studies and remember that you were sent to Paris to fulfill a serious task, therefore do not waste the money that has been such an effort for me to earn.

(AK, 1: 127)

The short passage highlights Amerbach's worries for his children, pursuing their studies far from home, and sheds a first light on the contents of the communication between him and his sons in the period between 1497 and 1508. The passage also reveals significant issues on which to focus the analysis of the unfolding relationship between parents and children living so far apart.

Physical and material well-being

The typically formal style of Amerbach's correspondence is mitigated in the letters to his children. This is evident right from the first lines of some of the letters. The introductory stereotypical phrases about health sometimes give way to expressions of feelings inspired by the love that binds parents and children. Delay in the delivery of a letter or the lack of an answer to one generated, for example, anxiety in those who awaited news. A very worried Amerbach wrote to Basilius in 1505: "Nibling [the servant] brought me [no letter] from you, and your brother made no mention of you in his letter"; and he continued: "I was very surprised, and it occurred to me that something terrible had happened to you", adding, "that you were no more among the living and that your brother and Nibling wanted to keep it from me" (AK, 1: 266). Sometime later, because of the silence of his father, the same doubt was testified by Bruno who wrote: "I am worried that something may have happened to you," and begged: "Please relieve me of this worry, if you love me" (AK, 1: 344).

Those working at the Basel printing shop also worried about the good health of Amerbach's sons with whom, sometimes, they developed an affectionate relationship, as in the case of Conrad Leontorius. When Basilius fell seriously ill, Leontorius intervened decisively and insisted on a surgical operation, against the wishes of his father. After visiting the Amerbachs in Basel, during the summer of 1508, Leontorius broached the question in a letter to Amerbach: "Your fine and splendid son Basilius, who is ill and has suffered a great deal, has remained in my mind." He suggested to his printer friend: "The sooner you take care of having your son operated on, the better you will do and will return him quickly to his interrupted studies", and he assured him at the end: "This operation will bring you and his mother happiness and your son health in body and spirit" (AK, 1: 387).

The welfare of the sons would be assured not only by providing appropriate medical care, but also by supplying material means adequate to their needs. The boys asked spontaneously and directly for what they wished or needed, whether books, clothing or money, even when they were studying in the nearby Schlettstadt. In January 1499, Bruno reassured his parents: "We need nothing at this time." But then he added: "We ask that you send us as a New Year's present the *Varia Carmina* by Sebastian Brant" (AK, 1: 89). A year after, Bruno communicated briefly to his parents: "Basilius [...] and I are well and without money" and he continued by asking with some impatience: "Send us the *Pharsalia* by Lucan, boots and other things I wrote to you about as soon as possible" (AK, 1: 107). The firm tone of the requests did not change when Amerbach's sons were studying in Paris. In 1502, Bruno wrote: "There is a certain book available in Basel called *Parvulus logyce* [...] by Master Bartholomeus de Usingen of Erfurt. We urgently request that you get it to us as soon as possible" (AK, 1: 158). In October 1504, he hastily recommended to his father: "If you have a trustworthy carrier, send us some money. We need a lot for the principal and for the steps to the baccalaureate" (AK, 1: 238).

The parents did their best to satisfy all the sons' requests: "May God [...] grant you the best in soul and body!" (AK, 1: 227). This wish, sent by their mother in June 1504, echoed the solid reassurances already given by their father in a letter dated June 1501: "I will spend everything I have for you", but, he adds, only if "[you] apply yourselves completely to your work" (AK, 1: 128).

The cost of education

To provide a good education for his sons represented for Amerbach not only the "fullfill[ment] [of] my every wish", but also a matter of pride. He could not permit his fame as a *humaniste imprimeur*, which he had built up with great effort through his publications over the years, to be diminished by his sons' inadequate academic achievement. He reminded them of this in an ironic wish that sounds like a warning at the same time: "It can't be said that I sent young asses to Paris and got full-grown asses back" (AK, 1: 128). In full agreement with her husband, Barbara Ortenberg also recognized the importance of academic success as well as the necessity of proper behaviour for her sons in order to secure a position of respect in the future. Thus she urged: "I beg you [...] to use your time well and study and do the best you can and behave properly so that no one can say 'they are bad boys who don't obey their father and will always be nobodies'" (AK, 1: 227).

Quite apart from declarations of principle, Amerbach realized how much he had underestimated the cost of supporting his sons. Shortly after their arrival in Paris, he was forced to scale down the range of possibilities he could offer them. He made them aware of the realities: "I am not so wealthy that I can afford to keep a private tutor for you", and, hoping better to control the expenses, he added in a peremptory tone: "I want each of you to keep a record and write down what you spend for every little thing, even for pens, and make an account" (AK, 1: 130). In an attempt to recall them to a sense of responsibility, even their mother intervened, urging: "Do your best and think of the labor your father does early and late for your sake" (AK, 1: 152). Initially, the parents' admonitions seem to have had positive effects. Amerbach had entrusted Johann Heidelberg, an agent in Paris for Anton Koberger, with the management of his sons' finances. In a report dated June 1503, Heidelberg wrote in a reassuring tone: "Each one [Bruno and Basilius] writes [the money they spend] down in my account book and in his own too", assuring them: "This year it will not amount to as much as it did in the past [...] everything is going well", although "It is very expensive here" (AK, 1: 198). Amerbach, mollified by these reassurances, promised again with great enthusiasm: "I will very happily provide those things that you buy out of necessity", but, he stressed, "not for frivolity" (AK, 1: 225).

Obvious differences among parents and sons in their perceptions of necessity and of frivolity caused quite a few misunderstandings. Signs of this appear in June 1504, when Barbara makes her sons aware that "your father has scolded me and says that he has had great expenses on account of you, and that you have squandered more than your friends, [therefore] I [...] ask you to be careful with your money" (AK, 1: 226). Amerbach, via the same courier, sends a letter in which, bitterly surprised, he summarizes the amount of their expenses: "You and your brother have spent more than 300 florins for these three years, and each of you had at least 50 florins per annum [therefore] I wonder how or what you spent it [on]." The warnings to "be more frugal than you have been up to now" or the prohibition to "give anyone a single penny or pay a penny for anyone in an inn or tavern" came to nothing as the reminder that "it is not for you to clothe your servant or master or to buy decorations for your room" (AK, 1: 225).

Unfortunately, after one year, not only had the expenses not been reduced, but Amerbach came to hear all about the less than uplifting behaviour of his sons. Barbara underlined her husband's feelings: "Your father is indignant. He thinks this has gone too far" (AK, 1: 281). Amerbach's disapproval was total and his words final:

> You live wildly, without concern for how your parents earn the money they send you. Money doesn't grow on trees [...]. When I was in Paris I hardly spent five or six florins at most per year beyond the fee, and I lived decently. [...] I did not drink to all hours; I refrained from excessive drinking and lived soberly. [Therefore] if some in your group are drinkers, don't follow them by drinking with them [or] if others want to use their money foolishly, turn from them and spend yours wisely.

Amerbach concluded with a threat: "But truly, if you do not live more frugally than you have lived up to now, I will recall you to your paternal home, whether you are baccalaureates or masters, [...] I will settle you into manual crafts where you will educate yourselves by the labor of your own hands. Therefore take heed and eat and drink to live and do not live to eat and drink" (AK, 1: 246).

Faced with their father's harsh words, after a long, guilty silence, Bruno and Basilius asked forgiveness, made excuses and repented, seeking to regain the trust of their father. Basilius wrote in despair: "I [...] believe that your love for me, natural and fixed deep within the inmost chambers of your heart, has been torn out and destroyed" (AK, 1: 258). Bruno's response was more articulate, composed and astute:

> When I took up this task of writing to you, dearest father, I felt no less considerable emotional pain than on that most bitter and sorrowful day when I understood how angry and exasperated you are toward me. As I returned to this matter, seeking mentally and emotionally some subject for writing to you

[…], I began to reflect on the many letters you have sent to me. While I was reading them very carefully, your most recent letter arrived. I was struck with fresh regret and, moved to tears, I deplored my state like one bereft. For a son who has lost his father's regard is considered an orphan by everyone. Both the memory of times gone by, when you always surrounded me with love I could not easily describe in this letter, and the very unsettled state of affairs at this moment brought me sadness. For when I consider your paternal wrath, I am so troubled and so pained that neither hand nor foot perform their usual function. This, then, I ask (if there is any place for prayers): change your mind and put on a gentler spirit toward your penitent son (AK, 1: 256).

Amerbach's cold and detached tone persisted in subsequent letters, revealing all his bitter disappointment. In May 1505 he wrote: "What use is it to confess mistakes now that the ship has been sunk?" As though he were talking to himself, he added, "You slighted yourselves. I must be patient" (AK, 1: 265). The trust he had placed in his sons had been temporarily broken, up to the point that, even when they fell sick, he wrote:

You are both pitiful and to be pitied because you are sick. I might conclude […] that it happened to you because of your disorderly lives, […] [w]hen you have no money you live wretchedly, and when you have or can get money, you eat and drink too much and some of you run around taverns and drink to a point of drunkenness.

After having expressed all his disappointment, he ended with resignation: "I am going to disregard this for the time being", and he sends to Paris "bandages", "salve", "a root" and detailed instructions for their treatment (AK, 1: 283).

Dynamics of control

Due to his sons' prolonged absence from home, Johann Amerbach resorted to various ways of supervising Bruno and Basilius, their education and their behaviour. As an esteemed and cultured businessman of his time, he had no difficulty in utilizing the network of partners and associates of his printing works to support his sons' stay in Paris and to narrow, at least in the perception of parents and children, the distance between Paris and Basel. He turned first to Anton Koberger, thanks to the position he held both in international book trade and in the affairs of the Basel print shop, who answered him promptly in 1501: "I commended your sons to my agent and asked him to treat them as if they were my own",[11] showing how the trust and faith of a business partnership could extend to the personal sphere. Johann Heidelberger, Koberger's agent in Paris, accepted the task and, in turn, mobilized "other of my good friends" (AK, 1: 134) to monitor the boys and to keep Amerbach informed of their doings. Over the years, Bruno and Basilius received many visits from their father's colleagues: Johann Petri and Johann Froben, Basel printers and Amerbach partners, some of Amerbach's employees, Koberger's grandson Hans, other friends of the family, as well as the parents of other students from Basel. The education of Amerbach's sons in Paris became a topic of interest even among the monks of the Charterhouse of Freiburg im Bresgau (AK, 1: 157).

Because of their connection to Amerbach, everyone in this vast array of *literati* and businessmen sought to assist his sons by bringing money or paying the outstanding bills by delivering books and gifts, relaying news and greetings from the members of the family, making suggestions and giving advice. The most important function carried out by all this coming and going was, however, the carrying of letters, thus ensuring direct communication between parents and children.

If, on the one hand, Amerbach gave advice and reassurance, on the other, he sent instructions and orders, demanded obedience and, where appropriate, threatened punishment. He asked for detailed reports; he sent precise instructions; and he intervened in their course of study: "After you have mastered logic I suggest you to give your attention unwaveringly to the school of philosophy most widely studied" (AK, 1: 128). He expected to be informed promptly about their studies: "I also want you to inform me which professor's course you are registered in and where you are in the course. Do you hear other lectures in addition to those of your courses?" (AK, 1: 214).

Sometimes, his comments seem more pedantic, as, for example, when he approached the subject of learning Latin: "Be careful in speaking and in writing to speak properly and distinguish the tenses carefully so that when you want to speak in the past you don't speak in the future or the present and vice versa" (AK, 1: 130). Faced with letters full of mistakes, he stated: "I am not criticizing you for simple style. I do not care about that, but I do care about grammatical agreement" (AK, 1: 191). Bruno sought to justify himself: "The errors you were criticizing and scolding me for occurred through neglect not ignorance, and (if I am not mistaken) I should not be blamed for this but deserve your forbearance" (AK, 1: 197). Fully aware of the limited ability of his sons, on receiving a letter written in a "very elegant" style Amerbach was surprised and suspicious: "I doubt that it was original with you. […] I suspect that someone else composed it and you worked it out afterward with your own handwriting", insisting that "I want and expect you to write out of your own head" (AK, 1: 225). Leontorius also urged the boys to study and urged Amerbach: "Write your sons not to continue to disfigure their handwriting with barely civilized gothic script, but to apply a modest measure of attention to forming their Latin letters in Roman style, so that they will develop their hands as well as their minds" (AK, 1: 265). To stop his sons' habit of writing collective letters, Amerbach warned Bruno: "I do not want Basilius to write for you or you for him anymore" and ordered: "Each of you should write me on his own […] to allow me to see how each of you is progressing" (AK, 1: 171). By means of separate letters, Amerbach could grasp the weak points of each son and reply, in turn, with different instructions. For example, he urged Bruno to "restrain and discipline yourself to speak slowly and with moderation [because] you rush the words and want to say everything in one breath" (AK, 1: 191). Basilius, too, gave cause for concern, but due to weakness of character rather than of intellect. In a heartfelt letter, Barbara echoed her husband's worries, outlining the weakness of her son: "I have […] heard about your daydreaming, Basilius, my dear son […] you should stop it and study hard […]. I beg you to do so" (AK, 1: 227). The news about Basilius's laziness and carelessness reached his father, who immediately asked Bruno for explanations and, before receiving an answer, urged him to look after his younger brother: "Scold him harshly sometimes, sometimes persuade him with gentle words, and make an effort to turn him away from this stubbornness" (AK, 1: 191). Amerbach did not underestimate the problem and, a year later, in a letter to Basilius, returned to the subject: "You write […] that all your unhappiness has disappeared and all your laziness and daydreams or fantasies are gone." He then continued: "I congratulate you on putting every impediment to your study behind you, and I urge you now to give your complete attention to study and no longer allow daydreams to distract you" (AK, 1: 226).

Amerbach's attempts at exercising a careful control over his sons clashed frequently with the freedom that Bruno and Basilius claimed for themselves. Contravening the precise instructions sent by their father and by Heidelberg, the two boys decided on their own where and with whom they stayed, which master they engaged and which courses they followed. Amerbach, although angered, did not intervene at first: "I do not care whether you two are alone or in a college or with the others [students from Basel], only that you study hard" (AK, 1: 128). These words were echoed in Barbara's letter, in which, on the one hand, she reproached them because "[y]ou have defied him [your father]", and so "[h]e is disturbed that you don't obey his command"; but, on the other hand, showed a certain understanding for them: "If it is your wish to stay with the same [master], it is all right with me […] just as long as you learn well" (AK, 1: 137).

In time, however, the boys' behaviour left much to be desired and, in March 1504, they had to admit that the master they had chosen "is slacker and more negligent in his attention and effort toward us than he had been at the beginning". Bruno reported, for example, that "he has not finished Cicero's *Rhetoric*, which, if I recall correctly, he began almost three years ago [and] he did not just fail to complete his instruction in historical authors as he promised, he did not even begin" (AK, 1: 217). Faced with the capitulation of the boys, but above all aware of the wretched state of their education, Amerbach transferred them to another school, placing them under the guidance of another master, but did not hide his disappointment: "I read and reread your letters and feel saddened when I comprehend your disobedience […]; you did not obey to my instructions […]; even though I threatened to disinherit you […], you did not heed my command" (AK, 1: 265).

Family ties

The Amerbach letters are exceptional in that they give us the words of female family members, not only of the wife, Barbara Ortenberg, but also of the daughter, Margarete. In fact, among the correspondence are ten short letters written in German between 1499 and 1505 in the hand of Margarete Amerbach. It was quite common for printers' daughters to have a certain degree of literacy from an early age and, since they were able to read and write, for them to be employed in the family business.[12] It does not appear, however, that Margarete contributed directly to the work at the printer's, in spite of her keen involvement in family matters.

The first of her surviving letters, written in December 1498, probably from the Cistercian convent at Engeltal not far from Basel, is addressed to her mother. Margarete turned very trustingly to Barbara Ortenberg to ask for something, writing: "I dare not ask my father" because, quite simply, "I am afraid he will be very busy" (AK, 1: 87). This confirms the habit, noted for all the Amerbach children, of asking freely for whatever they wanted. Whereas books and money were sent to Bruno and Basilius, Margarete's requests involved accessories or clothing. Specifically, the girl asked her mother to send her "a pair of winter shoes and socks as well" and a new "collar" since "the blue one is all tattered". She also begged her to send a "thick handkerchief to wear to church" and, especially, "the New Year's gift". The repetition of such phrases as "my beloved mother", "my dear" or "dearest mother" at the beginning of each short sentence gives a tender, loving tone to the letter. The next letter, written in March 1499, contains a further request, this time for a "neckpiece" and, as a token of thanks for what had already been received, she sent "a nice prayer to God to pray this holy Lent" since "I have nothing else to send you". Just like her older brothers and, surprisingly, using the same language, Margarete expressed her concern that her father had failed to visit her, writing: "I waited a long time for my father, and was looking forward to his visit, but he didn't come and I wonder if he is ill or not." She asked her mother: "Let me know what kept him from coming" (AK, 1: 97). Finally, in the last two letters, Margarete addressed her father and mother respectively as "meister Hans trucker" and "frau Barbara truckerin". She signed herself "Margred trucker", meaning "printer" and not Amerbach, her family surname.

To avert the calamity caused by the earlier loss of a child, Amerbach and his wife proved themselves to be prudent and farsighted parents. During the frequent epidemics that struck Basel in 1502, they sent the youngest children away from the city and arranged for them to stay in a safer place. For a few months, Margarete found herself far from home. In spite of the fact that she was with her younger brother, Bonifacius, this time she was very homesick for her parents, friends and life in Basel. This may have had to do with the realization that the plague was so dangerous. "I hear that many people are dying", she began in a letter to her mother, and went on to write: "I wish that my father and you were here." Significantly, this time she asked merely to be sent "the large rosary and the pearl rosary" (AK, 1: 168), devotional objects that evidently accompanied her prayers in those sorrowful times. In a letter sent not long afterwards, she was no longer able to hold back her distress. "[You] know that I have a great longing for all of you […] that we would love to be home again if it were possible." In the meantime, she hoped that the situation "will soon get better"; but she begged her mother "with all due respect to come and see us soon" because, she said under obvious stress, "I never expected that you would be away from us for such a long time." Margarete reported that Bonifacius, too, was homesick: "He is wretched that you are away from him so long" and added: "He asks for you every day" (AK, 1: 169). Other letters from Margarete to her mother followed rapidly, one after the other (AK, 1: 171, 180, 181). The children sent "[a] hundred thousand greetings" to their father, friends and acquaintances and they asked for "wafers", "shoes", "a pair of slippers" and "boots". Perhaps to hasten their return home, Margarete informed her parents on the changeable state of their health: "I want you to know that I have been ill with a carbuncle that has hit me hard with chills and fever" (AK, 1: 171). She also hinted at a barber's apprentice who died of the plague in the convent where they are (AK, 1: 180).

A few years later, in 1504, Margarete reappears in the correspondence to share in her parents' concern and disappointment over her older brothers' behaviour in Paris. Partly repeating her parents' words, she wrote directly to them just when the parents' criticism was at its strongest, saying: "I beg you to study hard and soon come home because I have been longing to see you for a long time." The letter left room for the 14-year-old Margarete's own personality, however. In it, she asked, "My dear brothers, send us something French, because we have in Basel nothing but German things – or send whatever you wish" (AK, 1: 228).

The similarities between Margarete and her older brothers do not revolve only around the use of a common language in their family correspondence. Like Bruno and Basilius, Margarete showed great independence in her ability to make decisions. Her brothers decided to do what they wanted regarding their course of study in Paris, despite their father's instructions to the contrary, and Margarete showed similar initiative that went against the will of her parents. She decided, on her own, to get married before she reached the age of 16 in February 1506. Her parents did not approve of her chosen spouse, Jakob Rechberger (died 1542), a citizen and spice merchant of Basel. Margarete's choice was dictated by genuine love that bound her to the young man. This becomes clear in a letter that Jakob sent to his beloved a short time before their wedding. He began: "My most beloved darling, how great is my distress and sorrow that I cannot come to you to console you", and went on to say: "Don't let it get you down or let what happens trouble you now because of me." He tried to comfort her by promising: "I will put the rest of my life at your disposal and will in good faith never forget you." Jakob's words indicate that the Amerbachs "want to put you in a convent" and, full of despair at the thought of this, he implored her "not to give in to them, but keep the promise you have made to me". In the same way, he assured her that he "will also without question keep the promise I made to you". The letter allowed Rechberger scope to deny categorically that he was involved with another woman and he urged Margarete to leave the family home and go "to the bowmaker's house" until he found better accommodation (AK, 1: 297).

In spite of the intervention of Jakob Wimpfeling, a friend and associate of Amerbach, on behalf of the two young people, not only did Margarete's father not consent to the marriage, but he disinherited his daughter when it was celebrated. Amerbach's action aroused the indignation of Conrad Leontorius, who criticized his friend and colleague (AK, 1: 300), causing considerable emotional upset within the family. Bruno, in a heartfelt letter, tried to convince his father to retract his words. Although he did not deny the seriousness of his sister's slight on their father's authority and shared the "upset" and "pain" it caused, he asked his father: "That you temper and control your sorrow or shake it off altogether and be a comfort to my unhappy mother and be merciful to my sister" (AK, 1: 299). The words of Bruno, as well as those of Leontorius, achieved the desired effect, and Amerbach, driven by the need to restore peace and harmony within the family, forgave his daughter's behaviour and admitted her back into the family, granting her 500 florins as a dowry (AK, 1: 491a).

The emotional community of a printer

Although there is more to be said about these sources, this brief examination of the relationships in the Amerbach family allows some reflections on childhood and emotion.

First of all, the quality of the childhood of Amerbach's children must be considered. Undoubtedly, Bruno, Basilius and Margarete were fortunate. The great care and attention shown to them by their parents preserved them from those situations of violence, abuse and exploitation that were the common fate of many of their peers.[13] The prosperity of their father also guaranteed them good living conditions, and the sons had access to prestigious educational opportunities. The letters show, however, that the separation of Bruno and Basilius from the family created personal problems and complicated the achievement of complete personal self-sufficiency. There was a continuing need for guidance. Both sons and parents made mistakes in judgement about the students' levels of self-determination and maturity. If Johann Amerbach and Barbara Ortenberg allowed Bruno and Basilius too much freedom regarding practical and intellectual decisions during their stay in Paris, they also exercised forms of control that failed to curb the exuberance and initiative of the boys. There is no doubt, however, that the parents intended their disciplinary methods to facilitate the gradual strengthening of independent judgement in the boys, preparing them to face the challenges of everyday life. Significantly, Johann Amerbach's habit of pushing the boys to think and act independently had real implications for the business activity that he wanted them to undertake: the management of the publishing house. This can be gathered from the kind of admonitions sent by Amerbach on the study methods the sons should follow in order to acquire not only a sound knowledge of Latin grammar, but also the ability to produce original texts for use as comment or introduction to the printed works.

Whether it is the disappointment of the parents over the behaviour of the children or the report of the latter on the difficulties encountered, or, simply, mutual updates on each person's state of health, what is most striking about the epistolary relationship amongst the Amerbachs is the emotional tone of the communication that takes place. If the above evidence is examined in the light of Barbara Rosenwein's discussion of emotion words,[14] it is easy to see the broad array of emotions[15] reflected in the exchange of letters among the Amerbachs. First of all, the love and affection (*bene velle*)[16] binding parents and children are expressed in the letters by means of the repetition of "dear", "most dear", "beloved" and "most beloved". These are followed by the "pleasure" of Amerbach at being able to place his own resources at the disposal of his children for their studies; the "fright" and "terror" resulting from the occasional interruption of communication between Paris and Basel, which make them all fear the worst; the "lament" of the father about the excessive spending of the boys, which often bursts into "anger" and "indignation" to the point of "heatedness" when he threatens to make them manual workers in the printing works; the "sadness" felt by the father at their continued disobedience; the sorrowful "hope" expressed by the mother that her children would follow their father's instructions; the "wretchedness" or the "pitiful" state of Bruno and Basilius when they make themselves ill through their excesses; the "shyness" that makes Bruno speak too fast; the "sloth" and "laziness" of Basilius in his attitude towards study; the "happiness" that Leontorius wishes the parents for the return to health of Basilius; the "desire" on the part of Margarete that Bruno and Basilius come back home soon; the "sorrow", "pain" and "distress" that Margarete herself causes to the other members of the family by her ("courageous and daring") decision to get married without permission. The analysis of the emotion words to be found in the Amerbach correspondence could go on; but what is interesting here is that the emotions expressed in these letters do not change according to who is writing, male or female, parent or child, adult or young. If anything, the use of different ways of expressing the same emotions can be seen.

Finally, the habit of communicating emotions was a practice shared not only among the members of the family, but also among those who were involved in the family's affairs. Examples of this are the heartfelt intervention of Conrad Leontorius about Basilius's illness or his dismay at the over-reaction of Amerbach to his daughter's elopement and, in the same way, the zeal of Anton Koberger and Johann Heidelberg in taking care of Bruno and Basilius in Paris. The people who were connected to the Basel printing shop showed they had a wealth of emotion with which to express feelings, so much so that it is safe to talk about an emotional community[17] around the Amerbach family.

Johann Amerbach's interest in the renewal of faith and knowledge through his publishing programme attracted the collaboration of a *sodalitas* of clever and refined connoisseurs of the book that was animated by a cultural and spiritual yearning for the values and principles of the humanistic tradition as a safeguard against the degeneration of faith and knowledge. The history of emotions has done much over the last decade to try to clarify emotions, understood as the result of values and human evaluations.[18] This analysis of the values of a printer as seen from the emotional relationships that developed among the various members of the Amerbach family is intended to stimulate further studies on the emotional communities of modern European printers.

Notes

1 *Die Amerbachkorrespondenz*, vol I. *Die Briefe aus der Zeit Johann Amerbachs, 1481–1513*, A. Hartmann (ed) (Basel, 1942) (hereinafter, AK). The first volume of the Amerbach correspondence has been broadly summarized, and the letters translated and commented on by Barbara C. Halporn. See B. C. Halporn, *The Correspondence of Johann Amerbach: Early*

Printing in its Social Context, (Ann Arbor, MI, 2000). Her translation is used here in the quotations.

2 L. Febvre, "À Bâle eat à Paris avec les Amerbach", *Revue Historique*, vol 67 (1943): pp211–216. See also L. Febvre, *L'apprentissage parisien des Amerbach*, in idem, *Au coeur religieux du XVIe siècle* (Paris, 1957), pp185–192.

3 The article by Febvre, which marks the start of his interest in the historical reconstruction of how emotional life was expressed, was written about a year earlier. See L. Febvre, "La sensibilité et l'histoire. Comment reconstituer la vie affective d'autrefois?", *Annales d'histoire sociale*, vol 3 (1941): pp5–20.

4 The childhood of Bonifacius, the youngest of Amerbach's sons, is not mentioned in this chapter except by reference to Margarete's correspondence. The letters exchanged by Bonifacius and his parents during the time he was away for his studies refer mostly to a time subsequent to the period considered here.

5 B. H. Rosenwein, "Worrying about Emotions in History", *American Historical Review*, vol 107 (2002): pp821–845; idem, *Emotional Communities in the Early Middle Ages* (Ithaca, NY, 2006).

6 On Johann Amerbach, see M. E. Welti, "Amerbach, Johann", in: P. G. Bietenholz and T. B. Deutscher (eds) *Contemporaries of Erasmus: A Biographical Register of the Renaissance and Reformation*, 3 vols (Toronto, 1985–1987), I: p47.

7 The history of early printing in Basel is widely documented. See M. Steinmann, "Der Basler Buchdruck im 16. Jahrhundert. Ein Versuch", *Librarium*, vol 53 (2010): pp79–98.

8 L. Febvre and H.-J. Martin, *L'Apparition du livre* (Paris, 1956).

9 Ambrosius Mediolanensis, *Opera*, J. Heynlin and J. Amerbach (eds) (Basel, 1492), fol. 6r. Consulted copy: University Library Basel, sign.: FJ II 1.

10 *Biblia. Cum postillis Hugonis – de Sancto Caro* (Basel 1498–1502), 7 parts: I, fol. 1v. Consulted copy: Forschungsbibliothek Gotha, sign.: Mon. typ. 1498 2° 00001.

11 Anton Koberger to Johann Amerbach, 26 May 1501, in O. von Hase, *Die Koberger. Eine Darstellung der Buchhändlischen Geschäftsbetriebes in der Zeit des Überganges vom Mittelalter zur Neuzeit*, 3rd edition (Amsterdam, 1967), pXXXIX.

12 See A. Grafton, *The Culture of Correction in Renaissance Europe* (London, 2011), p64.

13 For an overview, see H. Cunningham, *Children and Childhood in Western Society Since 1500* (London, 2005); L. A. Pollock, "Parent–Child Relations", in D. I. Kertzer and M. Barbagli (eds) *The History of the European Family*, 3 vols (New Haven, CT, 2001), I: pp191–220.

14 B. H. Rosenwein, "Emotion Words", in P. Nagy and D. Boquet (eds) *Le Sujet des émotions au Moyen Âge* (Paris, 2008), pp93–106.

15 On definition of emotion as distinct from affection and feeling, see M. Wetherell, *Affect and Emotion: A New Social Science Understanding* (London, 2012), esp. pp1–26.

16 To the list of emotion words tracked down by Rosenwein in the works of authors of the classical Greek and Roman tradition, the *bene velle* of the Latin poet Catullus can be added here. As distinct from *amor*, from *dilectione* and from *affectus*, it is more suitable to express the bond of affection between parents and children because, unlike love in the passionate sense (*amor*, *dilectione*) and general emotion (*affectus*), it denotes a spiritual sharing and implies a relationship of reciprocal trust (*fides*). See Gaius Valerius Catullus, *Carmina*, H. Bardon (ed) (Stuttgart, 1973): p72.

17 Rosenwein's "Emotional community", more than the concept of "emotional regime" as drawn up by William Reddy, is better suited to the emotional framework concerning the Amerbach family and the *sodalitas* gravitating around the printing shop. See W. Reddy, *The Navigation of Feeling: A Framework for the History of Emotions* (Cambridge, UK, 2001). See also J. Plamper, "The History of Emotion: An Interview with William Reddy, Barbara Rosenwein, and Peter Stearns", *History and Theory*, vol 49 (2010): pp237–265.

18 On the relationship between emotion and values, see J. Deonna and F. Teroni, *The Emotions: A Philosophical Introduction* (London, 2012), pp40–51.

10

"NATURE HAD FORM'D THEE FAIREST OF THY KIND"

Grieving dead children in Sweden circa 1650–1810

Marjo Kaartinen

> On Thursday night Mr Plaan was met with the greatest accident. The wet nurse slept his 18 weeks-old-son to death [by which was meant, the caregiver accidentally smothered the child, Ed.] When I heard about this I was hit so hard that I cannot express it. They will let the child be buried in the evening without great ceremony. May God comfort those who receive such a great sorrow. They both mourn their lost child greatly.[1]

This is what Christina Wallenstedt wrote when she had heard about the death of her friends' baby in Stockholm in November 1673. This chapter discusses these horrible moments in life: the emotions and expressions of sorrow when a child died. In these situations the feelings of anguish, pain and loss mixed, and were expected to mix. When death occurred love acquired many anguished expressions. I will look at these expressions in early modern Swedish letters, diaries, occasional poems and epitaphs. Such sources are especially important for the study of emotions because their authors often recorded their personal feelings in them. Early modern poems and epitaphs are, to a great extent, formal and, in fact, tied to certain emotional codes; but even these codes talk to us about the ways in which emotions were understood to be felt and supposed to be felt. This chapter argues for strong early modern parental emotions for and attachment to their children. When a child died, early modern parents experienced great emotional turmoil, and their society had a certain way of understanding and dealing with this turmoil. On the one hand, this loosely reflects what Barbara H. Rosenwein has termed "emotional communities".[2] On the other hand, grief turned the mourner away from his or her community.

On grief

Early modern people understood grief to be a strong and dangerous emotion. Writing in the first half of the sixteenth century, Spanish humanist Juan Luis Vives commented that grief was a feeling of the presence of evil, and a sub-category of this was the feeling of loss.[3] Thomas Hobbes counted grief as one of his eight passions,[4] and his contemporary Robert Burton attested in his *The Anatomy of Melancholy*, citing ancient authors, that sorrow was an inseparable companion, "the mother and daughter of melancholy, her epitome, symptom, and chief cause".[5] Importantly, Burton noted that grief was a bodily passion:

> "It drieth up the bones," saith Solomon (Prov.xvii), makes them hollow-eyed, pale, and lean, furrow-faced, to have dead looks, wrinkled bows, rivelled cheeks, dry bodies, and quite perverts their temperature that are misaffected with it. [...] It hinders concoction, refrigerates the heart, takes away stomach, colour, and sleep; thickens the blood; contaminates the spirits; overthrows the natural heat, perverts the good estate of body and mind, and makes them weary of their lives, cry out, howl and roar for the very anguish of their souls.[6]

As Burton's thoughts reflect, early modern theory of emotions pointed towards an understanding of the functions between the mind and body that differed from modern Western notions. Different organs of the human body controlled different emotions.[7] Emotions were essential if one wanted to remain in good health, and few things could cause as much bodily trouble as emotions misused or abused. This is why moderation was considered extremely important. In Sweden in the latter part of the eighteenth century, the readers of Carl Dahlman's popular household advice book learned that nothing caused as much illness as ill usage of passions. Such abuse could cost a person his or her life.[8] Not only excess sorrow, all excess passion was considered life threatening. Everyone knew the effects of strong emotions. Catharina Wallenstedt wrote in August 1680 that her good friend Mrs Reenfelt had died after an illness of several weeks caused by grief.[9] A fright could make one ill for a long period of time. This happened to the noble lady Agneta Horn, who wrote in her seventeenth-century memoir that she had been ill for weeks after she had been frightened by a monkey.[10] Agneta Horn's example is especially illustrative since she mentions this event in a memoir, written a great while after the incident. It was a very significant event in her life, vividly remembered years afterwards.

The death of a loved one could be lethal, and it was widely accepted that the death of a child could cause such devastating grief. As we know, a high number of very young children died in pre-modern Europe. In Scandinavia the medium rate of infant mortality was 224 per 1000 live births.[11] To bring this into context, one can contrast the situation in today's Finland, for example, where this rate is less than 3 per 1000 live births.[12] Children died at birth, from complications, and from illnesses such as worms, teething, diarrhoea, typhoid, scarlet fever, pertussis, smallpox, malaria and other fevers, plague and rickets. Accidents were not unheard of, and children were lost by horse kicks, natural catastrophes or fires, and falling or drowning accidents.[13] As such, it was not highly unusual for early modern people to have had experience of this sorrow, either personally or vicariously. It was accepted that such grief could make a person lose his or her mind. Grief in itself was, however, simultaneously seen as a healthy sign; mothers who did not love their children were considered more or less insane.[14]

The grim realities of early modern life, the devastating infant mortality rates, have led many social historians of the 1970s and 1980s to argue that these demographic facts played a role in parents' emotional distance from their children. They viewed the past as emotionally cold towards children, and ideals that emphasized parents' attitudes towards children as toys, pets, servants or worse received much attention.[15] These theories have been recently criticized, and the current consensus is that most, but not all, parents loved their children, some greatly. One of the first revisionists of the pessimistic view was Clare Gittings who noted when studying English children's funeral and burial practices that parents invested much time and money in them. This could not be a signal of lack of emotions; parents mourned their children.[16] In Sweden, Karin Sidén has shown in her art historical study of seventeenth-century portraits of children that parents ordered portraits of children who only lived a day or two. They would not have done this if they had had no feelings for their children.[17] The age of the child at death also affected these feelings, as will become clear.

Confronting infant death

Typically, elite mothers who left autobiographical records of their lives commented on the losses of their children, and gave at least a hint that this put their souls in turmoil. Even very brief mentions of the death of children 30 years after the fact elaborate on emotion: on grief, loss, sorrow and, ultimately, of great love towards children. While studying childhood, Rudolf Dekker has noted how literary conventions of grief changed in mid eighteenth-century Dutch sources.[18] Literary expression became more discursive; I would like to suggest that his findings apply to Sweden as well. In her late eighteenth-century autobiography, Christina Charlotta Hjärne wrote, for example, about how her "lost son of sorrows had made her shed thousands of tears".[19] Tears were, of course, fashionable in the eighteenth century; but though Hjärne's words comply with it, we have no reason to doubt her feelings. It is important to accept that a cultural model does not preclude the possibility of genuineness. Writing on eighteenth-century political tears, Jonas Liliequist importantly notes that "Genuineness of intention could be as confounding and elusive as genuineness of emotional response."[20]

In July 1798 Sweden expressed its public mourning very grandly. Märta Helena Reenstierna wrote in her extensive diaries about the death of the new-born prince Carl Adolph: "Official mourning has been declared in the Royal Court for three weeks with wreaths etc.; but the sorrow of the Royal family must be tender as we can think about those ones who have lost a beloved child."[21] It is interesting that even though she does not know the parents who had lost the child, she expects the grief and sorrow to be great. Such an emotion was expected. The culture of mourning, sorrow and grief was an integral part of pre-modern culture and social discourse.

The expression of emotions through tears in the eighteenth century does not, of course, indicate that there were no tears in the eyes of earlier mourners. Catharina

Wallenstedt's letters to her daughter show a seventeenth-century world in which sorrow at the death of children was devastating. Catharina herself does not appear to have lost any of her own, but commented sorrowfully on the deaths of her friends' children and felt the deaths of these children closely. "When I heard this", she wrote, "I was hit so hard I cannot express it in writing."[22] As we see, not only parents were affected: the wider family and friends suffered as well. That friends commented on the death of babies speaks to us that even infants were cherished, and parents who lost children received empathy.

The spring of 1681 was hard in Sweden because of famine and epidemics. The death of the son of Catharina Wallenstedt's friend, architect Jean de la Vallée, made her very pessimistic and frightened. The loss of the child epitomized for her the catastrophic situation in the country, and seemed to her a punishment of God. She wrote that more such horrors were to follow eventually: when the drought ended, rains would return and people and cattle would start dying. She wrote: "May God help us and let us prepare to meet the sorrow caused by all these deaths."[23] If we can judge from her reaction, seventeenth-century Sweden was not an emotional void.

The last hope

Even today, a parent's grief at the loss of a child focuses, in part, on the unfulfilled future of the child who is lost. Many expectations might be attached to a new-born, even a foetus. All those possibilities collapse when a child dies.[24]

In a pre-modern, patriarchal culture, the expectations of parents, and especially of elite parents, could be similarly great.[25] When the noble Mätta Madgalena Palmskiöld died at the age of nine in Stockholm in 1710, the parents, Elias Palmskiöld and Katharina Magdalena Blixenkrona, were grief stricken; their hope for the future was gone. They had lost their only child. In an epitaph for the little girl, the great Swedish poet Sophia Elisabet Brenner emphasized the impact of the loss by noting in typical but elegant verse that in the grave lay a little body, a loved one, an only child, and a child of much hope, a joy to her father and an image of the mother (both in her countenance and looks):

> Stand still you wandering man/and let me tell you
> That here below/is buried a weak and a little body
> A loved, only child, a child of much hope
> Mr. Palmskiöld's only joy, his beautiful little Mätta.[26]

As Karin Sidén and others have shown, pre-modern Swedish parents seem to have loved their infants. Funerary monuments, grand tombs and epitaphs for babies speak for this.[27] As in Brenner's words cited above, the child is often depicted as a source of joy and happiness, and that it was a privilege to have that child. Often the future is at least attempted to be seen in optimistic terms: a dead child had escaped the evils of this world; in heaven the child enjoyed all the possible joys. It was important to ensure that the baby reached heaven and cleanse the fathers' sins from the new born.[28] Emergency baptisms were thought to be necessary in these terms, and the death of a new-born is considered to have been especially worrisome in this respect.[29]

Bodily grief

Grief and sorrow appear as gendered concepts in pre-modern Europe. It was a culturally given that parents were devastated and mothers especially suffered greatly when their children were in danger of death or died. Women especially could even lose their minds and, as noted earlier, die. In her study of Swedish nobleman Gabriel Kurck, Liisa Lagerstam proposes that the danger of death of her baby was at least a partial reason for his wife's mental illness.[30] A near drowning, putting her unborn child at risk, apparently brought on her melancholic illness. People around her were devastated but not surprised at this kind of reaction, as they understood that a mother's love had no limits. A loving mother was such a prevailing cultural image that many sermons suggested mothers should embrace moderation in their grief.[31] Englishwoman Dorothy Leigh's words from the seventeenth century encapsulate the early modern presupposition: "Euery man knowes, that the loue of a mother to her children, is hardly contained within the bounds of reason."[32]

Women and mothers were known to express their grief in bodily terms: in 1702, Sophia Elisabet Brenner wrote a sonnet to Mrs Schmedeman who had lost her little boy. Brenner wrote that a grieving mother would sigh or weep. Grief could take the whole body, and it would be felt in the whole body. Christina Charlotte Hjärne wrote about the feelings of sorrow after her father's death: "This my first deep grief went so close to the heart that it took the whole body and no one could comfort me; only God's word kept me up."[33] Melancholy was a bodily illness, and it is possible that melancholy was a way to express grief. Patricia Phillippy has referred to Thomas Brewer's play *Weeping Lady*, which "casts plague-ridden London as a mourning Rachel, a mother who, seeing death 'gorgd with/her/Sonnes and Daughters,' appears 'with nothing but grones, Sighs, teares, shreaks, folding of arms; beating of brests, wringing of hands, pale looks, dejected eies, bleeding heart, & most heavy and bitter condolement'". This was female mourning epitomized.[34] When a child died, a heart could be broken. In pre-modern terms, it was possible to ask if the heart literally broke; loss caused such a gripping pain. The poet Sophia Elisabet Brenner asked: "Who knows if the heart does not bleed."[35]

The pain of losing hope in the form of a child weakened the body. Brenner comforted parents who had lost both their children:

Fate has at one strike made us childless
And we with these corpses throw all our hope in the grave
Our grief is beyond compare
For crying constantly weakens us.[36]

Hedvig Charlotta Nordenflycht, too, wrote about the feelings grief caused: all one's senses were disturbed and the body was thrown into utter misery. She suffered fits, illnesses and sleeplessness.[37] Agneta Horn lost her lustre – that is, so much weight, that her husband did not recognize her when he returned home from war. Catharina Wallenstedt wrote that the grieving Helena Silfverstierna had lost so much of her body that her skin hung on her cheekbones.[38]

Pain that follows

Pain and sorrow lasted a long time. Parents were left to wait until the soil eventually covered them as it had their lost child.[39] Though it did not pass, grief changed its form, settled to live among the living. Märta Helena Reenstierna's extensive diaries reveal the role her departed played in her life. Over the years, she had lost her husband and seven of her eight children. Only one had reached adulthood. She not only remembered her dead children's birthdays, baptismal days and death days, but she often wrote about them in her diary while they were happening. Writing perhaps made her memories permanent, and she clearly thought it important to reminisce about them on paper. Writing about them in her diary was a specific action, and indicates that there were countless thoughts and memories of the lost children in her everyday life.

On 26 July 1793, she wrote how her own name day reminded her of the feelings of loss that the death of her son Adolph Fredric had caused. Three years later she used nearly the same words.[40] On 17 March 1795 she remembered what a happy day they had had 19 years earlier, when their now dead first-born daughter, Frederica Maria, was baptized. She wrote: "Thank you God for everything!"[41] Two years later, on 13 March 1797, she wrote how she had brought with such great pain her beloved firstborn into the world 21 years earlier.[42] And in the same spring, on 19 April, she wrote Adolph Fredric would have been 16 years old, had he been allowed to live.[43]

Märta Helena wrote about the remains of her dear departed. In May 1802, the family was in the process of transferring their family grave as the old one was in a dismal condition. She recorded that she had seen in Frederica Maria's dust the bridal crown which Märta Helena herself had used as a bride. She mentioned that the crown had been put in the grave on 10 March 1778, 24 years and two months earlier, and that it had been preserved perfectly while even the coffin made of oak had been decomposed.[44]

Such thoughts convey great love towards the lost children, who were not forgotten by their parents. Parents counted their dates of their children (and other deceased ones) backwards with hourly exactness: "My beloved died three months, two days and eight hours ago." In Märta Helena's case, it is especially significant that she had put her bridal crown in her daughter's coffin. It served to herald the arrival of the Christ's new bride in heaven and to tell later generations how dearly beloved the departed daughter had been. This too shows that parental love was not only directed to sons or even first born sons; even daughters could be apples of their parents' eyes.

Grief and gender

Thus far female expressions of grief have been given ample space here. How about men? Did Swedish fathers not grieve for their dead children? I argue that they did, deeply so.[45] In fact, like the grief of a mother, the grief of a father was a cultural expectation. Leon Battista Alberti wrote that fathers should guard their babies very carefully and think ahead how much pain it causes fathers even to think about how many infants die.[46] There are, however, many scholars who point out that the relationship of mothers to their children was more intensive than that of the fathers. Margaret R. Sommerville reminds that it was common for the early modern theorists to stress the greater love of mothers.[47] Laurel Thatcher Ulrich notes that the role of the mother was to be responsible for the young children, whereas the father's role would grow with the children when questions of adulthood, property and sustenance became more central.[48] Kathleen M. Brown has suggested that the mother's role was weightier because there was no such web of duty as between father and child, especially between father and son. The father was responsible for the child's inheritance, both material and immaterial. Educating manhood was an especially important duty of the father.[49] These ideals and the division of responsibility in the family are doubtless true, but they do not mean that all fathers were distant from their children. Evidence from elite families in Sweden and England does not support a pessimistic view of the emotional repertoire of fathers.

Even though many have argued otherwise, fathers, too, grieved in a great and palpable way. They loved their children as they were, if one looks closely. Patriarchal society, however, placed on fathers the burdens of dynasties: they had the duty to carry on the family and heritage. A lost child was in very concrete terms a lost future for a father.

We can find mourning fathers in the sources. They do not always offer explicit expressions of grief. In diaries, for instance, silence can be read as a sign of extreme mourning rather than emotional distance. Words often reveal pain, and we can see that a father's grief could be gripping. In the Swedish kingdom's eastern border, in the remote Finnish Carelian city of Viborg,[50] nobleman Johan Rosenhane (1611–1661) wrote in his diary about the deaths of his children. He was the county governor from 1644 to 1655 and was later transferred to a more central position as the county governor of Linköping. He became a privy councillor (*rikdsråd*) in 1658.[51] He married Brita Ribbing in 1644. Tragedies followed as all their children died and were buried in the Viborg cathedral before they left town. It appears the mother finally refused to live in the Viborg Castle. The deaths of the children shook the father's world, too. When one of his children died, his entries in his otherwise laconic diary became more discursive and emotional, suggesting that these events had a special kind of force. Daily affairs were not granted similar space in the diary's pages.

Unfortunately, Rosenhane's diary does not begin before 1652, when the couple already had lost their sons Roderik and Wilmer, and their daughter Brita. The exact dates of their births and deaths are not recorded. On 16 September 1652, another son, Carl, was taken ill with a chest disease and cough. He suffered and languished until, on 30 September at eight in the evening, the boy (his age is not known) died. Rosenhane wrote that "his blessed son Carl was buried with proper ceremony in the Viipuri Cathedral" to join his brother Wilmer and sister Brita. (This suggests that the firstborn Roderik died before the couple moved to Viborg.) He asks in his diary for

Christ to give this child a happy resurrection but also to comfort and preserve those who remained.[52]

Another son, Adam Rosenhane, died on 14 October 1653, only a year after Carl's death. Adam was only eight weeks old. He, too, died of a chest disease, having been ill for eight days. The father wrote that little Adam died "quietly and peacefully" – that is, according to contemporary ideals of a good death, without any disturbance of the limbs and without great suffering. He mentioned that Adam was not the only child he had lost and that his death caused great sorrow. And as if to emphasize how appropriate it was for a father to feel great grief, he explains that on 18 October the Bishop of Viborg and Major Leffwe, among others, came and comforted the mourning parents. The following day Johan wrote that his wife took seriously ill and that "the body of their little boy was put in his coffin".[53]

Brita Ribbing's illness proved to be lengthy and so serious that the father had to postpone Adam's funeral for months. It was in the spring, on 17 March, that he mentioned that he had let his son's body be buried in the cathedral with his two brothers Wilmer and Carl, and their sister Brita. Their mother had now recovered so that she was able to leave the castle and travel to the cathedral for the funeral.[54] Unfortunately, Johan Rosenhane does not explain the nature of his wife's illness in his diary. It is possible that the birth had been difficult and complications caused her illness; it is also possible that her loss made her ill.

Nils Gyldenstolpe's grief

Johan Rosenhane's sorrow has to be read from brief accounts in his diary, but Nils Gyldenstolpe's case requires reading other people's texts. Studying his life's great tragedy takes us back to the family of Catharina Wallenstedt[55] and to the war year of 1709. The kingdom of Sweden and Charles XII dramatically lost the 20-year Great Northern War to Russia and Peter the Great at Poltava in July; the price the kingdom had to pay was horrible, not least in the lives of the thousands who were killed in battle. I propose that Nils Gyldenstolpe (1642–1709), the most powerful man in the kingdom after the king, at the age of 66, died in his Stockholm home because of what happened on the march towards Poltava. This is what the contemporaries may easily have thought and accepted as a fact.

The Gyldenstolpe family expressed its emotions strongly, and Nils's father, Michael, also expressed his overflowing love for his children in his letters.[56] Nils had been first married without issue, but he became father to three sons by his second wife, Greta (Margareta) Ehrensteen, Catharina Wallenstedt's beloved daughter. As a young nobleman he entered the service of the crown as a secretary to the law department in Stockholm. From there his career took flight. In 1679, he was sent to Holland as an envoy, a great moment in his career. Nils and Greta already had a son, Edvard, just before they moved to Holland, and they left him in Sweden with his grandmother. Because of her letters to her daughter in Holland, we know a great deal about little Edvard's childhood. He lived with his grandparents for several years, and they delighted in him, "a clever baby and a perfect boy", before he had to be sent to Holland, around the age of six, to get to know his parents and his little brother, Carl, who had been born in den Haag two years after Edvard's birth.

Nils was successful in Holland, and great positions followed his return home. He became president of the Privy Council in 1705 at the age of 63. This was the highest position in the country, even though practical power was bestowed upon the king and his war council. The Great Northern War, upon which Sweden was then embarked, caused the deaths of his two sons and, ultimately, it was probably thought by many, of their father as well.

Edvard grew to be a handsome, well-behaved, intelligent and learned man. We know that his father thought highly of him. Edvard was a perfect cosmopolitan; he was fluent in French, Latin, Greek, Italian, English and Dutch, among many others. After his university studies, he left for a Grand Tour with Carl and spent well his time in England, France, Holland and Italy. While Carl returned to Sweden, Edvard took part in a British embassy to the Orient to negotiate peace with the representatives of the Ottoman Empire. Among his companions was Edward Wortley Montagu, the future ambassador to Istanbul. Edvard was expected to have made a great career as a diplomat, blessed as he was with his linguistic talents, scholarly interests (for example, in archaeology) and social skills.

On his way home from the Ottoman Empire, he joined King Charles XII on a campaign somewhere in Eastern Europe. He volunteered and soon advanced to become a cornet, and later a captain of a dragoon regiment. His military career lasted from 1702 to 1709, when he was killed in a melee early in January 1709. Only a few months later, in April, his younger brother Carl died in the same campaign.

After Edvard was buried on the battlefield, a friend of his, Josias Cederhielm, wrote to his brother Germund about Edvard's death:

> I am sorry for his relatives, and fear that His Excellency [that is his father Nils Gyldenstolpe] will take this sorrow too highly to his heart. I do not know if that sorrow would increase or decrease if I told him all about his dear departed son's great acts. *Je perdis en lui un très sincere ami, mais en verité la patrie y perdit d'avantage.*[57]

It is interesting that Josias Cederhielm should ponder upon Nils Gyldenstolpe's feelings in a letter to his brother. Were these not hardened men who had seen sudden, violent death on the battlefield? Why should Nils Gyldenstolpe take his son's death "too highly?" In pre-modern terms it would have been logical to think that to lose his beloved sons in war could have broken Nils Gyldenstolpe's heart beyond any possibility of repair. He died soon after he heard the news – of causes unknown. Cederhielm's short yet revealing words indicate an acceptance of the idea that a father, too, could take his loss "too highly to his heart". Interestingly, Cederhielm does not ponder on the grief of Edvard's mother Greta at all. It was his friend's father whom he considered to be at risk.

If we go back in time some 30 years, to 1685, we find at the Swedish court a mourning king. Charles XI had lost a son. His biographer, Göran Rystad, notes that even though Charles very rarely revealed any emotions, he did so when his children died. The most beautiful of Charles and Ulrika Eleonora's children was considered to be Prince Gustaf, who died in 1685. Heartbroken, the king noted in his almanac with very customary seventeenth-century promptness that his son had died at the age of one year, ten months and 12 days.[58] As this kind of elaborate counting is so customary, I tend to interpret is as a sign of emotion. Charles wrote to his friend a month later that he could not have earlier believed that he would feel so strongly about a death of a child. Two weeks before the letter, he had lost another son, Ulrik, who was only one year old. In his sorrow the king locked himself up in his apartment.[59]

Conclusion

In many instances, mothers gave especially strong expression to their sorrow at the loss of their children. When the Duchess Charlotta (Hedvig Elisabet Charlotta of Holstein-Gottrop) lost her infant son, Karl Adolf, the Duke of Värmland, on the day of his baptism in July 1798, she wrote:

> It is impossible for me to describe how I mourn for my little baby and how limitless is my unhappiness. Oh, this can only be felt by a mother. *I see no end to this*; this grief will remain as long as I live.[60]

Her words perhaps reflect her experience of her husband's emotions: they grew more and more distanced from each other as years passed. But, as we have seen, fathers were also expected to feel deeply their children's deaths, and it was not considered unsuitable for a man to express grief. It has been shown that the deaths of many early modern children caused devastation, suggesting deep emotional attachment on the part of their parents. Both men and women mourned their sons and daughters, and they seem to have done so whether these children were new-born babies or full-grown adults.

Notes

1 Stockholm, 15 November 1673, in C. Wijkmark (ed) *Allrakäraste. Catharina Wallenstedts brev 1672–1718* (Stockholm, 1995), pp97–98 (hereinafter, *Allrakäraste*). All translations from Swedish to English are by the author.
2 B. H. Rosenwein, *Emotional Communities in the Early Middle Ages* (Ithaca, NY, 2006). On pre-modern history of emotions, and including Rosenwein's chapter "Theories of Change in the History of Emotions", see J. Liliequist (ed) *A History of Emotions, 1200–2000* (London, 2012).
3 J. V. Vives, *The Passions of the Soul. The Third Book of De Anima et Vita*, transl. C. G. Noreña (Lewiston, 1990).
4 S. James, "Explaining the Passions: Passions, Desires, and the Explanation of Action", in S. Gaugroger (ed) *The Soft Underbelly of Reason: The Passions in the Seventeenth Century* (London, 1998), p27.
5 R. Burton, *The Anatomy of Melancholy*, H. Jackson (ed) (New York, 2001), p259.

6 Ibid, pp259–260.
7 R. Porter and D. Porter (eds) *In Sickness and in Health: The British Experience 1650–1850* (London, 1988), p46.
8 K. Dahlman, *Swenska Red-Dejan Eller Wälöfwada Hushållerskan [–]och med en bifogad tilöfning eller en för alla menniskör wäl inrättad Sundhets-Bok* (Wästerås, 1772), p55. The liver controlled passions, the kidneys the temperament and the heart was the location of emotions. See also R. Porter and D. Porter, *In Sickness and in Health*, p46.
9 *Allrakäraste*, p183. On grief as the cause of death, see also L. M. Beier, *Sufferers & Healers: The Experience of Illness in Seventeenth-Century England* (London, 1987), p138; R. Porter and D. Porter, *In Sickness and in Health*, p64; A. Laurence, "Godly Grief: Individual Responses to Death in Seventeenth-Century Britain", in R. Houlbrooke (ed) *Death, Ritual, and Bereavement* (London, 1989), p75.
10 A. Horn, *Agneta Horn Lefverne*, E. Fries and S. Leijonhufvud (eds) (Stockholm, 1910), p139.
11 Christine Bladh notes that in 1750 infant mortality in Stockholm was 40 per cent. C. Bladh, "Women and Family Structure in Late 18th Century Stockholm", in M. Hietala and L. Nilsson (eds) *Women in Towns: The Social Position of European Urban Women in a Historical Context* (Stockholm, 1999), p89. See also L. Pollock, *With Faith and Physic: The Life of a Tudor Gentlewoman. Lady Grace Mildmay 1552–1620* (New York, 1993), p5; H. Wunder, *He Is the Sun, She Is the Moon: Women in Early Modern Germany*, transl. by Thomas Dunlap (Cambridge, MA, 1998), p18; M. Laharie, "L'enfant au Moyen Âge: Images et réalités", in E. Berriot-Salvadore and I. Pébay-Clottes (eds) *Autour de l'enfance* (Biarritz, 1999), p18; M. Lindemann, *Medicine and Society in Early Modern Europe* (Cambridge, UK, 1999), p25; W. Coster, "Tokens of Innocence: Infant Baptism, Death and Burial in Early Modern England", in B. Gordon and P. Marshall (eds) *The Place of the Dead: Death and Remembrance in Late Medieval and Early Modern Europe* (Cambridge, UK, 2000), p285.
12 See *Infant Mortality 1751–2007*, Statistics Finland: http://www.stat.fi/til/kuol/tau.html, accessed 14 September 2012. This rate has gone down in Finland at a constant rate. The rate of 3 deaths per 1000 births was first reached in 2002, and again in 2005. In 2006 the rate was 2.8 and in 2007, 2.7. In the eighteenth century, infant mortality rates varied greatly each year, but they remained very high and never went lower than 170 deaths per 1000 births. The worst year was the war year, 1808, when 360 infants died out of 1000 births. See K. Moring, "Motherhood, Milk, and Money: Infant Mortality in Pre-Industrial Finland", *Social History of Medicine*, vol 11 (1998): pp177–196. To compare these to today's developing countries, in 2010 the highest infant mortality rate according to the World Bank was in Sierra Leone: 112 deaths per 1000 births: http://data.worldbank.org/indicator/SP.DYN.IMRT.IN?order=wbapi_data_value_2010+wbapi_data_value+wbapi_data_value-last& sort = asc, accessed 15 September 2012.
13 L. M. Beier, "In Sickness and in Health: A Seventeenth Century Family's Experience", in: R. Porter (ed) *Patients and Practitioners. Lay Perceptions of Medicine in Pre-Industrial Society* (Cambridge, UK, 1985), pp107–110, 184, 191; R. Porter and D. Porter, *In Sickness and in Health*, pp2–3; E. Shorter, *Women's Bodies. A Social History of Women's Encounter with Health, Ill-Health, and Medicine* (New Brunswick, NJ, 1991), pp22–23; B. Moring, "Motherhood", p185; L. Haas, *The Renaissance Man and His Children: Childbirth and Early Childhood in Florence 1300–1600* (New York, 1998), p159; R. C. Finucane, *The Rescue of the Innocents: Endangered Children in Medieval Miracles* (London, 1997), pp101–149.
14 M. Macdonald, *Mystical Bedlam: Madness, Anxiety, and Healing in Seventeenth-Century England* (Cambridge, UK, 1981), pp80–84. On Swedish infanticides, see I. Lövkrona, *Annika Larsdotter barnamörderska. Kön, makt och sexualitet i 1700-talets Sverige* (Lund, 1999). On Finnish ones, see M. Rautelin, *En förutbestämd sanning: Barnamord och delaktighet i 1700-talets Finland belysta genom kön, kropp och social kontroll* (Helsingfors, 2009), http://urn.fi/URN:ISBN:978-952-10-5802-8.

15 On classic histories of family history and the history of childhood, see L. Stone, *The Family, Sex and Marriage in England 1500–1800* (Harmondsworth, UK, 1990), p57; P. Ariès, *Centuries of Childhood*, transl. by R. Baldick (London, 1960); E. Badinter, *Den kärleksfulla modern*, transl. by B. Gröndahl (Stockholm, 1980/1981), pp31–47. See also S. Ozment, *Ancestors: The Loving Family in Old Europe* (Cambridge, MA, 2001); H. Berry and E. Foyster (eds) *The Family in Early Modern England* (Cambridge, MA, 2007).

16 C. Gittings, *Death, Burial and the Individual in Early Modern England* (London, 1984), pp80–81. See also N. S. Dye and D. B. Smith, "Mother Love and Infant Death, 1720–1920", in *Journal of American History*, vol 73 (1986): pp329–353; J. J. H. Dekker and L. F. Groenendijk, "The Republic of God or the Republic of Children? Childhood and Child-Rearing After the Reformation: An Appraisal of Simon Schama's Thesis About the Uniqueness of the Dutch Case", *Oxford Review of Education*, vol 17 (1991): pp317–336; L. Haas, *The Renaissance Man*, pp157, 170, 176; G. Avery and K. Reynolds (eds) *Representations of Childhood Death* (Basingstoke, UK, 2000); R. Woods, *Children Remembered: Responses to Untimely Death in the Past* (Liverpool, UK, 2006); R. Houlbrooke, "Death in Childhood: The Practice of the 'Good Death' in James Janeway's *A Token for Children*", in A. Fletcher and S. Hussey (eds) *Childhood in Question: Children, Parents and the State* (Manchester, UK, 1999); H. Newton, *The Sick Child in Early Modern England, 1580–1720* (Oxford, UK, 2012), pp121–157; L. McMahon, "'So Truly Afflicting and Distressing to Me His Sorrowing Mother': Expressions of Maternal Grief in Eighteenth-Century Philadelphia", in *Journal of the Early Republic*, vol 32, no 1 (2012): pp27–60.

17 K. Sidén, *Den ideala barndomen. Studier i det stormaktstida barnporträttens ikonografi och funktion* (Stockholm, 2001), passim. She also notes that portraits of dead children were more usual than portraits of dead adults. Ibid, p214.

18 R. Dekker, *Childhood, Memory and Autobiography in Holland: From the Golden Age to Romanticism* (Houndmills, UK, 2000), p138.

19 C. C. Hjärne, *Självbiografi* (Stockholm, 1880), p23. See also C. Sjöblad, *Min vandring dag för dag. Kvinnors dagböcker från 1700-talet* (Stockholm, 1997), p204.

20 J. Liliequist, "The Political Rhetoric of Tears in Early Modern Sweden", in J. Liliequist (ed) *A History of Emotions, 1200–1800* (London, 2012), p204.

21 "Onsdag 11.7.1798", in M. H. Reenstierna, *Årstadagboken. Journalen från åren 1793–1839*, edited by S. Erixon, A. Stålhane and S. Wallin, urval och förklaringar av Gunnar Broman, vol I (Stockholm, 1966), p172 (hereinafter Reenstierna, *Årstadagboken*).

22 Stockholm, 15 November 1673, in *Allrakäraste*, pp97–98. To her great sadness Catharina Wallenstedt had to comment on many childhood deaths in the families that were close to her. Her steward Måns lost a little girl in the spring of 1674, and Catharina wrote that she had never seen such a good child. The girl had been a great joy to her. She noted that Måns's son probably would not live long either. Stockholm, 2 May 1674, ibid, p149.

23 Stockholm, 28 May 1681, in *Allrakäraste*, p254.

24 H. Laakso, *Äidin suru alle seitsenvuotiaan lapsen kuoleman jälkeen* (Tampere, 2000), p16.

25 See also K. Sidén, *Den ideala barndomen*, p223.

26 "Epitaphium öfweer sin lilla gudotter", in S. E. Brenner, *Poetiske dikter*, vol I (Stockholm, 1732), pp186–187:

> Stå stilla Wandrings-Mann/så skal jag dig berätta
>
> At härinunder/göms en späd och liten kropp
>
> Et kiärt/et enda Barn/et Barn af mycket hopp/
>
> Herr Palmskiölds Änga-frögd/hans täcka lilla Mätta.

27 W. Coster, "Tokens of Innocence", pp267, 280, 286; K. Sidén, *Den ideala barndomen*; L. Lagerstam, *A Noble Life: The Cultural Biography of Gabriel Kurck (1630–1712)* (Helsinki, 2007), pp184–185.

28 C. Jarzebowski, "Loss and Emotion in Funeral Works on Children in Seventeenth-Century Germany", in L. Tatlock (ed) *Enduring Loss in Early Modern Germany* (Leiden, 2010), pp187–213.

29 R. C. Finucane, *The Rescue of the Innocents*, pp42–46; E. Fudge, *Perceiving Animals: Humans and Beasts in Early Modern English Culture* (Basingstoke, UK, 2000), pp40–41.

30 L. Lagerstam, *A Noble Life*, pp190–194.

31 A. Lahtinen, *Sopeutuvat, neuvottelevat, kapinalliset. Naiset toimijoina Flemingin sukupiirissä 1470–1620* (Helsinki, 2007), pp88–89. See also O. Hufton, "Women, Work, and Family", in N. Z. Davis and A. Farge (eds) *A History of Women in the West. Part III. Renaissance and Enlightenment Paradoxes* (Cambridge, MA, 1993), pp35–36.

32 D. Leigh, *The Mothers Blessing or The godly counsaile of a Gentle-woman not long since deceased, left behind for her children: Containing many good exhortations, and godly admonitions, profitable for all Parents to leaue as a Legacy to their Children, but especially by those, who by reason of their young yeeres stand most in need of Instruction* (London, 1616), p12.

33 S. E. Brenner, "Till fru Schmedeman öfwer hennes lilla Son, 1702", in S. E. Brenner, *Poetiske dikter*, pp157–58; C. C. Hjärne, *Självbiografi*, p9.

34 P. Phillippy, "London's Mourning Garment: Maternity, Mourning and Royal Succession", in: N. J. Miller and N. Yavneh (eds) *Maternal Measures: Figuring Caregiving in the Early Modern Period* (Aldershot, UK, 2000), p320. See also L. Babb, *The Elizabethan Malady. A Study of Melancholia in English Literature from 1580 to 1642* (East Lansing, MI, 1951), pp12–13, 103.

35 S. E. Brenner, "Samtal Emellan De sörjande Föräldrarne, 1698", in S. E. Brenner, *Poetiske dikter*, p136. See also V. Lindgärde, "Ett sött gift. Kärlekens bild i Sophia Elisabet Brenners bröllopsdikter", in V. Lindgärde and E. Mansén (eds) *Ljuva möten och ömma samtal. Om kärlek och vänskap på 1700-talet* (Stockholm, 1999), pp69–70.

36 S. E. Brenner, "Samtal Emellan De sörjande Föräldrarne, 1698", in S. E. Brenner, *Poetiske dikter*, p236.

37 H. C. Nordenflycht, *Skrifter*, Torkel Stålmarck (ed) (Stockholm, 1966), p12.

38 A. Horn, *Agneta Horn Lefverne*, pp138–139.

39 S. E. Brenner, "Samtal emellan de sörjande föräldrarne, 1698", in S. E. Brenner, *Poetiske dikter*, p136.

40 Reenstierna, *Årstadagboken*, pp45–46, 117–118.

41 Ibid, p87.

42 Ibid, p142.

43 Ibid, p144.

44 Ibid, p272.

45 See also L. Wilson, *Ye Heart of a Man: The Domestic Life of Men in Colonial New England* (New Haven, CT, 1999), pp132–139; S. Ozment, *Flesh and Spirit: Private Life in Early Modern Germany* (New York, 1999), pp97–98. Ozment studies the family of Georg Scheurlin in sixteenth-century Germany and shows how grief stricken Scheurlin was after losing his many children.

46 Cited in L. Haas, *The Renaissance Man*, p158.

47 M. R. Sommerville, *Sex & Subjection: Attitudes to Women in Early-Modern Society* (London, 1995), pp61, 120.

48 L. T. Ulrich, *Good Wives: Image and Reality in the Lives of Women in Northern New England 1650–1750* (New York, 1980/1991), p155.

49 K. M. Brown, *Good Wives, Nasty Wenches, and Anxious Patriarchs: Gender, Race, and Power in Colonial Virginia* (Chapel Hill, NC, 1996), pp347–348.

50 In Finnish: Viipuri. The town was the second largest town in Finland until 1944 when it was lost to the Soviet Union. The written form of Vyborg often refers to the Russian name of the present town.

51 Biographical information from Georg Haggrén's entry in *The Finnish National Biography*: http://www.kansallisbiografia.fi/kb/artikkeli/6228/, accessed 30 September 2012.

52 On Carl's illness and his death, see J. Rosenhane, *Dagbok 1652–1661*, A. Jansson (ed) (Stockholm, 1995), pp43–46 (hereinafter Rosenhane, *Dagbok*).

53 Rosenhane, *Dagbok*, p85.

54 Ibid, pp100–101. It is important to notice the cultural meaning of this long waiting to bury the child. The mother's presence at the cathedral was considered so essential that the funeral could not be performed without her. In the seventeenth century, it was not unusual to have a coffin waiting for a burial for a long time, and, of course, in the northern cold climates, inhumations could not customarily be carried out in winter when the ground was frozen. In Adam Rosenhane's case, this was not the reason for the wait since he was buried in the cathedral.

55 Catharine Wallenstedt's beloved daughter Margareta Ehrensteen married Nils Gyldenstolpe and they had three sons.

56 I wish to thank Dr Raija Sarasti-Wilenius for the information regarding the family. She is currently editing the Wexonius family correspondence.

57 On Edvard's military service and this letter, see A. Lewenhaupt, *Karolinen Edvard Gyldenstolpe* (Stockholm, 1941), passim, esp. p186. (The French sentence translates as follows: I lost a very good friend in him but in reality Sweden lost in him much more.)

58 G. Rystad, *Karl XI. En biografi* (Lund, 2001), p296.

59 Ibid, pp296–297. For similar conclusions in early America, see L. Wilson, *Ye Heart of a Man*, p139, and in England, P. Phillippy, "'I might againe have been the sepulcure': Paternal and Maternal Mourning in Early Modern England", in J. C. Vaught and L. D. Bruckner (eds) *Grief and Gender 700–1700* (Basingstoke, UK, 2003), p203.

60 C. Sjöblad, *Min vandring dag för dag*, p247 (italics in the original).

11

DESERTERS' VOICES ON CHILDHOOD AND EMOTION IN EIGHTEENTH-CENTURY FRANCE

Naoko Seriu

Those who are interested in military history know quite well that desertion was a chronic phenomenon in the army of the Old Regime.[1] In so far as mass patriotism was "invented" during the revolution and came to be shared progressively and not without conflict[2] by a large number of people in the process of nation-building, we can understand how little, or rather how differently, early modern soldiers were attached to their military service.[3] However, even if it was commonplace, desertion was not a choice without risk. During the eighteenth century, under the French absolute monarchy, the crime was punishable by the most severe penalties, such as galley servitude or death.[4] Although the sentence was mostly pronounced in absentia, arrests certainly occurred and therewith the likelihood of sanction. The fact that family constituted one of the major causes of desertion deserves, therefore, the attention of historians interested in the relationship between men and their families. Records of military desertion can be read as a somewhat unexpected source to be integrated within the history of family. In this chapter, the analysis is based on records of interrogations of deserters by the highway police in the second half of the eighteenth century, and the aim is to shed light on the meaning that deserters attached to family ties, and in particular to their relationship with children.

Regarding the subject under consideration, some brief preliminary remarks are necessary on the historiographic investigation of childhood and emotion, which has been in progress for half a century. The study of childhood owes much to Philippe Ariès's *L'Enfant et la vie familiale sous l'Ancien Régime*, published in 1960.[5] As many historians have acknowledged,[6] he was the first to argue that a concept of childhood slowly emerged and came to be considered a separate phase of human life in the sixteenth century. Only then did the notion of childhood as a valuable stage in life, inciting emotions, and the idea of "coddling" children become acceptable. Ariès further highlighted the development of the concept of childhood in the eighteenth century, when it became associated with innocence needing to be protected and ignorance or weakness needing to be removed. According to Ariès's hypothesis, this emotional view of children and childhood is something that arose in the Early Modern Period and grew over time. The importance of Ariès's work in promoting a historical understanding of emotion is undeniable, but the reception of his work has produced a simplified interpretation: a lack of feeling for children in the pre-modern family and especially among the poor. Emblematic in this regard is the famous book by Edward Shorter, which made the "luck of love" the key to understanding the "traditional family" in both its conjugal and filial dimensions.[7]

Since this conceptualization of childhood and emotion as attributes of an early modern elite, many critical studies have directed our attention to other historicities and other social spaces initially thought to have ignored childhood. We can highlight the efforts of medieval historians, such as Danièle Alexandre-Bido, Monique Closson and Didier Lett, who mobilized a variety of sources – iconographical, archaeological, hagiographical, literary, etc. – and analysed the various forms of attention to children in different social contexts in pre-modern Europe.[8] We can also note the methodological remarks of Hans Medick and David Sabean who stressed the importance of historians not separating material concerns from the emotional dimensions of the family experience.[9] Interestingly, they also pointed out the difficulties in approaching the affective experience of working-class people due to the implicit dimension of their language; for them, these historians suggested, silence and what is untold could be important elements of language, the meaning of which can be understood only with difficulty by outsiders.[10] Since people do not have the need or the habit of expressing themselves explicitly in order to communicate with other members of the same community, an absence of affective expression cannot in any way be read as proof of a lack of it.

Without doubt, this question of language – brought to light as early as 1988 – encourages historians to work closely on the faint traces of expression. Through resort to "ego-documents" and other autobiographical sources, historians have shed light on the complexity and the richness of parent–child relationships for those who are likely to produce such a written testimony.[11] The difficulty of locating such sources for low-literacy people of the working classes remains.

In the Early Modern Period, writing a life story was a practice of better educated people. However, there were some individuals who, despite their modest origins, were brought to write about themselves. In these sources, traces of feelings for children are sometimes explicit. Ulrich Bräker, for example, who was obliged to enlist as a soldier in the army of Frederick II in the middle of the Seven Years' War, wrote an extensive autobiography. It forms an interesting source for military history, revealing much about the hardness of discipline in the Prussian army, from which he deserted to return to his native village in Switzerland.[12] In the context of this chapter, his life after his return to his village in Switzerland is also very interesting.[13] After his marriage he had seven children, of which two died young. He recalls the death of these two children as the saddest days of his life. Describing the agony of his eldest son suffering from dysentery, he wrote: "God only knows what I felt at this calamity: to see such a sweet-tempered child whom I loved like my own soul, patient as a lamb, suffering day and night … ."[14] When the boy passed away, he recalled: "I felt as if my heart would shatter into a thousand pieces."[15] He did not, however, devote so much space to the death of his eldest daughter, which occurred shortly afterwards, because she died suddenly while he himself was sick with contagion. Nevertheless, both of them continue to occupy an important place for their father, a poor and indebted worker. In his memoirs, Bräker forgets none of his children: the comment and advice he gave to them are surely gendered.[16] Yet, he expressed emotion towards all of them, both daughters and sons alike.

This kind of sentimental confession towards children might seem exceptional for the popular French autobiographical writers of the same period, and for Jean-Antoine Rossignol, in particular. His memoirs are also well known to military historians as a testimony of army life at the end of the Old Regime.[17] He privileges the description of manly friendship and writes little about his childhood. Moreover, he remained unmarried and without children. Yet, one passage in his life story says something of affection. It concerns his mother, who – according to Rossignol – "did not cajole" him.[18] This expression reveals the expectations of a child who is claiming some attention. The indication of his disappointment illustrates the possibility of the tenderness that should affect the relationship between mother and son.

The life story of Jacques-Louis Ménétra provides rich material with many more numerous indications of family affection.[19] As Daniel Roche points out,[20] whereas Ménétra highlights the conflictual dimension of his relationship with his father, he speaks with affection of his mother, who passed away when he was still small, and of his grandmother, who raised him thereafter.[21] Ménétra's description of his adult life certainly tends to focus on his numerous and compulsive sexual conquests.[22] Yet, this faithless husband reveals himself to be a responsible father. While he is hardly expressive of his feelings towards them, he specifies what he was led to do for them; looking after his small son in his sickness and supporting his daughter in her divorce proceedings are the topics approached in this popular autobiography.[23] If he was endowed with fatherly love, his affection finds expression more in actions than in words. Thus, by including details about the perception of children, "ego-documents" are undoubtedly important materials for the study of childhood and emotion. Their scarcity, however, requires the use of other more abundant sources.

Court records produced by the tribunals of the Old Regime have been used not only by historians working on crime and so-called deviance, but also by those who are interested in popular culture and practices.[24] Through a close reading of the words of often nameless people, we can analyse the various attitudes – from neglect and indifference to compassion and affection – towards non-elite children. A series of works by Arlette Farge has demonstrated convincingly the importance of integrating such traces in the process of history writing.[25] According to her, the desire to protect children played a role in the rebellion in 1750 of Parisian men and women against the "kidnapping" of children by the police.[26] While other historians have highlighted the abandonment of children as illustrating a lack of love for them,[27] an analysis of letters and words left in the clothing of children abandoned at the hospital leads Farge to grasp the feelings of those unhappy parents for their babies.[28] In light of the recent development of the history of emotion,[29] civil and criminal court records offer rich materials for examining expressions of emotion constructed about children.[30]

The archives of the *maréchaussée*

Following the path outlined above, this chapter focuses on the expressions of army deserters, who mentioned their children as grounds for their criminal actions during interrogations by the *maréchaussée*. Originally a military police force, the *maréchaussée* dealt much with crimes committed by soldiers on the road.[31] During the eighteenth century, checking identity became another one of its activities,[32] and deserters came to constitute an important part of the mobile population it had to monitor. When arrested and taken to jail, deserters were questioned by a lieutenant of the *maréchaussée* before being conducted back to their regiment by order of the minister of war.[33]

Interrogations by the *maréchaussée* reveal the tensions that the soldiers might have suffered in the army. Prompted by a question, each man explained why he deserted. The reasons and circumstances that led men to do so were various. Based on an analysis of a corpus of 900 cases, mostly in the second half of the eighteenth century and during the period of peace,[34] three of the most frequent reasons are abuse at the time of enlistment, mistreatment and punishment, and family circumstances.[35] The latter cases, of which there are 116, allow an analysis of how men constructed their relationships with the members of their families, which they had left in order to carry out their military duty. Because the military authorities regarded desertion as a crime, deserters had to justify their returning home to the police and to speak of their families in explicit terms. In so doing, they engaged in a "presentation of self"[36] that they hoped would convince the authority.

Historians interested in father–child relationships have highlighted the importance of the fatherly duty to feed and educate children, constructed as legal and Christian obligations from the Middle Ages to the Early Modern Period.[37] At the same time, they have analysed the expressions of fatherly tenderness found essentially in the ego-documentals left by materially and socially privileged fathers, from King Henry IV to Montaigne.[38]

Admittedly, in the century of Enlightenment, the family is portrayed more and more as a site of emotional exchange. The theme of a father's curse, exalted by writers such as Diderot and Retif de La Bretonne, illustrates the strong attachment that a man can develop towards his son.[39] Even if all children – sons and daughters alike – were dependent on paternal authority, the writers' attention focused on conflicts within the male lineage and set aside conflict between fathers and daughters. By contrast, the theme of filial piety indicates a form of earthly happiness that a man can experience within his family, not only with male descendants but also with other family members – spouse, daughters and servants – as Jean-Baptiste Greuze represented in his famous painting "Piété filiale".[40] Literature of the eighteenth century also gives a central place to the issue of seeking affiliation.[41] For example, Louis Sébastien Mercier, in his play *The Deserter*, narrated a history of separation and reunion between a son – a soldier and then deserter – and his father – an officer receiving the order for his execution.[42] This work, well known as an appeal for the abolition of the death penalty for deserters,[43] owes its success to the dramatic intensity Mercier created in tune with the public's expectation of what historians used to call "family romance".[44]

Contemporary to these developments, deserters spoke of their families. When arrested, they spoke of their children, their reasons for joining and deserting the army. All the statements elicited in a judicial process – from interrogation by the police to the verdict of the court – have a strategic dimension.[45] Yet, deserters' words still capture some of the reality of the military profession, their precarious circumstances and their difficulty in organizing family life.[46] The archives of the *maréchaussée* therefore allow a contribution to the history of the family, generally, and of childhood and emotion, specifically, through the testimonies of deserters who were fathers and husbands.

Wives and children in poverty

When deserters spoke of their children, their evocation was generally inseparable from that of their wives. Indeed, it is she who had to assume the responsibility for feeding and raising the children during the husband's absence. As more and more historians emphasize, the life of working-class people was far from sedentary, and mobility and separation were integral parts of their day-to-day experience.[47] Paradoxically, the profession of arms, which obliged soldiers to move with the regiment, considerably reduced freedom of movement because permission was required every time the soldier was absent from the army.[48] For married men, therefore, choosing the military profession in some cases meant abandoning the family. The famous case of Martin Guerre, analysed by Natalie Zemon Davis, is not an isolated one.[49] Young Martin, who was sexually impotent, suffered from social pressure and "dreamt of"[50] another life. He found himself in the army of Philip II after leaving behind his father's house and wife and only child. The army needed men, and those who desired to change their lives could find a new one in it.[51]

Some deserters, indeed, cast the abandonment of a wife and children as an almost ordinary episode in the soldier's life. Speaking of this potentially fateful separation could, however, provoke strong emotions. In 1775, Joseph Jabeau, a farm labourer, states that "having learnt that his father-in-law, who had guaranteed the farm that the respondent was running, sold – without regard for his guarantee – for the third time the heritage that his wife could hope to receive, the grief with which he was overwhelmed made him abandon his wife and children and come to Rennes, where he entered the army".[52] A conflict of interest with the father-in-law is presented here as the reason for his becoming a soldier: for a desperate husband with children, the army offered an alternative living. This man served six months before deserting from the Royal Marine Corps of Brest for the reason that "the regret for having abandoned his wife and his four children made so much impression on his spirit".[53] Here, the emotional language relieved him of responsibility, first towards the family, and then towards the army.

Becoming a soldier could also be synonymous with abandonment because of the precarious economic conditions of the military. A soldier's pay, which was hardly sufficient to meet his own needs,[54] could not be considered a source of revenue for others. When speaking of the circumstances of his enlistment, if the deserter frequently mentions drunkenness,[55] it is not only to underline the invalidity of the contract but also – in the case of a married man with children – to excuse himself abandoning his family and placing them in need. In 1781, Pierre Gardon served in the Royal Marine Corps for seven months before deserting. Arrested on the road, this pit sawyer by trade explained: "the reason for his desertion is that he enlisted through drunkenness. He repented of having done so, having a wife and children whom he knew to be in hardship […]."[56] His statement illustrates the fragility of a family structure which men were able to abandon in favour of the army. According to his testimony, enlistment was a fault committed against his wife and his "five children, all of small ages". Desertion then becomes an act of reparation towards the family.

The significance of the action – that of becoming a soldier – is not fixed once and for all. Others evoke enlistment as their last chance when confronted with their families' suffering from poverty. Jean-Louis Cullot, 29 years old, states that "the hardship to which he was reduced with his family obliged him to enlist" and that "he gave the amount of the enlistment premium to his wife in order to help her to subsist with his children".[57] A day labourer, he declared that he received 72 livres – the equivalent of 120 days' work for him – out of the promised amount of 120 livres.[58] Payment of the premium for enlistment that the soldier should receive at the moment of signing the contract was most uncertain, although it was stipulated by various royal ordinances.[59] When the recruit was paid correctly, as is the case here, the amount could serve as a resource, albeit limited, for the family. We can thus understand that the prospect of receiving money for enlistment must have been attractive to married men in extreme necessity, even though in reality there was the risk of being manipulated by a hollow promise from the recruiter.

Having been attracted by the possibility of receiving money, some married men claim that they both entered the army and then deserted for the sake of their families. François Lainé became a soldier in the Vermondois regiment, "finding himself without bread and without any means to support his wife and his children, who were perishing from unfulfilled needs".[60] On temporary leave from the army, he went home to see his wife "in childbirth" but did not return to the army afterward. When arrested, the 28-year-old day labourer explained that "he stayed to provide support for his wife, whose illness has been long and dangerous, and to give bread to his two small children, who would have perished from their needs without him".[61] The man's presence is justified by the incapacity of his wife, sick in childbirth. At the end of the interrogation, when asked about his place of domicile, he does not miss this occasion to specify that he lives in a village called Menière "with his wife who is pregnant and his two children" in order to highlight his need to stay with them.

Other deserters present returning home on leave as an occasion during which they discover the destitution of their families. Scenes of supplication by wives and children are both central and recurring in their testimonies. The men state they remained with their families out of compassion. In 1774, Pierre Guihart, 40 years old, became a soldier in the Corps of the Royal Artillery "under the effects of drunkenness". After six weeks of service, he was authorized to return from Brest to Rennes to help his family, who were "sick and in poverty". When it was time to return to the army, "his wife and his children threw themselves at him, which moved him, so that, touched by their tears, he stayed in his city to work in order to give them bread and to raise them".[62] The impossibility of separation from the wife and especially children is thus presented as the reason for desertion. By putting forward a manifestation of a father's empathy with his own family – as in a "serious comedy" by Diderot[63] – the deserter sought to influence the authorities. According to a note in the margin of the document, the deserter was to be released by ministerial order. Several other similar cases of release suggest that the monarchy may have been receptive to this argument, which centred on a sense of duty.

Claims of fatherly duty

When men talk about their wives and children, the role of small children is particularly important. This means that a wife is supposed to be economically autonomous without the husband's help when he is away from home. To justify her inability to work, the deserters therefore need to mention circumstances such as illness, pregnancy or nursing. In so doing, they stress the idea that children, regardless of their sex, cannot exist without the presence and care of an adult, male or female, an idea for which they ask the authorities' understanding.

In this respect, the case of Gilles Guerin is exemplary. This deserter was arrested in 1778 and then again in 1780, and each time he put his fatherly duties at the centre of his statements. In 1778, he explained that he joined the Royal Roussillon regiment a bit "drunk" and received the sizeable sum of 168 livres. He declared that:

> […]he served in the army for about one year, after which time he lost his wife, who left him with two small children. He requested a three-month leave in order to settle his affairs and that due to pity for his two small children without bread or support, he did not return (to the regiment) and has stayed until this day in his village in order to take care of them.[64]

While the death of his wife explains the need to settle his affairs, the mention of the children encourages *pity*. This feeling conforms to the norms regarding the expression of emotion towards children. Here, the mention of children legitimates the father's duty to protect them. As Nicolas Baudeau, an economist of the eighteenth century, writes: "The natural powerlessness of children is too obvious; you would have to not be a human being to be insensitive to the misfortune of those who are needy."[65] Not re-joining the regiment turns out to be a necessity in order to take care of the children, who have been deprived of their mother. The fact that Gilles Guerin was released by ministerial order suggests that a certain consensus among deserter and authorities existed on this point.

After this first experience, Guerin, a day labourer by trade, had another opportunity to enter the army. Shortly after his release, he enlisted in the Toul regiment and deserted three months later. When arrested in 1780, he explained:

> He got a short permit to go home and to bring back with him his child as the commander of the detachment staying in Grandville in Normandy had told him to do, but on arriving home he received a letter from this commander indicating that he could bring his child, who, however, would not be received into the regiment, and that as his intention was to have his son enter this army so that he would learn some profession in order for him to earn his bread honestly, the refusal he had received determined him to not go back so as to ensure the subsistence of his child.[66]

This time, the reason is a child that he wants to take with him in the regiment. The presence of children and women in the army of the Old Regime is a well-known fact for historians.[67] Examining troop registers, André Corvisier specifically notes the existence of children "enlisted and paid at young ages".[68] According to the rule established by Choiseul in 1766, a soldier's son could be admitted on a half wage as early as the age of six.[69] According to Guerin, his intention was to have his son integrated as one of these "soldier's children" (*enfants des troupes*). If he did not return to the regiment, it was because his superior withdrew his offer in regard to the promised status of his child. Here again, a sense of fatherly duty constitutes a justification for desertion. As is recommended in Diderot's and d'Alembert's *Encyclopédie*: "it is not sufficient for a father to feed his children. He must also bring up and conduct them".[70] When Guerin mentioned his son "who has to earn his bread honestly", he met the expectation of a working-class father.

In contrast with the first interrogation, which focused on his duty to feed his family, Guerin's preoccupation seems to have moved on to educational matters. His initial experience of dealing with the highway police, which resulted in him being released, may have encouraged this vision of a father's duty, which he understood as having some chance of being listened to and accepted by the authorities. When asked to explain his previous desertion, Gilles Guerin claimed that "His Majesty, taking into consideration his righteous situation, had the goodwill to grant him his Grace."[71] The crossing out of the word "righteous" is interesting. Like a Freudian slip,[72] it might reveal that the fatherly preoccupation conforms to the social expectations.

Desire and affection as justification

When deserters speak about their children, a sense of duty appears as a central element of the justification for desertion. In general, they don't mention their affection as fathers. It would be interesting, therefore, to turn our attention to deserters' words, referring to their relationships with other family members, particularly their parents. While some justified their desertion on the basis of material duty or need, others indicate only their *desire* to be with their kin. Some expression of attachment then appears as a justification for the desertion.

Concerning their parents, deserters, especially those not yet married, quite often assigned a clear objective for their return home. They specified that they had gone back to their parents in order to request some material support, such as underwear or money – for instance, to reimburse a debt contracted with other soldiers. They also argued regularly that they deserted in order to assist aged parents, especially after the loss of a spouse. As with children and wives, a sense of duty appears important. When it comes to parents, particularly mothers, however, men speak more easily of their attachment. Asked his reason for leaving the Beaujolais regiment in 1775, Antoine Bullet, 21, explained that "no other reason than the desire to see his father and mother of whom he had received no news made him desert".[73] According to René Yvons, 23, he abandoned the Vermondois regiment in 1766 because "after serving for 4 months, he had the misfortune to remember his mother who had written to him in Brest, and, hoping to go and see her, he left Brest in order to return to her house".[74] In 1779, Jacques Auguste David, a 27-year-old woodworker who deserted the Condé regiment, affirmed that "the love he has for his bed-ridden mother overwhelmed what he owed to his prince".[75]

In the corpus of interrogations of deserters, expressions of family feelings certainly increase in the second half of the century, and especially with regard to parents. Deserters who mention children at all, whether with or without their mothers, are, generally speaking, less expressive of their affective feelings towards them than they are towards their parents. Concerning this differentiation in ways of describing family relations, we may remember, with Jean-Louis Flandrin, that Christian doctrine, which initially gave privilege to the language of duty, stressed the duty of the son towards his parents more explicitly than the duty parents have towards their children.[76] As Flandrin remarked, to honour one's parents is one of the Ten Commandments, while there is no equivalent commandment regarding the attitude of parents towards children. Through his analysis of confessional manuals, in particular, he showed how this dissymmetry was corrected in the post-Tridentine era by an expansion of parental duties, related notably to material assistance and educational matters, and also by the emergence of the explicitly formulated imperative for parents to love their children.[77]

During the eighteenth century, enlightened discourse gave particular prominence to the question of affection. The previously mentioned entry "father", written by Jaucourt, in the *Encyclopédie* puts forward the importance of fatherly love.[78] According to the author, fatherly love makes all the care and fatigue spent by a father on his children bearable: while it may be considered a source of grief, in the case of loss or unhappiness, this emotional state is closely related to pleasure, with "a great advantage of softening the horror and the image of death".[79] Here, fatherly love appears as the essential meaning of life, allowing even the threat of death to be overcome. Interestingly, the tone seems to change when it comes to describing the attitude of children towards their parents. The entry "child" is on this issue very explicit:

> […] they must have for their fathers and mothers feelings of affection, esteem, and respect, and display these feelings through their behaviour. They must give

all the support they are able to, advise them on their business, give them con-
solations for their misfortunes, bear with patience their bad character and their
flaws. There is no age, no rank, no dignity, which could relieve a child of these
duties. Finally, a child must help, assist, feed his father and mother, when they
are in need and poverty.[80]

Children therefore appear to have a duty of affection towards their parents, but con-
versely the love parents may feel towards their children is not viewed as a duty.
Concerning affective issues, this imbalance between parents and children, noticed by
Jean-Louis Flandrin with regard to duty, is sometimes reflected in the words of the
deserters: more expressive when it comes to parents; more restrained regarding children.

As sons, deserters had more leeway for expressing their various relationships with
their parents: they expected both to help them and to be helped by them. They
described their relationships with them in terms of assistance and affection. As fathers,
they tend to express the concept of duty, which is implied by manifestations of strong
emotions such as *regret*. Confronted by the *maréchaussée*, deserters speak differently of
their emotions according to their position in the family.

On the whole, however, family reasons emerge as an effective strategy, when
compared, for example, with the other important type of argument: mistreatment by
superiors. Although it is difficult to give a statistical account,[81] those who give family
reasons for desertion may be released by ministerial order, which is rarely the case for
those referring to some abuse suffered at the hands of officers. Thus, calling into
question the legitimacy of the military hierarchy did not result in a positive conclusion, while focusing on the family with an argument efficiently supported by mention
of a health problem allowed the deserter to remove any doubt concerning a potential
intention to criticize the army. Needing to re-join one's family was a comprehensible
motive from the monarchical point of view. In some sense, explaining desertion by a
sense of duty to, or affection for, family members, or by a simple desire to see them,
constituted another way of avoiding conflict with authority.

A deserter occasionally invented his own language to qualify his relationship with
his wife and children, on the one hand, and with the army, on the other. The
interrogation of François Deveu, a wigmaker, is quite exceptional, evoking each
moment of his itinerary in relation to his feelings for his family.[82] In doing so, he
underlined the legitimacy of love, the sentiment binding him to his wife and children. He enlisted in July 1788, when he had no work, out of disappointment that he
could not support his wife and children. His desertion came after ten months spent in
the army. When asked if he requested leave to return home, he asserted that he saved
the effort because "he was aware that it would not have been given to him". For
him, the only motivation for his desertion was related to his family: "He had such a
strong desire to see his wife and children, whom he loves, that this only reason
enticed him to behave this way, and also to make them feel that his enlistment in the
troops of the colonies had not suppressed in him this friendship: he had contracted
this enlistment only out of despair, seeing that he could not make them happy in
spite of the good desire he had to do so."[83]

This testimony reveals what a man of the working class is capable of expressing in terms of desire for his wife and the children he "loves". Aspiring to their happiness,[84] he suffers from his own incapacity to achieve this goal. Here, the language of affection came to prevail without any conflict with the material concern for the family. According to some, one of the goals of military discipline consists in controlling or even suppressing soldiers' emotions.[85] Against this imperative, emotion seems to be overflowing here. Deveu's words describe the colour of his sentiment towards his family with acuity. Enlisted and separated far away from them, he wishes to show that he has not forgotten them and conserves what he calls the sentiment of *friendship*. This is the only purpose he assigned to his desertion before the court.

This intention is also confirmed in his reply to a question about his uniform. Deveu stated that "he was wearing civilian clothes when he went absent from the Corps in Lorient, and he had with him nothing belonging to the state of a soldier, not desiring to appear in military dress in his wife's presence and to increase her sorrow".[86] After ten months living with the troops, he had grown to dislike the army, the traces of which he yearned to erase. Deserters often changed their uniforms for civilian clothes to better disguise their status,[87] but François Deveu claimed to have done so in order to signal his rejection of his affiliation with the army and his care for the woman he loved.

Deveu's words seem all the more meaningful, given that they were chosen instead of reasons that might have exonerated him, such as a health problem. Indeed, it is the lieutenant of the *maréchaussée* who notices an anomaly and asks about a "lump or abscess" on his body. The deserter replied that "he does not know but when he entered the army it was not bigger than a hazelnut but has since grown. He is troubled much by this and by his chest, which he feels infected […]."[88] This statement is followed by the deserter showing the growth, which is "bigger than a goose's egg". Yet, instead of putting forward his putative physical fragility, the deserter seems to take advantage of the moment of interrogation to express the sentiment of love towards his children and wife in order to make it a basis for rejecting military life.

Conclusion

Questioned by the police, the individuals – here the deserters from the French army of the late eighteenth century – tried to justify themselves, delivering their version of their own experience. In this corpus, the significances that men attached to their children are various, but still converged on some commonly shared notions of what they should feel towards their children, who are small and dependent. Predominantly, deserters emphasized the concept of fatherly duties. When they were not in a position to fulfil them, they spoke in terms of emotions, which appear as a form of self-indictment. While abandonment was a reality for some men, speaking of sentiments such as regret, they acknowledged their incapacity or fault as fathers. By so doing, they also aimed to justify their transgressing military norms without calling into question military authority. Here, there is surely a guiding rule for the deserters' words about their children to the police, which are generally more expressive of fatherly duty than of fatherly love. However, the archives – produced by a confrontation between state power and a fragile individual – show how a different language based on fatherly love can be invented. Even if its expression is exceptional, its emergence should be highlighted as one of the myriad moments in the history of family.

Notes

1 A. Corvisier, *L'armée française de la fin du XVIIe siècle au ministère de Choiseul. Le soldat* (Paris, 1764), 2 vols, p737; concerning the Prussian army, see M. Sikora, *Disziplin und Desertion* (Berlin, 1994).

2 A. Forrest, *Déserteurs et Insoumis sous la Révolution et l'Empire* (Paris, 1988).

3 See, for example, G. Parker, *The Military Revolution: Military Innovation and the Rise of the West, 1500–1800* (Cambridge, UK, 1988), ch. 2; S. Loriga, *Soldats* (Paris, 1991).

4 The death penalty for desertion, which was replaced by galley servitude in 1687, was restored in 1716. Criticized by enlightened opinion, it was "abolished", except in cases of desertion in wartime, in 1775. The penalty of hard labour (called *chaîne* or *galère de terre*) was imposed on an experimental basis until 1786.

5 P. Ariès, *L'enfant et la vie familiale sous l'Ancien Régime* (Paris, 1960), p3.

6 For historiographical surveys see, for example, D. Julia, "L'enfance entre absolutisme et Lumières", in E. Becchi and D. Julia (eds) *Histoire de l'enfance en Occident*, vol 2 (Paris, 1998), pp7–119; S. Ozment, *Ancestors: The Loving Family in Old Europe* (Cambridge, MA, 2001), pp5–21; A. Defrance, D. Lopez and F.-J. Ruggiu, "Introduction", in A. Defrance, D. Lopez and F.-J. Ruggiu (eds) *Regards sur l'enfance au XVIIe siècle* (Tübingen, 2007), pp11–30.

7 E. Shorter, *Naissance de la famille moderne* (Paris, 1977). See also, E. Badinter, *L'amour en plus: l'Histoire de l'amour maternel (XVIIe-XXe siècle)* (Paris, 1980).

8 D. Alexandre-Bidon and M. Closson, *L'enfant à l'ombre des cathedrals* (Lyon, 1985); D. Lett, *L'enfant des miracles. Enfance et société au Moyen Age* (Paris, 1997).

9 H. Medick and D. Sabean, "Interest and Emotion in Family and Kinship Studies: A Critique of Social History and Anthropology", in H. Medick and D. Sabean (eds) *Interest and Emotion: Essays on the Study of Family and Kinship* (Paris, 1988), pp9–24.

10 Ibid, p11.

11 S. Beauvalet-Boutouyrie, "Le travail de deuil à travers un ensemble de lettres de consolation du XVIIe siècle", in J.-P. Bardet and F.-J. Ruggiu (eds) *Au plus près du secret des cœurs? Nouvelles lectures historiques des écrits du for privé en Europe du XVIe au XVIIIe siècle* (Paris, 2005), pp111–129; S. Mouysset and D. Rives, "Bon fils, bon mari et bon père? Antoine-Jean Solier par lui-même (1760–1836)", *CLIO: Histoire, femmes et sociétés*, vol 34 (2011): pp137–152.

12 M. Dinges, "Soldatenkörper in der Frühen Neuzeit", in R. van Dülmen (ed) *Körper-Geschichten* (Frankfurt/Main, 1996), pp71–98.

13 U. Bräker, *The Life Story and Real Adventures of the Poor Man of Toggenburg*, translated [from German] by D. Browman (Edinburgh, 1970).

14 Idem, p166: "Nur Gott weiss, was ich bey diesem Unfall empfunden: Ein so guttartiges Kind, das ich wie meine Seele liebte, unter einer so schmerzhaft Krankheit geduldig wie ein Lamm Tag und Nacht", in U. Bräker, *Der arme Mann im Tockenburg* (Zürich, 1993), p230.

15 Idem, p167: "Mir war, mein Herz wollte mir in tausend Stücke Zerspringen" (*Der arme Mann …* , p231).

16 Idem, pp205–207. For his two sons, the question of profession is broached. For two of his daughters, he speculated on their future as wives or mothers. One daughter remained, whom he regretted not being able to give a good education according to her intelligence.

17 V. Barrucand (ed) *La vie véritable du citoyen Jean Rossignol* (Paris, 1896).
18 Ibid, p3.
19 D. Roche (ed) *Journal de ma vie: édition critique du journal de Jacques-Louis Ménétra, compagnon vitrier au XVIIIe siècle* (Paris, 1982).
20 Ibid, pp285–405.
21 Ibid, pp287–292.
22 Ibid, pp323–330.
23 Ibid, pp306–307.
24 Among precursory works, see Y. Castan, *Honnêteté et relations sociales en Languedoc (1715–1780)* (Paris, 1974); R. Muchembled, *La violence au village* (Turnhout, 1989); N. Castan, *Les criminels du Languedoc* (Toulouse, 1980).
25 A. Farge, *La vie fragile* (Paris, Hachette, 1986), cf. ch. IV, "Entre parents et enfants".
26 A. Farge and J. Revel, *Logiques de la foule* (Paris, 1988).
27 E. Shorter, *Naissance de la famille moderne*, pp215–218.
28 A. Farge, *Effusion et tourment: Le récit des corps* (Paris, 2007), pp177–200.
29 See, for example, the two special issues of *Ecrire l'histoire* devoted to emotion (nos 1 and 2, 2008); P. Nagy and D. Boquet (eds) *Le sujet des émotions au Moyen Age* (Paris, 2009).
30 S. Steinberg, "Le droit, les sentiments familiaux et les conceptions de la filiation: à propos d'une affaire de possession d'état du début du XVIIe siècle", *Annales de démographie historique*, vol 2 (2009): pp123–142.
31 J. Lorgnier, *Maréchaussée: Histoire d'une révolution judiciaire et administrative* (Paris, 1994), vol 2.
32 V. Denis, *Une histoire de l'identité, France, 1715–1815* (Seyssel 2008).
33 When brought back to the regiment, the deserter was tried before the *Conseil de Guerre*. The archives produced by this military institution are badly preserved and relatively poor in content.
34 The analysis was made in the archives of the *maréchaussée* of Bretagne, preserved in the departmental archives of the Ille-et-Vilaine (hereinafter A. D. Ille-et-Vilaine).
35 See N. Seriu, *Faire un soldat: Une histoire des hommes à l'épreuve de l'institution militaire (XVIIIe s.)* (PhD thesis, EHESS, Paris, 2005).
36 E. Goffman, *The Presentation of Self in Everyday Life* (Edinburgh, 1956); E. Goffman, *Worlds of Talk: The Presentation of Self in Everyday Conversation* (Cambridge, 1979).
37 J. Delumeau and D. Roche, *Histoire des Pères et de la Paternité* (Paris, 2000). See different contributions to this volume, particularly D. Lett, "Tendres souvenirs", pp17–40; J. Mulliez, "La désignation du père", pp43–72; and A. Molinier, "Nourrir, éduquer et transmettre", pp115–142.
38 Ibid. For this topic, see another set of contributions to Delumeau and Roche's *Histoire des Pères*, particularly S. Melchior-Bonnet, "De Gerson à Montaigne, le pouvoir et l'amour", pp73–88; O. Robert, "Porter le nom de Dieu", pp145–167; and M. Foisil, "En son for privé", pp193–218.
39 J.-C. Bonnet, *Naissance du panthéon: Essai sur le culte des grands hommes* (Paris, 1998), pp19–24; P. Hartmann, *Rétif de la Bretonne. Individu et Communauté* (Paris, 2009), pp73–113.
40 See the comments made by Diderot, "Salon de 1763", in: D. Diderot, *Oeuvres esthétiques*, (Paris, 1959), pp524–529.
41 L. Hunt, *The Family Romance of the French Revolution* (Berkeley, CA, 1992).
42 L.-S. Mercier, *Le déserteur* (Paris, 1770).
43 J. Chagniot, *Paris et l'armée au XVIIIe siècle* (Paris, 1985), p627.
44 *Supra*, note 41; M. Robert, *Roman des origines et origines du roman* (Paris, 1972); F. Magnot-Ogilvy and J. Valls-Russel (eds) *Enfants perdus, enfants trouvés: discours et littérature sur lénfane délaissée dans l'Europe d'Ancien Régime.* (Paris, 2013).
45 This question was explored at the three-day conference "Argumentation at the Heart of the Judicial Process, from the Middle Ages to the Present", held on 28 September, 26 October and 23 November 2012 at Lille (organized by S. Dauchy and C. Deny in the framework of the project on "Argumentation, Decision, Action"; Maison européenne

des sciences de l'homme et de la société). See also the classical work by N. Z. Davis, *Fiction in the Archives: Pardon Tales and Their Tellers in Sixteenth-Century France* (Cambridge, MA, 1987).

46 Even though the army of the Ancien Regime sometimes tolerated soldiers' families as camp followers: see J. Lynn, *Women, Armies, and Warfare in Early Modern Europe* (Cambridge, UK, 2008).

47 D. Roche, *Humeurs vagabondes* (Paris, 2003), pp923–1007; A. Farge, *Le bracelet de parchemin: L'écrit sur soi au XVIIIe siècle* (Paris, 2003).

48 Royal ordinance of 2 July 1716, art. IV.

49 N. Z. Davis, *The Return of Martin Guerre* (Cambridge, MA, 1983).

50 Ibid, p21.

51 J. Chagniot, "Quelques aspects originaux du recrutement parisien au milieu du XVIIIe siècle", in *Recrutement, mentalités, sociétés* (Montpellier, 1975), p112.

52 A. D. Ille-et-Vilaine, 8B 555, 27 May 1775: "Ayant apris que son beau père qui l'a cautionné pour la ferme que le répondant tient sans avoir égard à son cautionnement avoit vendu pour la troisième fois le bien que la femme du répondant pouvoit espérer le chagrin dont il fut accablé luy fit abandonner sa femme et ses enfants et venir à Renne où il s'engagea." Unless otherwise indicated, translations are those of the author.

53 A. D. Ille-et-Vilaine, 8B 555, 27 May 1775: "[…] le regret d'avoir abandonné sa femme et ses quatre enfants fait sur son esprit tant d'impression".

54 H.-J. de Buttet, "La dépense du soldat en 1772", in *Actes du 90ème congrès national des société savantes (Nice, 1965)* (Paris, 1966), vol I, pp141–149.

55 The use of alcohol by recruiters to "encourage" enlistment was quite common. See G. Girard, *Racolage et milice* (Paris, 1921), p78.

56 A. D. Ille-et-Vilaine, 8B 558, 20 November 1781: "La cause de sa désertion vient de ce que s'étant engagé dans l'yvresse, il s'est repenty de l'avoir fait, ayant femme et enfant qu'il sçait être dans la misère […]".

57 A. D. Ille-et-Vilaine, 8B 560, 7 June 1784: "C'est la misère où il se voit réduit avec sa famille, qui l'a porté à s'engager qu'il a donné le prix de son engagement à sa femme pour luy aider à subsister et ses enfants."

58 The wage of a day-worker (*manœuvrier*) can be estimated at between 12 to 15 sols (see H.-J. de Buttet, "La dépense du soldat en 1772", p147).

59 *Encyclopédie méthodique: Art militaire*, 4 vols (Paris 1784–1797), vol II, p253.

60 A. D. Ille-et-Vilaine, 8B 554, 21 January 1772: "[Il s'est engagé] se trouvant sans pain et sans aucun moien de faire subsister sa femme et ses enfans qui perissoient de besoin."

61 A. D. Ille-et-Vilaine, 8B 554, 21 January 1772: "Il a resté à procurer des secours à sa femme dont la maladie a été longue et dangereuse et a donner du pain à ses deux petits enfants qui auroient péry de besoin sans luy."

62 A. D. Ille-et-Vilaine, 8B 555, 1 September 1774: "Sa femme et ses enfants se jetterent à luy et ce qui l'attendrit de telle sorte qu'étant touché de leur larmes, il est resté en cette ville pour travailler à fin de leur donner du pain et de pouvoir les élever."

63 J. Siess, "Un modèle des Lumières: la comédie sérieuse de Diderot", in M. Buffat (ed) *Diderot, L'invention du drame* (Paris, 2000), pp15–26.

64 A. D. Ille-et-Vilaine, 8B 556, 16 March 1778: "Il y a servi environ un an au bout de ce temps ayant perdu sa femme qui lui laissoit deux petits enfants il demanda un congé de trois mois pour aller vaquer à ses affaires que la pitié de laisser ses petits enfants sans pain et sans secours il n'a pas rejoint et a resté jusqu'à ce jour dans son pays pour avoir soin d'eux."

65 N. Baudeau, *Idées d'un citoyen sur les besoins, les droits et les devoirs des vrais pauvres* (Amsterdam, 1765), p10: "l'impuissance naturelle des enfants est trop évidente; il faudroit n'être pas homme pour se montrer insensible au malheur de ceux qui sont dans l'indigence".

66 A. D. Ille-et-Vilaine, 8B 557, 31 March 1780: "Il obtint un petit congé pour aller chez lui chercher son enfan que le commandant d'un détachement qui était à Grand ville en Normandie, lui avoit dit d'ammener et qu'il auroit été reçu dans le Régiment; qu'étant

chez lui, il reçut une lettre du même commandant qu'il lui marquoit qu'il pouvoit emmener son enfant, mais qu'il n'eut pas été reçu dans le Régiment; que l'intention de l'interrogé ayant été de faire entrer son fils dans ce corps pour lui faire apprendre quelque état afin qu'il put gagner un pain honnêtement, le refus qu'on lui faisoit, le détermina à ne pas rejoindre pour faire subsister son enfant et sans cela il eut retourné au regiment."

67 The prints and pictures of Watteau, the northern French painter, represent these figures at the side of soldiers as they march or camp. See A. Farge, *Les fatigues de la guerre* (Paris, 1996).

68 A. Corvisier, *L'armée française*, vol II, p761.

69 Ibid, p757.

70 D. Diderot and J.-B. le Rond d'Alembert, *Encyclopédie ou dictionnaire raisonné des sciences des arts et des métiers par une société de gens de lettre* (Paris, 1751–1780), vol 34, p338: "Il ne suffit pas aux pères de les nourrir, il faut encore qu'ils les élèvent & qu'ils les conduisent."

71 A. D. Ille-et-Vilaine, 8B 557, 31 March 1780: "Sa Majesté en considération de ses justes situations voulut bien lui accorder sa Grâce."

72 Concerning the use of psychoanalysis in history, see A. Cavazzini, "L'archive, la trace, le symptôme. Remarques sur la lecture des archives", L'Atelier du Centre de recherches historiques, vol 5 (2009): http://acrh.revues.org/1635.

73 A. D. Ille-et-Vilaine, 8B 555, 2 October 1775: "(Interrogé quels sont les motifs qui l'ont engagé à déserter) – dit qu'il n'en avoir aucun, que l'envie seule de voir son père et sa mère dont il n'avoit point de nouvelles, l'a engagé à deserter."

74 A. D. Ille-et-Vilaine, 8B 552, 7 November 1766: "après y avoir servi pendant environ quatre mois il eust le malheur de se rappeler le souvenir de sa mère qui luy avoit écrit à Brest, et dans l'espérance d'aller la voir il quitta Brest pour se rendre chez elle".

75 A. D. Ille-et-Vilaine, 8B 556, 4 May 1779: "l'amour qu'il a pour sa mère grabataire l'ayant emporté sur tout ce qu'il devait à son prince".

76 J.-L. Flandrin, *Famille: Parenté, maison, sexualité dans l'ancienne société* (Paris, 1984), pp160–163.

77 Ibid, p162

78 D. Diderot and J.-B. le Rond d'Alembert, *Encyclopédie*, pXII, 338 sq.

79 Ibid, ppXII, 338: "[L'amour paternelle] [...] a l'avantage d'adoucir les horreurs & l'image de la mort."

80 Ibid, ppV, 652: "Ils doivent avoir pour leurs père & mère des sentiments d'affection, d'estime et de respect, & témoigner ces sentimens par toute leur conduite. Ils doivent leur rendre tous les services dont ils sont capables, les conseiller dans leurs affaires, les consoler dans leurs malheurs, supporter patiemment leurs mauvaises humeurs & leurs défauts. Il n'est point d'âge, de rang, ni de dignité, qui puisse dispenser un enfant de ces sortes de devoirs. Enfin un enfant doit aider, assister, nourrir son père & sa mère, quand ils sont tombés dans le besoin & dans l'indigence."

81 The ministerial decision is not systematically noted in the deserters' files.

82 A. D. Ille-et-Vilaine, 8B 562, 25 May 1789.

83 A. D. Ille-et-Vilaine, 8B 562, 25 May 1789: "Il avait une si forte envie de voir sa femme & ses enfants qu'il aime que ce seul motif l'excita à faire cette démarche, et pour leur faire sentir que son engagement pour les troupes des colonies n'avoit point étouffé en lui cette amitié; engagement qu'il n'a contracté que par désespoir, voyant ne pouvoir les rendre heureux malgré la bonne envie qu'il avait de le faire."

84 We can note that happiness is one of the intentions of the Enlightenment. See R. Mauzi, *L'idée du bonheur au XVIIIe siècle* (Paris, 1960).

85 As Souillart, an officer of the Condé regiment, stated: "The most important point of the hard discipline is to choke the voice of passion. The soldier submitted to discipline and stripped of sentiments is now only capable of purely mechanical organization" ("Le propre d'une discipline dure est d'étouffer la voix des passions, le soldat qui s'y trouve soumis dépouillé de sentiments n'est plus susceptible que d'une organisation purement mécanique"). Service Historique de la Défense, 1M 1712.

86 A. D. Ille-et-Vilaine, 8B 562, 25 May 1789: "Il était vêtu d'un habit Bourgeois lorsqu'il s'absenta du Corps à L'orient, et n'avait rien de l'ordonnance, ne voulant pas d'ailleurs paraître sous un habit militaire devant sa femme pour augmenter son chagrin."

87 Civilians who agreed to exchange their clothes for deserters' uniforms were tried by the *maréchaussée*.

88 A. D. Ille-et-Vilaine, 8B 562, 25 May 1789: "[Interrogé] comment lui est provenu cette loupe ou dépôt – Répond qu'il n'en sait rien mais que lorsqu'il entra au Bataillon elle n'était pas plus grosse qu'une noizette et a profité ainsi depuis, de ce dont il est fort gêné, outre sa poitrine qu'il se sent affecté […]."

SELECTED READINGS

Alexandre-Bidon, D. and Closson, M., *L'enfant à l'ombre des cathédrales* (Lyon, 1985).

Amelang, J. S., *The Flight of Icarus: Artisan Autobiography in Early Modern Europe* (Stanford, CA, 1998).

Ariès, P., *L'enfant et la vie familiale sous l'Ancien Régime* (Paris, 1960).

Avery, G. and Briggs, J. (eds) *Children and Their Books: A Celebration of the Work of Iona and Peter Opie* (Oxford, UK, 1989).

Avery, G. and Reynolds, K. (eds) *Representations of Childhood Death* (Basingstoke, UK, 2000).

Baggerman, A., "The Moral of the Story: Children's Reading and the Catechism of Nature around 1800", in B. Schmidt and P. Smith (eds) *Making Knowledge in Early Modern Europe: Practice, Objects, and Texts, 1400–1800* (Chicago, IL, 2008), pp143–163.

Baggerman, A. and Dekker, R., *Child of the Enlightenment: Revolutionary Europe Reflected in a Boyhood Diary* (Leiden, 2009).

Baseotto, P., "Theology and Interiority: Emotions as Evidence of the Working of Grace in Elizabethan and Stuart Conversion Narratives", in J. Liliequist (ed) *A History of Emotions, 1200–1800* (London, 2012), pp65–77.

Becchi, E. and Julia, D. (eds) *Histoire de l'enfance en Occident*, 2 vols (Paris, 1998), II: pp7–119.

Berriot-Salvadore, E. and Pébay-Clottes, I. (eds) *Autour de l'enfance* (Biarritz, 1999).

Berry, H. and Foyster, E. (eds) *The Family in Early Modern England* (Cambridge, UK, 2007).

Blussé, L., *Strange Company: Chinese Settlers, Mestizo Women and the Dutch in VOC Batavia* (Dordrecht, 1986).

Borchardt, N., "Euro-asiatische Kindheit im Batavia der VOC", in E. Streifeneder and B. Rickum (eds) *Quo Vadis, Indonesien? Neueste Beiträge des Doktoranden Netzwerk Indonesien* (Berlin, 2009), pp61–92.

Boros, G., De Dijn, H. and Moors, M. (eds) *The Concept of Love in 17th and 18th Century Philosophy* (Leuven, 2007).

Bosma, U. and Raben, R., *De oude Indische wereld. 1500–1920* (Amsterdam, 2003).

Briggs, J. L., *Inuit Morality Play: The Emotional Education of a Three-Year-Old* (New Haven, CT, 1998).

Brown, S. A. (ed) *Women, Gender and Radical Religion in Early Modern Europe* (Leiden, 2007).

Davies, R. T. (ed) *The Corpus Christi Play of the English Middle Ages* (London, 1972).

Davis, N. Z., "Boundaries and the Sense of Self in 16th-Century France", in T. C. Heller and C. Brooke-Rose (eds) *Reconstructing Individualism: Autonomy, Individuality, and the Self in Western Thought* (Stanford, CA, 1986), pp53–63.

Defrance, A., Lopez, D. and Ruggiu, F.-J., "Introduction", in A. Defrance, D. Lopez, F.-J. Delumeau and D. Roche (eds) *Histoire des Pères et de la Paternité* (Paris, 2000).

Deonna, J. and Teroni, F., *The Emotions: A Philosophical Introduction* (London, 2012).

Eisenberg, N., Cumberland, A. and Spinrad, T. L., "Parental Socialization of Emotion", in A. S. R. Manstead (ed) *Psychology of Emotions*, 5 vols (Los Angeles, CA, 2008), V: pp157–212.

Farge, A. and Revel, J., *Logiques de la foule* (Paris, 1988).

Finucane, R. C., *The Rescue of the Innocents: Endangered Children in Medieval Miracles* (London, 1997).

Flandrin, J.-L., *Famille: parenté, maison, sexualité dans l'ancienne société* (Paris, 1984).

Fletcher, A. and Hussey, S. (eds) *Childhood in Question: Children, Parents and the State* (Manchester, UK, 1999).

Girvan, R. (ed) *Ratis Raving and Other Early Scots Poems on Morals* (Edinburgh 1937/1939).

Gordon, B. and Marshall, P. (eds) *The Place of the Dead: Death and Remembrance in Late Medieval and Early Modern Europe* (Cambridge, UK, 2000).

Gowing, L., Hunter, M. and Rubin, M., *Love, Friendship and Faith in Europe, 1300–1800* (Basingstoke, UK, 2005).

Haas, L., *The Renaissance Man and His Children: Childbirth and Early Childhood in Florence 1300–1600* (New York, 1998).

Holodynski, M., "Milestones and Mechanisms of Emotional Development", in B. Rottger-Rossler and H. J. Markowitsch (eds) *Emotions as Bio-Cultural Processes* (New York, 2009), pp139–163.

Immel, A. and Witmore, M. (eds) *Childhood and Children's Books in Early Modern Europe, 1550–1800* (New York, 2006).

Jancke, G. and Ulbrich, C. (eds) *Vom Individuum zur Person: Neue Konzepte im Spannungsfeld von Autobiographietheorie und Selbstzeugnisforschung* (Göttingen, 2005).

Jarzebowski, C., "Loss and Emotion in Funeral Works on Children in Seventeenth Century Germany", in L. Tatlock (ed) *Enduring Loss in Early Modern Germany* (Leiden, 2010), pp187–213.

Jones, E., *Wives, Slaves, and Concubines: A History of the Female Underclass in Dutch Asia* (DeKalb, IL, 2010).

Knuuttila, S., *Emotions in Ancient and Medieval Philosophy* (Oxford, 2005).

Lett, D., *L'Enfant des miracles: Enfance et société au Moyen Age* (Paris, 1997).

Leverenz, D., *The Language of Puritan Feeling: An Exploration in Literature, Psychology, and Social History* (New Brunswick, NJ, 1980).

Lutz, C., "Emotion, Thought, and Estrangement: Emotion as a Cultural Category", *Cultural Anthropology*, vol 1 (1986): pp287–309.

Lutz, C. and White, G. M. "The Anthropology of Emotions," *Annual Review of Anthropology*, vol 15 (1986): pp405–436.

Magnot-Ogilvy, F. and Valls-Russel, J. (eds) *Enfants perdus, enfants trouvés: discours et littérature sur lénfance délaissée dans l'Europe d'Ancien Régime.* (Paris, 2013).

Martin, L. H., Gutman, H. and Hutton, P. H. (eds) *Technologien des Selbst* (Frankfurt/Main, 1993).

Medick, H. and Sabean, D. (eds) *Interest and Emotion: Essays on the Study of Family and Kinship* (Paris, 1988).

Niemeijer, H. F., "Slavery, Ethnicity and the Economic Independence of Women in Seventeenth Century Batavia", in B. W. Andaya (ed) *Other Pasts: Women, Gender and History in Early Modern Southeast Asia* (Honolulu, 2000), pp174–194.

Niemeijer, H. F., *Batavia: Een koloniale samenleving in de zeventiende eeuw* (Amsterdam, 2005).

Newton, H., *The Sick Child in Early Modern England, 1580–1720* (Oxford, UK, 2012).

Orme, N., *Medieval Children*, (New Haven and London, 2001).

Parish, D. L., "The Power of Female Pietism: Women as Spiritual Authorities and Religious Role Models in Seventeenth-Century England", *Journal of Religious History*, vol 17 (1992): pp33–46.

Pearson, J., *Women's Reading in Britain, 1750–1835: A Dangerous Recreation* (Cambridge, UK, 1999).

Pitkin, B., "'The Heritage of the Lord': Children in the Theology of John Calvin", in M. J. Bunge (ed) *The Child in Christian Thought* (Grand Rapids, MI, 2001), pp160–193.

Plamper, J., "The History of Emotion: An Interview with William Reddy, Barbara Rosenwein, and Peter Stearns", *History and Theory*, vol 49 (2010): pp237–265.

Pollock, L. A., *Forgotten Children: Parent–Child Relations from 1500 to 1900* (Cambridge, UK, 1983).

Reynolds, D. F., "Childhood in One Thousand Years of Arabic Autobiography", in *Edebiyât. Journal of Near Eastern Literatures*, Special issue: "Arabic Autobiography", vol 7 (1996): pp379–392.

Rosenwein, B. H., *Emotional Communities in the Early Middle Age* (Ithaca, NY, 2006).

Rosenwein, B. H., "Emotion Words", in P. Nagy and D. Boquet (eds) *Le Sujet des émotions au Moyen Âge* (Paris, 2008), pp93–106.

Ruggiu (eds) *Regards sur l'enfance au XVIIe siècle* (Tübingen, 2007).

Safley, T. M., *Charity and Economy in the Orphanages of Early Modern Augsburg* (Atlantic Highlands, NJ, 1997).

Safley, T. M., *Matheus Miller's Memoir: A Merchant's Life in the Seventeenth Century* (Basingstoke, UK, 2000).

Safley, T. M. (ed) *Die Aufzeichnung des Matheus Miller. Das Leben eines Augsburger Kaufmanns im 17. Jahrhundert* (Augsburg, 2003).

Safley, T. M., *Children of the Laboring Poor: Expectation and Experience among the Orphans of Early Modern Augsburg* (Leiden, 2005).

Sander, D. and Scherer, K. R. (eds) *The Oxford Companion to Emotion and the Affective Sciences* (Oxford, UK, 2009).

Schmid, B., *Schreiben für Status und Herrschaft. Deutsche Autobiographie in Spätmittelalter und früher Neuzeit* (Zürich, 2006).

Schücking, L. L., *The Puritan Family: A Social Study from the Literary Sources* (London, 1969).

Seaver, P. S. (ed) *Wallington's World: A Puritan Artisan in Seventeenth-Century London* (London, 1985).

Seymour, M. (ed) *On the Properties of Things: John Trevisa's Translation of Bartholomaeus Anglicus De Proprietatibus Rerum; A Critical Text* (Oxford, UK, 1975).

Sidén, K., *Den ideala barndomen. Studier i det stormaktstida barnporträttens ikonografi och funktion* (Stockholm, 2001).

Sommerville, C. J., "The Distinction between Indoctrination and Education in England, 1549–1719", *Journal of the History of Ideas*, vol 44 (1983): pp387–406.

Stannard, D. E., "Death and the Puritan Child", *American Quarterly*, vol 26 (1974): pp456–476.

Stearns, P. N. with C. Z. Stearns, "Emotionology: Clarifying the History of Emotions and Emotional Standards", *American Historical Review*, vol 90 (1985): pp813–836.

Stitziel, J., "God, the Devil, Medicine, and the Word: A Controversy over Ecstatic Women in Protestant Middle Germany, 1691–93," *Central European History*, vol 29 (1996): pp309–337.

Strohl, J. E., "The Child in Luther's Theology: 'For What Purpose Do We Older Folks Exist, Other Than to Care for … the Young?'", in M. J. Bunge (ed) *The Child in Christian Thought* (Grand Rapids, MI, 2001), pp134–159.

Taylor, J. G., *The Social World of Batavia* (Madison, WI, 1983).

Taylor, J. G., "Europese en Euraziatische vrouwen in Nederlands-Indië in de VOC-tijd", in J. Reijs, et al (eds) *Vrouwen in de Nederlandse koloniën* (Nijmegen, 1986), pp10–33.

Taylor, J. G., "Meditations on a Portrait from Seventeenth-Century Batavia", *Journal of Southeast Asian Studies*, vol 37 (2006): pp23–41.

Ulbrich, C., Medick, H. and Schaser, A. (eds) *Selbstzeugnis und Person. Transkulturelle Perspektiven* (Cologne, 2012).

Von Greyerz, K., *Passagen und Stationen. Lebensstufen zwischen Mittelalter und Moderne* (Göttingen, 2010).

Von Greyerz, K., Medick, H. and Veit, P. (eds) *Von der dargestellten Person zum erinnerten Ich. Europäische Selbstzeugnisse als historische Quellen (1500–1850)* (Cologne, 2001).
Wetherell, M., *Affect and Emotion: A New Social Science Understanding* (London, 2012).
Woods, R., *Children Remembered: Responses to Untimely Death in the Past* (Liverpool, 2006).

INDEX